PRAISE FOR *THE TRUTH OF MANKIND*

"This engaging book of memories and reflections by a former student and close friend of René Girard radiates the warmth of remembrance and admiration. It also turns an affectionately critical gaze on the scientific character of Girard's theory and tries to integrate his thought within a traditional Christian framework. It is an intellectually stimulating and deeply personal look at Girard, his ideas, and the Catholic faith that animates him."

—**JEAN-MICHEL OUGHOURLIAN**, author of *Alterity* and *Psychopolitics: Conversations with Trevor Cribben Merrill*

"Cesáreo Bandera's critical reflection is a brilliant sequel to what may one day be called the 'Buffalo Controversy.' A historic interlocutor of René Girard and scandalized reader of *Battling to the End*, Bandera understands his friend's teaching as follows: Christ will only return when we truly realize that Christian revelation has failed. This radical reading 'finishes off' the scientism that threatens mimetic theory and refocuses it on the person of Christ. It is in this way the voice of the 'last Doctor of the Church' who Bandera masterfully restores and makes heard."

—**BENOÎT CHANTRE**, author of *The Time Has Grown Short: René Girard, or the Last Law*

"Cesáreo Bandera's book challenges the anthropological apology of Christianity that his friend René Girard undertook in his unfolding of mimetic theory by showing how it depends on a theocentric or even Christocentric origin. Even if one doubts this strong thesis, the book leads to a better understanding of mimetic theory by its engagement with authors like Lucretius, Virgil, and Cervantes."

—**WOLFGANG PALAVER**, author of *René Girard's Mimetic Theory* and *Transforming the Sacred into Saintliness*

"Bandera ranges widely and deeply over René Girard's writings and up-to-date commentary on them. He deftly probes the issues of religion and science, faith and reason, persuasively challenging many an uncritical conception of this fraught entanglement. As a result, the relations of mimetic anthropology and Biblical revelation are on reset."

—**ANDREW J. MCKENNA**, author of *Violence and Difference: Girard, Derrida, and Deconstruction*

"Cesáreo Bandera's *The Truth of Mankind* focuses on the relations between René Girard's mimetic theory and his Christian faith. At the heart of Bandera's reflection and memories is why a man he remembers as a close friend and devout Christian decided to present his anthropological discovery as purely scientific, while arguing that it is a direct consequence of Christian Revelation, which alone made it possible. Challenging Girard's repeated claim that his theory is exclusively scientific with the help of wonderful analyses of Virgil's *Aeneid*, Bandera, like the Latin poet, asks the right questions; but unlike him, provides answers."

—**PAUL DUMOUCHEL**, author of *The Ambivalence of Scarcity and Other Essays* and *The Barren Sacrifice: An Essay on Political Violence*

"Cesáreo Bandera understands the work of René Girard better than most of Girard's ardent admirers. His critical appraisal of his longtime friend, carried out in defense of the Girardian legacy—'probably the most important anthropological discovery of our time'—is filled with brilliant insights. A reader may disagree with the premise of Bandera's critique, as I do, while still profiting from the author's faith, passion, and erudition. If Girard had not argued for the scientific validity of his work, the *apocalyptic* crisis he foresaw might have been mistaken for an *apologetic*—one paradoxically less likely to inspire conversion. And if it took the 'scandal' of Girard's insistence on scientific validity to compel Bandera to write this book, it was a 'happy fault' that brought about this passionate defense of the Girardian legacy and its indispensable Christian ramifications."

—**GIL BAILIE**, author of *God's Gamble: The Gravitational Power of Crucified Love* and *The Apocalypse of the Sovereign Self: Recovering the Christian Mystery of Personhood*

"*The Truth of Mankind* might more aptly be titled *Mimetic Theory and Christ*. From the book's opening pages, Bandera makes clear that he wishes to explore 'the deeply problematic relationship between Girard's perfectly orthodox understanding of Christian doctrine, on one hand, and the scientific findings of his anthropology on the other.' He does so in a provocative and erudite fashion that will be sure to generate discussion among those familiar with Girard's theory. This excellent study takes a clear stand on the question of the connection, in Girard's thought, between faith and reason, and religion and science."

—**JOHN J. RANIERI**, author of *Disturbing Revelation: Leo Strauss, Eric Voegelin, and the Bible* and *Eric Voegelin and the Good Society*

THE TRUTH OF MANKIND

The Truth *of* Mankind

REFLECTIONS ON GIRARDIAN THEORY

CESÁREO BANDERA

Angelico Press

First published in the USA
by Angelico Press 2024

For information, address:
Angelico Press, Ltd.
169 Monitor St.
Brooklyn, NY 11222
www.angelicopress.com

ppr 979-8-89280-029-7
cloth 979-8-89280-030-3
ebook 979-8-89280-031-0

Book and cover design
by Michael Schrauzer

in memoriam,
dilectissime

CONTENTS

You may freely eat of every tree of the garden; but of the tree of knowledge of good and evil you shall not eat, for in the day that you eat of it you shall die.

Gen. 2:16–17

[Poets] must realize that prayers are requests to the gods, and they must apply their intelligence to the utmost in order to avoid ever mistakenly requesting evil in place of good . . . but the race of poets are not entirely capable of understanding well what things are good and what things are not.

Plato, *The Laws*

Good and evil seem to be so inseparable, that like two converging lines . . . they spring from different beginnings, yet both end in the same point.

Cervantes, *The Trials of Persiles and Sigismunda*

If deceit cannot be distinguished from true friendship, the world will soon revert to its primeval chaotic violence.

Cervantes, *Don Quixote*

This is the true day of God,
blessed with serene light
by which the sacred blood washed away
the shameful crimes of the world.

Ambrosian Chant

This is why the Son of God became man, suffered, died, and was raised again: because divine wisdom has ordained and divine goodness has willed, not to do away with evils of the human race through power, but to convert those same evils into a supreme good according to the just and mysterious law of the cross.

Bernard Lonergan

❧ OLD MEMORIES

I MET GIRARD IN 1968 IN ITHACA, NY, AT THE HOME OF John Freccero, who had directed my doctoral dissertation at Cornell. Girard was on his way from Johns Hopkins to SUNY/Buffalo, where he had accepted a faculty position as Distinguished Professor. I followed him there a year later, in 1969. It was my first tenured appointment at the rank of Associate Professor.[1]

We became close friends. In those early years at SUNY/Buffalo, there were periods when we would meet almost daily, usually for lunch at the faculty club. We talked enthusiastically about the great literary masters, Shakespeare, Cervantes, Molière.... Fascinating details we had just discovered; things we learned from them, incredible suggestions. We had practically no interest in questions of style or literary theory, which was the talk of the town those days. I introduced him to Calderón, with whom he was less familiar. Mostly, though, I listened. We were frequently joined by Eugenio Donato, who had been his student at Johns Hopkins. He died very young.

We looked forward to our meetings with anticipation. However, it was also clear to me that those moments of friendly conversation were for him something like a welcomed break, a relaxing pause, in the midst of something bigger, of which, at the beginning, he hardly ever spoke. I felt I could not pressure him on that. It appeared to be something deeply personal, not

---

1 I take this opportunity to correct a chronological detail in James Williams's Biographical Sketch in *The Girard Reader*, where we read the following: "In 1971 Girard accepted a distinguished professor position at the State University of New York at Buffalo, where he remained until 1976. During this period, he became a close friend of Cesáreo Bandera, now University Distinguished Professor of Spanish Literature at the University of North Carolina [Chapel Hill]. Bandera was and has remained an important conversation partner for Girard.... In 1976 Girard accepted a second appointment at Johns Hopkins University..." As I said, Girard moved to Buffalo in 1968. When I, in turn, moved to Buffalo in 1969, he was already there. In fact, that was one of the reasons why I decided to accept Buffalo's offer. Chris Fleming repeats the same error in *René Girard. Violence and Mimesis* (Cambridge: Polity Press, 2004).

your ordinary scholarly project. On the rare occasions when he said something about it, which I could not fully understand for lack of context, his tone changed; vivacious enthusiasm would give way to something quieter, more intense, meditative. Clearly it was something not to be treated lightly. As I learned much later, those years, the late sixties and early seventies, were a crucial period in his intellectual trajectory, "the most hyperactive period of my life I have known [he said], at the end of the 1960s, when I alternated between elation and depression in the face of what I was trying to construct."[2]

All I knew was that it was some kind of anthropological project, which at some point he thought of calling "Anthropologie fondamentale." One day, at his home in East Aurora, south of Buffalo, relaxing over a cup of coffee, I finally asked him, "what is it all about?" These were his words, I remember vividly, as he looked straight into my eyes, very seriously and very calmly: "I am convinced I can explain the transition from animal to man." That was it, nothing else. Everything came down to that one phrase: the transition from animal to man. I had no idea. It sounded crazy. Not knowing what to say, I tried to make light of it: "René, you shouldn't say those things in a loud voice, people may think you are crazy." He insisted, "I am serious. I am convinced I can do it." The rest is history. *La violence et le sacré* was published in 1972. *Des choses cachées depuis la fondation du monde*, which came out in 1978, had been in the works for some time, even before he left Buffalo to go back to Johns Hopkins in 1976. I remember occasionally joining him, Jean-Michel Oughourlian and Guy Lefort at their hotel in Cheektowaga[3] after one of their sessions. Apparently, the title of the book had not been decided

2 René Girard, *Battling to the End: Conversations with Benoît Chantre*, trans. Mary Baker (East Lansing, MI: Michigan State University Press, 2010), 124.

3 The "Foreword" to the English translation of *Des choses cachées depuis la fondation du monde* (*Things Hidden Since the Foundation of the World* [Stanford, CA: Stanford University Press, 1987]) begins with the words: "The texts collected in this work derive from research undertaken at Cheektowaga University." To the best of my knowledge, there never was such an institution.

yet, for there was some joking about calling it "Les entretiens de Cheektowaga."

"I am convinced I can do it," he said. That was almost fifty years before his death in 2015. Did he do it? Did he actually "explain the transition from animal to man"? No, not completely. Does that mean that *Violence and the Sacred* was a mistake? Not at all, since he did explain, in a perfectly rational, scientific, way, the fundamental violence at the origin of all known myths and rituals: the scapegoat or victimizing mechanism. Furthermore, he understood why such violence had been consistently misunderstood, misrepresented, in the language of myths. In other words, he could explain why the mythical is indeed mythical; an explanation which includes knowledge of why, as he put it, "the Bible is not a myth." He knew that what made possible the scientific approach, in a book such as *Violence and the Sacred*, was Christ, the culmination of the Biblical perspective.

Yet Christ is not even mentioned in the book. Half-jokingly, with a tinge of irony, he would say that *Violence and the Sacred* was the first atheistic explanation of the historical importance, the centrality, of religion in human history. In fact, he boasted about it. He was convinced that his insight into the violent origin of religion was made possible by that which was out of it, untouched by the violence, infinitely distant from it: that is to say, Christ. Hence the paradox: that which made the scientific insight possible is totally outside the original violence that explains everything. Christ reveals the originating violence as he moves away from such a revelation, which can now stand on its own rationality. The very uniqueness of Christ, the only one untouched by the violence, takes him out of the picture. The uniqueness of Christ disappears, moves out of sight, in favor of a rationality that needs no further explanation. Christ communicated something which everybody could understand. Once the message was delivered, the messenger was no longer necessary. In fact, his absence from the scene enhanced the scientific character of the message. In this scientific context, Christ's sacrifice is the proof of his expulsion from the foundational violence, the proof that he did not belong there. And it is also an indictment of such violence, because his innocence prevailed against the overwhelming power of the violent crowd—which is also proof of his divinity. The crucified reveals the structure and functioning of the foundational violence, as well as his divinity. But the rational explanation can stand on its own rationality; the divinity of Christ, on the other hand, is a question of faith. It makes the rational explanation possible, but it is not an integral part of such an explanation. You can ignore it. That is what Girard did in *Violence and the Sacred.* And yet he saw that book as an *apologia christiana*, a demonstration of the profound rationality of religion in general and of Christianity in particular. He was carried away. He forgot Christ's words: "I am the truth," not the one who tells the truth; not a reliable witness to the truth, but truth itself. Which means you cannot separate Christ from the truth or the truth from Christ. All the rational knowledge in the world is useless without Christ. The devil is extremely knowledgeable, but it does not benefit him at all.

Violence and the Sacred became the basis for a purely "epistemological Christianity," which attracted the interest of some prominent Girardians, as we will see. However, one must wonder why Jesus the Christ took such a personal, such a bloody, interest in something which was alien to him. This paradoxical view of Christ, ready to die for something in which he had no part, would haunt Girard for the rest of his life. We should not be surprised to hear him say: "In *Violence and the Sacred*, I wanted to write a book about both archaic religion, which I did, and Christianity. But on Christianity I just gave up, I just couldn't do it." The book on Christianity came a few years later. Did it solve the problem? We will explore here the deeply problematic relationship between Girard's perfectly orthodox understanding of Christian doctrine, on one hand, and the scientific findings of his anthropology, on the other.

Nevertheless, he was never a prisoner of his own theory. He was convinced that, in reality,

> no experience of a purely philosophical nature can secure the individual the slightest victory over mimetic desire and its victimage delusions.... For there to be the slightest degree of progress, the victimage delusion must be vanquished on the most intimate level of experience; and this triumph, if it is not to remain a dead letter, must succeed in collapsing... all the things that are based upon our interdividual oppositions—consequently everything that we can call our "ego," our "personality," our "temperament," and so on.[4]

The only irony in this situation is that it was somebody like René Girard who originated such a purely "epistemological Christianity." For he was not only a devout Catholic but a saintly man. Those of us who had the privilege of knowing him as a friend can testify to that. Gil Bailie, for example, remembers the following question and answer at a meeting of biblical scholars: "What is to be done?" he was asked; in other words, in view of everything you have been telling us about sacrifice and the Bible, "what is to be done?" And this is what he said: "We are each called to different tasks, so perhaps we should begin by striving for personal sanctity."

Many years later, toward the end of his life, one of his biographers, Cynthia L. Haven, reports this conversation:

> —So, given this long apocalypse you say we're going through, what would you advise?
> —What do you mean...?
> —What do we do?
> —Nothing.
> —We just sit it out?
> —We just sit it out. Yes. [...]
> —God is taking care of it. Yes. Yes.

4 René Girard, *Things Hidden Since the Foundation of the World* (Stanford, CA: Stanford University Press, 1987), 399.

The biographer wonders: "Does that throw us back, helplessly, on passivity and quietism, powerless witnesses to war, confusion, and terror?"[5] This is what I think Girard meant: "Yes, there will be war, confusion, and terror. Christ himself announced it. He also warned that our faith will be sorely tested by the war, the confusion, and the terror. But we must hold to it as our only hope." Implicitly, this answer has an essential element in common with the earlier one: look inside of you; the voice of the faith speaks to you inwardly; beware of the ever-rising noise outside. False prophets will spring up everywhere selling false solutions. They are part of the noise. Do not add to it. Just keep the faith. In other words, whatever you do, strive for sanctity. There is, of course, no sanctity, without the love of your neighbor, without caring for him or her, whoever and wherever they may be.

The biographer adds the following comment:

> Girard frequently cited the New Testament passages about how, were these [apocalyptic] times not abridged, "no one would be saved." But saved in what sense? One cannot assume, in Girard's case, he meant the term in a strictly theological context, rather than an anthropological one.[6]

I think she misses the point. Apocalyptic violence is a threat both to the survival of the species and to the survival of the faith. The two are intimately connected. Unless God comes to the rescue, humanity will self-destruct, but at that point it would be a faithless humanity. If God does not intervene, the faith will disappear and so will humanity. The whole point is that salvation and survival are inseparable. There will be human formulas for survival preached all over the place. They are all worse than useless, a threat to your faith. So, ultimately, if the question is, what do you propose that we do, given everything that you have been saying about human violence? The answer is nothing. In other words,

5 Cynthia L. Haven, *Evolution of Desire* (East Lansing, MI: Michigan State University Press, 2018), 273–74.
6 Haven, *Evolution of Desire*, 261.

Girardian theory should in no way be taken as a human formula for survival, or a blueprint for the construction of a new society.

He was profoundly humble as a human being. But there was also, by no means unrelated to the question of sanctity, something Quixotic about him, a certain audacity without bitterness, without resentment. Jean-Pierre Dupuy, who knew him very well, called him a "madman":

> Only a madman [could claim today] that the truth of mankind is religious in nature. That of all religions, only one possesses full knowledge of the human world . . . that this religion is Christianity . . . founded on the Gospels, which is to say on the accounts of the death and the resurrection of Jesus Christ.[7]

It bears repeating: "the truth of mankind is religious in nature." That is at the basis of the entire Girardian edifice. No rational and scientific way of dealing with the truth of mankind can disregard its fundamental religious expression. But for a Christian, this fundamental religious expression is Christ Himself; not Christ the teacher, not even the Christ who comes in glory at the end of time to judge the living and the dead, but Christ on the Cross, inseparable. It is Christ on the Cross who makes the Cross meaningful, the basis of all knowledge about "the truth of mankind." It is Christ on the Cross who makes all rational, scientific, knowledge, not only possible, but historically relevant as well, capable of changing the course of history. Therein lies the fundamental difference between pre-Christian classical science, Aristotelian or Lucretian science, for example, and modern science, the one that flourishes (after a long gestation) in the thought of a Descartes, a Bacon, a Pascal, or a Newton. Knowledge is, indeed, the engine of human history. But it only benefits humanity, only reveals a transcendental truth

7 Jean-Pierre Dupuy, *The Mark of the Sacred* (Stanford, CA: Stanford University Press, 2013), 39.

which gives meaning to everything, because it is good and only good. Without Christ knowledge is ultimately in the service of violence.

Girard, the deeply Christian man, forgot about it. There is something missing in Girard's scientific explanation of his famous "transition from animal to man," an original unexplained gap, an arbitrary assumption: the sacred character of the original victim, its meaningful uniqueness, without which there is no original victim, no originality, they are all the same. What did those hominids see in "the original" victim? What turned it into the "ur" symbol, the origin of symbolicity itself, of language? Yet Girard told us that the Eucharistic Body and Blood of Christ point back to the human flesh consumed at that most primitive of origins. Christ is the original victim. He cannot possibly be excluded from the sacrificial origin of humanity, from Girard's anthropological explanation of "the transition from animal to man."

I could well understand Girard's commendable purpose: to prove that the Biblical text is perfectly compatible with the most rigorous scientific scrutiny. Theology and science support each other. But there is danger in this apparently innocent pairing. Christ owes absolutely nothing to science; science owes everything to Christ. The power of Christ, the formidable historical power of Christ, transcends all scientific boundaries. Science without Christ falls hopelessly short of "the truth of mankind."

CHAPTER 1
A Question of Sanctity

> René Girard did not have much interest in miracles. But he came back often to Peter's tears or Paul's conversion. Cervantes said it all, when his character, together with Sancho, broached the question of sanctity on a Castilian desert.[1]

THE QUESTION OF SANCTITY, EXPLICITLY OR IMPLICITLY, is everywhere in Cervantes's *Don Quixote*,[2] particularly in the second part. It comes up in connection with the amazing news that Samson Carrasco, the bachelor from Salamanca, brought with him to the village. The adventures of Don Quixote and Sancho were already in print and circulating widely. Don Quixote feels rather uneasy about it. He has already experienced the malice of the sage enchanter who can turn giants into windmills to rob him of the glory that defeating the giants would accrue to him, as to any other worthy knight errant. Sancho, on the other hand, does not care about that.

> But let them say what they like; naked was I born, naked I find myself, I neither lose nor gain; nay, while I see myself put into a book and passed on from hand to hand over the world, I don't care a fig, let them say what they like of me.[3]

As we can see, not even Sancho is immune to the attraction of popular fame, even if it is somewhat infamous. Don Quixote is quick to expand on that attitude of Sancho's with numerous historical examples of people who did crazy things, even terrible, infamous, things out of a "desire of acquiring

---

1 Benoît Chantre, *Les derniers jours de René Girard* (Paris: Grasset, 2016), 37 (my translation).

2 Miguel de Cervantes, *Don Quixote*, translated with an introduction by John Ormsby. Digireads, 2015. II, 259.

3 Ibid., 269.

fame, [which] is a very powerful motive." Of course, we "Catholic Christians and knights-errant look more to that future glory that is everlasting... than to the vanity of the fame that is to be acquired in this present transitory life; a fame that, however long it may last, must after all end with the world itself, which has its own appointed end" (II, 269). Sancho understands all that, but he still has doubts and keeps asking questions. For example:

> "Which is the greater work, to bring a dead man to life or to kill a giant?" "The answer is easy," replied Don Quixote; "it is a greater work to bring to life a dead man." "Now I have got you," said Sancho; "in that case the fame of them who bring the dead to life, who give sight to the blind, cure cripples, restore health to the sick, and before whose tombs there are lamps burning, and whose chapels are filled with devout folk on their knees adoring their relics be a better fame in this life and in the other than that which all the heathen emperors and knights-errant that have ever been in the world have left or may leave behind them?" "That I grant, too," said Don Quixote.

The master is getting a bit impatient:

> "What wouldst thou have me infer from all thou hast said, Sancho?" asked Don Quixote. "My meaning is," said Sancho, "let us set about becoming saints, and we shall obtain more quickly the fair fame we are striving after."

There it is, in the simple words of the illiterate peasant, Sancho, the whole question of sanctity. If it is true that we are pursuing the same end as the saints, why on earth do we not become saints instead of knights-errant? Why do we have to go looking for evil giants to kill, or damsels in distress to save, while being beaten all over the place?

Don Quixote's reply is a bit evasive, yet extremely significant: there are many ways of serving God. "Chivalry, knight-errantry, is a form of religion."

We should pay attention. This is more than rhetoric in the general context of Cervantes's novel. The idea is repeated in a more serious way much later. Knight and squire are already on their way to Barcelona when they see a group of men, "dressed as labourers," sitting on the grass and eating their meal. As it turns out, they are carrying some religious images "carved in relief for a retablo." Each image is covered with a white sheet for protection. They graciously agree to remove their cover and show them, one by one, to Don Quixote. The last image is that of Saint Paul falling from his horse.

> When Don Quixote saw it, rendered in such lifelike style that one would have said Christ was speaking and Paul answering, "This," he said, "was in his time the greatest enemy that the Church of God our Lord had, and the greatest champion it will ever have; a knight-errant in life, a steadfast saint in death, an untiring labourer in the Lord's vineyard, a teacher of the Gentiles, whose school was heaven, and whose instructor and master was Jesus Christ himself." There were no more images, so Don Quixote bade them cover them up again, and said to those who had brought them, "I take it as a happy omen, brothers, to have seen what I have; for these saints and knights were of the same profession as myself, which is the calling of arms; only there is this difference between them and me, that they were saints, and fought with divine weapons, and I am a sinner and fight with human ones. They won heaven by force of arms, for heaven suffereth violence; and I, so far, know not what I have won by dint of my sufferings; but if my Dulcinea del Toboso were to be released from hers, perhaps with mended fortunes and a mind restored to itself I might direct my steps in a better path than I am following at present." "May God hear and sin be deaf," said Sancho to this. (II, 269)

"These saints and knights were of the same profession as myself." This is true, in a sense, because it points to the very nature of Don Quixote's madness; to that which, by definition, he cannot see, unless it is revealed to him. There is a reason why Cervantes insists on the idea. He knew that his Don Quixote, like Lady Macbeth for Shakespeare, "is more in need of the divine than the physician."

René Girard, truly the spiritual heir to the Cervantes who wrote *Don Quixote*, goes straight to the point at the center of his reflection on Cervantes's novel, a point which was also central for Cervantes. "Chivalric existence," says Girard, "is the imitation of Amadís in the same sense that the Christian's existence is the imitation of Christ."[4] In the eyes of Don Quixote Amadís was not just a famous knight-errant but was

> I should say, the only, the first, the unique, the master and lord of all those who existed in the world.... I think ... that, when a painter wants to become famous for his art he tries to imitate the originals of the best masters he knows; ... thus the man who wishes to be known as careful and patient should and does imitate Ulysses, in whose person and works Homer paints for us a vivid portrait of carefulness and patience, just as Virgil shows us in the person of Aeneas the valor of a pious son and the wisdom of a valiant captain.... In the same way Amadís was the pole, the star, the sun for brave and amorous knights.... Thus, my friend Sancho, I reckon that whoever imitates him best will come closest to perfect chivalry.

Clearly Don Quixote is fooling himself. His imitation of Amadís goes far beyond the rationally defined and well-focused imitation of a master by his apprentice. He does not simply want to imitate Amadís's actions; he is fighting for glory and fame, he wants to be Amadís. He wants to be "the only, the first, the unique, the master and lord of all." That is what he sees in Amadís, and that is what he is after. Let me repeat here what I said in *The Humble Story*: Don Quixote was lucky that he never met his idol in the flesh, because there can only be one who is "the only, the first, the unique." In other words, Amadís is not only god-like in the eyes of Don Quixote, he is also the ultimate rival and obstacle, the one he could not defeat without defeating himself. Quixotic adoration of the model is inherently ambivalent. It can and will eventually turn into envious hatred. The adoring subject will eventually

4 *Deceit, Desire, and the Novel. Self and Other in Literary Structure*. Translated by Yvonne Freccero (Baltimore, MD: The Johns Hopkins University Press, 1965), 2.

feel his own unbearable inadequacy, for which he will hate his God-like model. Don Quixote will eventually turn into Dostoyevsky's "eternal husband," a transformation anticipated, in his own way, by Cervantes himself—as Girard brilliantly demonstrates—in "The Story of the Curious Impertinent," to which everybody (except Don Quixote) listened as it was read aloud at the famous inn in Part I.

The idolatrous fascination of the deified human model is the fascination of the obstacle: only that attracts you which is denied to you. That was not discovered by Cervantes or any other of Girard's literary masters. It was well known to the Graeco-Roman classics. Lucretius, as we will see when we examine *De rerum natura* (On the nature of things), knew much about mimetic desire and occasionally uses metaphors to describe it that are clearly Shakespearian *avant la lettre*, as when he speaks of "savouring things through somebody else's mouth" (*ex ore aliena*), or "choosing by hearsay" (*ex auditis*) (Book V, 1120). Virgil's description of the terrible wars on Italian soil is a classic example of the perfect reciprocity between the violent contending parties, each one violently becoming a mirror image of the other. And, of course, there is Ovid, a real master in the manipulation of mimetic desire, the desire of the obstacle in particular. His *Erotic Poems* are all about that. Here is a sample, as he addresses the husband or boyfriend of the woman:

> You may not feel any need (and more fool you) to guard that / Girl of yours—but it sharpens my desire / So would you oblige? What's allowed is a bore, it's what isn't / That turns me on . . . We lovers need hope and despair in / Alternate doses. An intermittent rebuff / Makes us promise the earth. / Who wants a beautiful woman / When she never deceives him?[5]

But something formidable happened between these classics and the literary masters who told Girard everything about mimetic desire, something that radically changed the

5 *The Erotic Poems*, trans. Peter Green (Penguin Classics, 2004), 134–35.

historical significance of mimetic desire. It went from being a typical feature in the make-up of a human being to being the deciding factor in the very existence and destiny of humanity on earth. What happened was Christ. Human history was "gospelled." And Christ did not come so much as a teacher, or a wise man, but as an example, or rather, *the* example, the one to be followed and imitated. The famous devotional book *The Imitation of Christ* begins with the following words from John's gospel:

> "He who follows Me, walks not in darkness," says the Lord. By these words of Christ we are advised to imitate His life and habits if we wish to be truly enlightened and free from all blindness of heart.

And later:

> What, therefore, have we to do with questions of philosophy? He to whom the Eternal Word speaks is free from theorizing. For from this Word are all things and of Him all things speak—the Beginning Who also speaks to us. Without this Word no man understands or judges aright. He to whom it becomes everything, who traces all things to it and who sees all things in it, may ease his heart and remain at peace with God.[6]

All of a sudden the sacred is no longer untouchable, *horrendus*, terrifying. The sacred has become *holy*, *saintly*, and it lives among us. What for Lucretius could only be the very definition of an apocalyptic catastrophe, god and human together, has become our only way to salvation and survival. Christ is the only model who will never become your rival. He will die for you so that you can be saved from yourself, from your attachment to the obstacle.

Unaided, in and of itself, mimetic desire is unavoidably ambivalent. Cervantes may describe this situation in different ways. In the *Persiles*, for example, as we will see in a moment,

6 Thomas à Kempis, *The Imitation of Christ*, trans. Aloysius Croft and Harold Bolton (Milwaukee, WI: Bruce Publishing, 1949), 1, 5.

it appears to him in the image of two radically different things, good and evil, converging in time toward a single point, where it becomes impossible to clearly separate the one from the other. Or as it appears in a sonnet sung by mad Cardenio in the Sierra Morena. These are the last two stanzas:

> Leave heaven, oh friendship, do not allow
> Deceit to wear thy robes,
> With which it destroys an earnest will.
> If you do not take your semblance from deceit
> The world will soon return to the violence
> Of its primeval chaotic confusion. (I, chap. XXVII)

If reality cannot be clearly separated from fiction, or a good intention from an evil one, peace will be impossible. We are entirely in God's hands. Only Christ as model and mediator can take humanity beyond "the violence of the primeval chaos." When Jesus says to the disciple "come, follow me, do as I do," he means "me and only me." In his own words, "I am the way, the truth, and the life" (John 14:6). There is no other one: "Whoever is not with me is against me" (Matt. 12:30). It is either a saint or a hero. Amadís (the fake god, the man-made substitute) or Christ. They mirror each other, because "[envy] is the reverse image of divine love."[7] But by simply suggesting this ultimate contrast, Cervantes is giving Don Quixote's madness a universal scope and meaning. It takes divine love to cure Don Quixote of his madness. It is, therefore, not something accidental, affecting some but not all human beings. In the eyes of Cervantes, Don Quixote is the face of humanity. In this sense, it is something like original sin: substituting the human other for God:

> The false prophets proclaim that in tomorrow's world *men will be god for each other* . . . They do not perceive the irony of their own formula; they think they are heralding paradise but they are talking about hell, a hell into which they themselves are already sinking.[8]

---

7 *Deceit, Desire, and the Novel*, 61. "Hate is the reverse image of divine love."
8 Ibid.

"Either a saint or a hero," I said. But this requires further elaboration. Old heroes, Homer's heroes, even Virgil's Aeneas, are gone. They are profoundly out of place in Renaissance Europe.[9] Chivalry novels, *novelas de caballería*, are their last, distant, and rather mediocre relatives. All literary attempts to create a Christian epic that would mean in Renaissance Christian Europe what the old epic meant to their original audiences—and there were many such attempts—failed; even Milton, probably the best and the last, could not fit the Christian story to the epic format. Christ is definitely not the stuff epic heroes are made of. Cervantes's *Don Quixote* is the story of their belated burial. Its explicit aim, as we read in the author's prologue, is "nothing more than to destroy the authority and influence which books of chivalry have in the world and with the public."

Cervantes is particularly sensitive about the fake authority of such books, which claim to be history. The author of the chivalric book pretends to have found a real manuscript describing such chivalric adventures. Cervantes parodies this false pretense, by creating his own Cidi Hamete Benengeli (or "berenjena," for Sancho), whose Arabic manuscript he found in Toledo, and paid a morisco to have it translated to Castilian. So, given the fact that neither the Arabic author nor the morisco translator can be expected to show proper reverence for the truth of history, we should not be surprised if not everything we read really happened.

Cervantes's irony hides a real concern. Humankind faces a real problem given the mimetic character of human desire: the ease with which appearances can be deceiving; the ease with which fiction can be mistaken for reality. And that, Cervantes is convinced, poses a real threat to the survival, not to speak of the salvation, of humankind. That is the problem behind Don Quixote's madness.

---

9 Cesáreo Bandera, *The Sacred Game. The Role of the Sacred in the Genesis of Modern Literary Fiction* (University Park, PA: Pennsylvania State University Press, 1994), 29 ff.

I do not mean to say that Cervantes blamed such a silly pretense to be history for driving a naïve Alonso Quijano into madness. But it was, nevertheless, the power of the poetic fiction itself; the powerful attraction of the desire to which poetic imagination gives form and expression. The desire itself is the bait. The poet does not have to make any silly declaration about the historical reality of what he is writing. If he does it, as authors of books of chivalry do, it only proves he doesn't know what he is doing. He doesn't know that he is playing with fire. And he must share in the responsibility for Don Quixote's madness. He or she cannot throw the first stone. Nobody can throw the first stone. Cervantes learned that in his own novel. His *Don Quixote* is a reflection on the Manchegan knight and on itself as a poetic creation. As Girard also discovered, what separates the great masters from the not so great is this awareness of their own complicity in creating the condition for the Alonso Quijanos of the world to become Quixotic. The first and greatest modern novel is the story of a man who went crazy reading novels. There is a lesson to be learned there. It takes something similar to a religious conversion not to fall for the *mensonge romantique*, "the romantic lie."

"The romantic lie" is anti-Christian, in spite of the fact that it became historically possible because of Christ. Let me explain. The romantic lie is a form of hero worship in a world in which the old heroes have become utterly irrelevant; there is no longer anything sacred about them. *Amadís* is the shining cover-up of a horrible emptiness. It is a lie; there is no truth behind it. But we know that because such knowledge is an integral part of the Christian revelation. Homer's original audience never saw Ulysses or Achilles as anything exemplary, something to be imitated. The old heroes carried the mark of the old sacred, the terrifying, hair-raising, overpowering violence of the old sacred. The very thought of becoming a second Achilles or a second Ulysses would have sent shivers down the spine of an old sacred worshipper. We will find that out when we study Lucretius. Christ transforms the old sacred into the holy. With Christ the terror is gone. In consequence, the old sacred rituals were set on their way to becoming the fascinating poetic fiction of today. "Art is magic delivered from the lie of being truth," said Theodor Adorno.[10] I would modify this statement: Art is magic delivered from its anxious, terrified need of hiding the truth, of substituting for an unspeakable truth.

We, belated heirs to Cervantes or Shakespeare, know nothing about that. We have forgotten the old terror. But Cervantes and Shakespeare still remembered. Even Voltaire, as we will also see, still remembered "the [old] heinous monsters the trembling world made into gods."

It was Christ, the Messiah, the Son of the Living God, who was the first one ever to say such an extraordinary thing: "Imitate me, do as I do." A god inviting a human being to be god-like. What could that possibly mean in the domain of the old sacred other than a terrifying invitation to become the scapegoat, the sacrificial victim? To become, that is, the one to be blamed, the carrier of that which is unbearable, *horrendus*, which must be expelled, killed, for the rest to be able to function.

Only Christ could do that, could offer such an invitation, "follow me," because he is the one who has already triumphed over the horror of the old sacred, the sacred fear of death. Which also means that he has triumphed over the power of the crowd. His invitation is not addressed to the crowd, but to each and every human individual, to every single member of the crowd. "Imitate me in order to be yourself." Christ is a crowd breaker: "Look inside yourself"—he said—"before you throw the first stone." Which also means that if you want to hear his voice you must listen within yourself: "harden not your heart" (Hebrews 3:15). When you follow Christ you discover, not only Christ, but yourself. Because Christ is the only model, the only mediator of your desire, who will not become

10 See Cesáreo Bandera, *A Refuge of Lies. Reflections on Faith and Fiction* (East Lansing, MI: Michigan State University Press, 2013), 132 ff.

your rival, your enemy. Therefore, it is either the old sacred, the defeated old sacred, now living "romantically" under the cover of artistic or poetic creation, or Christ. That is what the great masters discovered; and that is what Girard learned from them. What he said about the theater can be extended to cover any form of poetic fiction, first of all, the modern novel.

> At their most radical and pessimistic, all great playwrights, including Molière and Racine, have more affinity for the enemies of the theater than for its pious friends. . . . Great theater has never flourished except in periods when it was distrusted and ostracized.[11]

Calderón, the greatest playwright of the Spanish Golden Age, concurs: "There is no better window on the stage than the one every man brings with himself; for when he looks on, what he sees on the stage is his own shame in the nude."[12] The desire that brings a man to the theater is of the same kind as the "impertinent curiosity" portrayed in Cervantes's story at the inn. If that is so, what should we think of the poet who fabricated the farce for the stage, the one who profits from such a desire?

In the beginning was mimetic desire. In its most radical sense, what this means is that there is nothing that can be called human prior to mimetic desire. Humanity begins at that point where everything rests on the fact that human individuals depend on other human individuals in a unique and totally unprecedented degree, that is to say, where everything is ultimately a question of interindividual relationship. Everything is at stake in the way we relate to one another. We could say that humanity is not an essence but a relationship. What I am, what I am destined to be, rests entirely on how I relate to my neighbor, my *proximus*; and Christ is the model, the mediator.

The existential intensity of our most personal desires is not a measure of their autonomy or of our individual independence.

11 René Girard, *A Theater of Envy. William Shakespeare* (New York, Oxford: Oxford University Press, 1991), 159.

12 *Life Is a Dream*, act 2, sc. 2.

It could be the very opposite, as is the case with Don Quixote. His madness testifies to his complete dependence on his model Amadís. If, additionally, this dependence on the model is itself inherently ambivalent—unbounded admiration easily turns into rivalry—then what we see at the very beginning of humanity is a radically unstable and violent situation. Which is exactly what Cervantes sees behind Don Quixote's madness.

In primitive societies the sacred character of madness was frequently associated with some sort of primeval chaos, out of which the world was made. This old idea is reflected to some extent in the way Cervantes describes Cardenio's madness and behavior in the mountains.[13] But Cervantes goes beyond that to define the primeval chaos as a state of violence in which all differences between the human contenders disappear, and it becomes impossible to differentiate reality from fiction.

But now, thanks to Christ, free from the ever present menace of the old sacred, it becomes possible to contemplate and analyze in a perfectly rational way the problem of origins, the violent beginning as best as scientific rationality can determine. Sacred terror, the terror of the sacred, had made such a scientific analysis impossible. The first and urgent task of any scientific endeavor was to keep the mind unperturbed, as Epicurus would say.

To the follower of Christ, on the other hand, the question of origins is a quest for understanding that from which Christ has saved humankind: faith seeking understanding, not in order to believe, but because we believe. That is ultimately what led Girard from the study of the great literary masters to the anthropology of religion; from *Deceit, Desire and the Novel* to *Violence and the Sacred.*

---

13 See "Don Quixote's Madness and Modernity," in Cesáreo Bandera, *The Humble Story of Don Quixote. Reflections on the Birth of the Modern Novel* (Washington, DC: The Catholic University of America Press, 2006), chapter 4.

CHAPTER 2

From Don Quixote's Madness to Sacrificial Violence

THIS IS WHAT WE FIND ON THE VERY FIRST PAGE OF *VIOlence and the Sacred*: "[Ritual] sacrifice resembles criminal violence . . . there is, inversely, hardly any form of violence that cannot be described in terms of sacrifice."

Girardians are familiar with this transition from the study of the modern novel to the study of the violent origin of humanity and the discovery of the scapegoat mechanism. But has anybody noticed a surprisingly similar transition in Cervantes from *Don Quixote* to the primitive and sacrificial violence described on the very first page of the *Persiles*, Cervantes's last novel, the successor to *Don Quixote*, published posthumously, in 1617? Before he had even finished the *Quixote*, he announced that he was finishing the book that would follow *Don Quixote*, the book that he thought was going to be his *magnum opus*.

In his dedication of the Second Part of the *Quixote* to the Duke of Lemos, he also offered to the Duke *Los Trabajos de Persiles y Sigismunda* (*The Trials of Persiles and Sigismunda*), "which [he says] will be either the worst or the best ever written in our language, I mean among those for entertainment; in fact, I regret saying the worst, because in the opinion of my friends it will reach the highest level of goodness." It is done in the style of a group of Hellenistic novels, which became popular again during the Renaissance. "It dares to compete with Heliodorus," said Cervantes. Fourth-century Heliodorus was the author of *Theagenes and Cariclea: An Aethiopian Story*. The *Persiles* has been called, quite appropriately, a "Christian romance."[1] It is Cervantes's Christian response

1 Alban Forcione, *Cervantes' Christian Romance: A Study of 'Persiles y Sigismunda'* (Princeton, NJ: Princeton University Press, 1972).

to the violence of a world dominated by endless rivalries fed by the violent reciprocity of mimetic antagonists.

It emerges from the same profound reflection that sustains and gives meaning to *Don Quixote*. Stylistically, it appears to be the very opposite. It has baffled the critics, and they are right, if you remain on the surface. This is not the place for such a discussion. What I am saying is that we do not fully understand what Cervantes saw in the universal story of Don Quixote if we do not see its profound connection with the *Persiles*.

The same thing can be said of Girard's interest in the anthropology of religious origins following his profound reflection on the modern novel, and the *Quixote* in particular. It is no accident that the very first thing that both Cervantes and Girard contemplate, beyond their understanding of literary fiction, is the question of violence at the origin. In the case of Cervantes this happens in the most literal sense: the very first sound on the very first line in the *Persiles* is the terrible and frightening roaring of a primitive voice, that of "barbarian Corsicurbo" speaking into the opening of an underground dungeon, "more like a tomb for many living bodies," one of which is that of Persiles, a captive of primitives still living in the stone age, and destined to be sacrificed to one of their deities. I believe that what led Girard to the anthropological study of human sacrifice at the very origin of religion is intimately related to what Cervantes heard beyond "the terrible roaring of Corsicurbo's primitive voice" asking for the human victim who is about to be sacrificed.

Cervantes called it "A Northern Story," because that is where it begins. It is the story of a journey, or rather, *the* journey, the human journey. Its destination is Rome. For Cervantes it couldn't be anywhere else. And it begins at the beginning, the North, the Septentrion, a cold, frigid cold, that is to say, loveless, desolate, violent region, a hellish place, reminiscent of the frozen immobility of Satan at the center of Hell, infinitely removed from *l'amor che move il sole e l'altre stelle.* Dante called it *vedovo sito* (*Purgatorio* 1:26): widowed, that is, sad, lonely. It is deprived of the light coming from the stars that form the Southern Cross, a light that "gladdens" the southern sky.

Persiles and Sigismunda are held captives in such a terrible place. That is where their human journey begins. Their destination is Rome, the historical center of Christianity. They are of royal blood, and have been promised in marriage. Their union will take place when they reach their destination and are further instructed in the Christian faith. While travelling, they hide their identity under the assumed names of Periandro and Auristela, posing as brother and sister. In other words, in the fairly obvious symbolism of the novel, what is at stake here is not only their survival and their Christianity, but their personal relationship as well. Will their loving relationship survive? The inner obstacles can be just as deadly as the outer ones.

A dispute arose among the barbarians about who owned the beautiful couple, which quickly became a chaotic mayhem and generalized butchery extending all around the terrified group of captives that included Periandro and Auristela.

The way Cervantes describes this primitive violence merits attention:

> All flew to arms, and soon, incited by vengeance and rage, the arrows flew on all sides, dealing death far and wide. When the arrows were spent, as hands and poignards did not fail, they fell upon each other without respect of kindred. The son respected not the father nor the brother his brother, and as among them were many enemies who owed one another grudges for former injuries, they fell to work tearing to pieces with their nails, and cutting with their knives, without anyone attempting to restore peace.[2]

Notice the main features of the violence: they are all possessed by "vengeance and rage" as if by madness; all social or

---

2 Miguel de Cervantes, *The Trials of Persiles and Sigismunda.* Translator L. D. S. (1853). Digireads, 2014.

natural differences are destroyed: son against father, brother against brother; it involves anybody who ever had a grudge against anybody, in other words, everybody; and it is endless: when their primitive arms are spent, "they fell to work tearing to pieces with their nails," and nobody makes any "attempt to restore peace." There is nothing but violence feeding on itself endlessly for as long as there is any pair of rivals standing. Of itself it can only lead to the complete destruction of the group. If this was, as we must assume, "the primeval violence" mentioned in the *Quixote*, only God could save violent humanity from itself. There is no awareness of any other possibility for the survival of the group. Just like Don Quixote's madness, or Shakespeare's Lady Macbeth's disease, it can only be cured by the grace of God. In the Christian faith there is only one scapegoat, one victim, capable of saving humanity, and that is Christ. There can be no purely human scapegoat to do what Christ did, according to the faith.

As I just said, and as I pointed out in *Mímesis conflictiva*, the obstacles the two lovers must overcome are not only physical, but they are also spiritual, emerging from their own mutual relationship. In the end, perhaps the most difficult obstacle will turn out to be the very absence of obstacles. Once they have reached their destination, Rome, there is nothing preventing their union, for which they have yearned all along. The fulfillment of their saintly desire is within easy reach.

But the devil has one last trick. Sigismunda becomes sick after drinking a potion prepared by a sorceress intent on preventing the marriage. She is near death, but finally recovers. It was the last obstacle, apparently. All of a sudden, convalescent Sigismunda feels the powerful attraction of the spirit in her role as Auristela, sister of Periandro. She feels the attraction of her victorious persona. She loves her own fiction. They have maintained their perfect, chaste, and loving relationship for so long through so many perils: why change? She would love to give herself entirely to God. There is only one obstacle. She gave her word and promise to him, her beloved Persiles.

Only he can give her back her freedom in order to go directly to God. Sigismunda pleads with him. She is not giving him up for another man, but for God, she says.

Persiles is devastated. He cannot believe what he is hearing. Without saying a word, he runs away in anguish and tears. Once alone, he turns over Sigismunda's words in his mind. And, in his mind, he responds to her. This is basically what he says: if you think that gaining access to Heaven is strictly something between you and God, and nobody else's concern, I want you to know that your decision will destroy me. I cannot be myself without you, and you know it. You gave me your word, I return it to you, if you need to be free. I renounce my freedom for your sake. But you cannot do this without sin.

It is at this point that Cervantes reflects on how close good and evil can be:

> Parece que el bien y el mal distan tan poco el uno del otro, que son como dos lineas concurrentes, que, aunque parten de apartados y diferentes principios, acaban en un punto.[3]

"It seems that good and evil are as close to each other as two converging lines are, which, though starting at separate and different beginnings, end at one single point." For a moment it looks like the sorceress's potion has done its job. In the end, by God's mercy, the diabolical spell is broken, Sigismunda comes to her senses, and they will get married.

The sorceress's presence in the narrative is a purely rhetorical device. Perhaps it is a way to suggest the diabolical character of the obstacle that all of a sudden threatens to derail the original Christian plan for the benefit of the two lovers. Ultimately, what is really at stake in Cervantes's "Christian romance," this symbolical journey of humanity from the violence of the origin to the historical presence of Christ in Rome, is the quality of the relationship between individual

---

3 Miguel de Cervantes, *Obras Completas*, ed. Rodolfo Schevill and Adolfo Bonilla, 2:277.

human beings, the amazing instability of the will, of human desire, the ease with which good intention ends up in the service of evil, as we heard in Cardenio's sonnet. That is always at the center of Cervantes's reflection on what lies behind Don Quixote's madness.

If Sigismunda had persisted in her sudden desire to break the original promise of marriage and "given herself directly to God," the story of Persiles and Sigismunda would have been just another typically frustrated and possibly tragic love story like those of Marcela and Grisóstomo, Cardenio and Luscinda, or that of the *Curioso impertinente.* Nothing but God's mercy prevented the frustration or the tragedy, as was also the case with Don Quixote.

Good and evil converging toward a single point: something good, even admirable, exemplary, ending up aiding and abetting, making it possible for something bad to develop, which can destroy the person. In Spanish Golden Age literature this archetypal situation, very often, takes the form of jealousy, *celos*. *Celos* are "the greatest monster in the world," which is actually the title of one of Calderón's best-known plays. And *celos* are the terrible force moving the husbands in Calderón's famous "honor" plays to murder their perfectly innocent wives. *El médico de su honra* (The Physician of His Own Honor) is perhaps the most terrible.

The way Cervantes deals with jealousy in the *Persiles* deserves special attention. At a certain point in the long narrative, Auristela (i.e. Sigismunda in her role as sister of Periandro/Persiles), who has been separated from "her brother" Periandro for several months, not knowing where he might be, hears from the captain of the ship in which she and other fugitive captives are sailing, that Periandro had participated in some sort of Olympic games, winning every prize and attracting the attention of beautiful Sinforosa, daughter of king Policarpo, the organizer of the games. All of a sudden, Auristela feels the terrible sting of jealousy. The narrator laments the presence of the disease:

> O mighty power of jealousy! O disease, that grips the soul in such a way, that can only be uprooted with life itself! Ah! beautiful Auristela, stay and reflect before you allow yourself to become a prey to this cruel suffering! But who can restrain thought within bounds, which is so light and subtle, that bodiless it passes through stone walls, enters human bosoms, and penetrates the deepest recesses of the soul? At that very moment, the wind rose all at once with such fury, that [the captain] was forced to leave Auristela . . . and call to his sailors to mind the sails, reef and secure them. All hands hastened to the work. The ship began to fly before the wind, over a tremendous sea. . . . At this point the author of this story leaves the first volume and passes to the second, wherein things will be related which although they do not surpass truth, yet go beyond what one could conceive, since they could scarcely enter into the most lively and expansive imagination.[4]

We turn the page and come to Chapter I of the Second Volume:

> Wherein it is related how the Ship was turned upside down, with all that were in it.

And this is how this chapter begins:

> It would seem as though the author of this history was more of a lover than an historian; for nearly the whole of the first chapter of his Second Book is spent in a definition of jealousies, caused by that which was shown by Auristela. . . . But, as it appears to me to be prolix, I shall omit it in this translation, and come to the facts, which were as follows:—The wind changing, and the clouds gathering, night came on very dark and gloomy, and the thunder sending forth the lightning as messenger, disturbed and bewildered the mariners. Then began the tempest with a fury that no power or skill could withstand, for it came all at once and without warning.
>
> The fury of the tempest was such that it turned the ship upside down, burying the topmasts in the depths of

4 *Persiles*, Book II, c. 1, digireads, 2014.

> ocean, and leaving its keel turned up to the skies, making it a tomb for all who were within it. "Goodby to all the chaste thoughts of Auristela! goodby to all her pious intentions! Rest in peace, honoured and holy one; no other mausoleum, no other monument can thou expect, except a few poor frail planks. . . . " Such were the words of the author of this most remarkable and pitiful history, in consequence of the upsetting of the ship, and the certain death of all who were in it; and what more he says, will be seen in the following chapter.[5]

The following chapter "narrates a strange event." At this point the nineteenth-century English translator of Cervantes's work gives up, obviously in complete disbelief of what he is reading. He probably thought he was doing Cervantes a favor, by changing the text and softening what appears to be absurd. I must beg the reader's indulgence to bear with me a little longer and see where all this strangeness is leading. It helps when you read Cervantes within a Girardian context. This is as literally close as I can get to Cervantes's text:

> It seems that the turning of the ship upside down also turned, or rather perturbed, the mind of the author of this story, because he wrote four or five beginnings to this second chapter, as if in doubt of what the end would be. In the end, he decided to say that good fortune and misfortune come usually so together that there is perhaps no way to separate them; that suffering and pleasure are so paired that it is silly for the sad one to despair or the happy one not to worry at all, as this strange event easily demonstrates. The ship buried itself in the water, as we have said; the dead bodies buried without a soil [*enterrados* without *tierra*]; *all hopes were dissolved; all remedies impossible; but merciful heaven, which from far way back is in the habit of remedying our misfortunes* [my emphasis], ordered for the ship to be carried little by little by the waves which were already calm at the seashore, to a beach so peaceful and tame that it could serve as a perfectly secure harbor.[6]

5 Ibid., Book II, c. 1.
6 Ibid., Book II, c. 2.

"All hopes were dissolved; all remedies impossible." The devastating violence of the storm is triggered and driven by jealousy, or, in Girardian terms, by human hypermimetic desire. And there is nothing human that can put a stop to it. There is not the slightest indication that such violence entirely on its own could evolve blindly, at random, into something like the scapegoat mechanism. The idea that violence could create its own saving god would probably sound incredibly far-fetched to Cervantes, except through Christ, the only saving victim conceivable to a Christian man like Cervantes.

As it turns out, the ship has just been gently laid down within sight of king Policarpo's city, where a miraculously revived Auristela and the rest of her companions will find Periandro and, of course, Sinforosa, Policarpo's younger daughter, the one who had unknowingly been the cause of Auristela's jealousy. She was indeed in love with Periandro, as she confided to Auristela, thinking she was talking to his sister.

But I am not trying to write a critical analysis of the *Persiles*. I am comparing Girard's transition from his literary analysis of the *Quixote* and the other masters of the modern novel to his anthropological interest in sacrificial violence, with Cervantes's own transition from the *Quixote* to something apparently so different in style and purpose as the *Persiles*.

We have already noticed that they both see at the beginning a state of chaotic violence without an end because of its mimetically self-feeding character. It is this inherent mimetism of the human, violently enhanced, that makes it ultimately impossible clearly to differentiate between opposites: fiction and reality, fortune and misfortune, suffering and happiness, love and hate. And Cervantes insists that such a condition is ultimately fatal; it cannot generate its own way out. It is radically in need of the divine: *los piadosos cielos que de muy atrás toman la corriente de remediar nuestras desventuras* (merciful heaven which from far way back is in the habit of remedying our misfortunes). We would not be here if "merciful heaven" had not remedied our self-destructive origin. There would have been no human origin without it.

Girard, on the other hand, believed that mimetism itself, which is the cause of the self-feeding expansion of human violence, is also the reason why it could blindly, at random, find its own solution in the violent formation of the scapegoat mechanism. Because human violence attracts human violence in direct proportion to its size, the bigger the violence the stronger its attraction, the general violence of all against all could snowball and become the violence of all against one. At least for the moment, as soon as all turn against the one and kill it, a *de facto* unanimity has been created, and peace, for the moment, is restored. What Girard said is that there would be a tendency to repeat this peaceful moment, because we may assume that human beings are naturally inclined to live in peace. Eventually the killing of the one, which holds the key to desirable peace, and, therefore, the key to everything made possible by the peace (which is everything), repeated over thousands of years, would become institutionalized, ritualized, made sacred.

This is an oversimplification, of course, but enough to suggest that the old sacred in the Girard of *Violence and the Sacred* was man-made; basically human violence deified, transcendentalized, if you will. Eventually the true sacred, God the Father, would send his only Son, Jesus Christ the Lord, to rescue humanity from its own violence. For our salvation, *propter nostram salutem*, he accepted being the victim in a process which was alien to him; a Satanic process, that is to say, based on a lie. He, the Messiah, had to embody and follow a process which humans could recognize, in order to show to them its arbitrariness, its injustice; for it was all based on a false accusation; the victim was innocent. In Christ all victims were innocent, at least no more guilty than anybody else. They were killed without cause. Christ defeated Satan because his innocence, the innocence of the victim, prevailed, could not be suppressed. He was the truth, the light, that shone in the darkness and the darkness did not overcome it (John 1:1–5).

In sharp contrast, there is nothing in Cervantes that could even remotely suggest that human beings could create their own god, their own sacred process; that they could survive on their own. I am sure he would have been immensely impressed, as so many of us were, by Girard's discovery of the scapegoat mechanism. Such a discovery could only confirm in a definitive way what Christians had always believed: Christ was there from the beginning, or in Cervantes's own words, again: "merciful heaven which from far way back [was] in the habit of remedying our misfortunes."

Can they both be right? Could human beings create a god of their own, capable of preventing their self-destruction, capable of sustaining for thousands of years complex civilizations? Could Satan, human violence deified, restrain, even expel, Satan? That is the real question. Could Satan be the "the stone that the builders rejected, [which] has become the cornerstone"? Could humanity survive without Christ? Where was Christ for thousands of years while human beings were sacrificing millions of their own to Satan in order to survive? These are not idle questions. Girard was well aware of them:

> Since the dawn of humanity, millions of innocent victims have been killed in this way in order to enable their fellow humans to live together, or at least not to destroy one another. This is the implacable logic of the sacred, which myths dissimulate less and less as humans become increasingly self-aware. The decisive point in this evolution is Christian revelation, a kind of divine expiation in which God through his Son could be seen as asking for forgiveness from humans for having revealed the mechanisms of their violence so late.[7]

Should we forgive God the Father for being tardy? This absurd, yet inevitable, question should teach us something about Girard. He was never a prisoner of his own theory. He knew self-satire. He knew how to stand back and accept his

---

7 *Battling to the End*, ix.

own theory's limitations. The Christian solution was always a matter of inner personal discovery and conversion.

Nevertheless, this saintly man, infinitely trusting in God's providence, forever ready and willing to put everything in God's hand, is also the anthropologist who said he could demonstrate the transition from animal to man without even mentioning God the Father or his only Son, Jesus the Christ. But he knew the truth hiding in the silence. He could do it without mentioning the Christian Trinity, but not without its invisible help, not without the formidable influence of the Christian revelation. The ironic smile on the face of this saintly man when he called his book "atheistic," says it all.

Girard was right. The rationality of the scapegoat mechanism is clearly supported by the Gospel text. The scapegoat mechanism makes sense in the light of the Gospel text, and *vice versa*. But to make sense in a purely rational way is one thing; to transition from the old mechanism to the new one with Christ at the center, is quite another, and far more important. A rational understanding of the old is one thing; being liberated from the old by the new is an entirely different matter. Virgil is the key. As we will see, he knew everything about the old sacrificial mechanism, but that only deepened his pessimism. It was knowledge without hope. We might say he was a Cervantes without Christ. Christ did not bring a new rational knowledge; he simply added hope to the old one when he became the victim. The Crucified made the old knowledge fruitful, liberating.

CHAPTER 3
Christ and the Scapegoat Mechanism

IT HAS BEEN SAID THAT "THE FOX KNOWS MANY THINGS, but the hedgehog knows only one big thing. The 'one big thing' that Girard knows has a name: the scapegoat."[1] That is to say, the human violence that kills the one that saves the many, which in Girardian anthropology accounts for the transition from animal to human as well as for the archaic, man-made, sacred. Everything begins with the scapegoat.

But there is another big thing, the Christian big thing, Christ, which cannot be avoided when you are talking about the sacrificial killing of the victim, the one that must be given up for the sake of many. If Girard knows only one big thing at the beginning of things human, so does Saint Paul, as he says in his *Letter to the Corinthians*: "The only knowledge I claimed to have was about Jesus, and only about him as the crucified Christ . . . The hidden wisdom of God which we teach in our mysteries is the wisdom of God predestined to be for our glory before the ages began" (1 Cor. 2:2–9).

Girard could say the same thing, because Girard's Christ, the crucified, reveals *Things Hidden since the Foundation of the World*, the biblical quotation furnishing the title of his major book on Christianity. But what Girard's anthropological Christ reveals as the origin or the beginning of humanity is not "the wisdom of God predestined to be for our glory," but Satan's lie (human violence sacralized) which blames the victim for the horrible violence of the scapegoat or victimizing mechanism:

---

1 René Girard, *Evolution and Conversion: dialogues on the origins of culture* (London: Bloomsbury, 2017), 1.

> The Passion is presented as a blatant piece of injustice. Far from taking the collective violence upon itself, the text places it squarely on those who are responsible for it.[2]

On a human level, it was indeed an injustice. They killed Christ without cause. He had committed no crime. But is that the Christian way to look at it? Christ himself rebuked Peter when he became scandalized by Jesus's announcement of the Passion. "Get behind me, Satan. Your way is men's way, not God's." That is indeed severe. Peter's way, men's way, is Satan's way. Peter will learn, though; he will enjoin the new Christians "to count the patient long suffering of Christ as salvation. [As] also our beloved brother Paul wrote to you, according to the wisdom given to him" (2 Peter 3:15).

This is definitely not the passion presented as "just plain murder," "a scapegoat killed to pacify a murderous crowd." Girard might argue that he is doing anthropology, not theology. But the truth ultimately can only be one, as Girard himself firmly believed. Besides, why is Peter an image of Satan in front of Jesus, a scandal, an obstacle on Jesus's path? Satan, we must remember, has no interest whatsoever in saving humanity from its own violence. Satan, through whom envy entered the world (Wisdom 2:24) has only one desire: to block Jesus's path to salvation, to prevent humanity from becoming Jesus-like, that is to say, Christian. Just like the bad prostitute in the judgement of Solomon (as Girard brilliantly explained): she was willing to accept the destruction of the child, anything to prevent the rival from getting the child. This being the case, can we trust Satan, or, if you will, human violence magnified beyond control, to provide the means for humanity to survive? Or, to put it differently, can Girard's Christless scapegoat do the job for the benefit of humanity, without help from the Crucified, "the hidden wisdom of God before the ages"? Can human science explain the beginning, the "foundation of the world," without help from revealed faith? How do you bring these two things together?

---

2 Girard, *Things Hidden*, 170.

On second thought, this is probably the wrong question. These two things are already together, the rationally defined scapegoat mechanism and Christ crucified. Girard saw that. No matter how you look at it, it is sacrifice on all sides. That was, once again, his monumental discovery. But is it the horror of what we do to the victim that should hold our scandalized attention? If we have been doing it for tens or even hundreds of thousands of years, we may not even understand what the scandal is all about. Here is an example of what I mean, taken from Fray Bernardino de Sahagún's *Historia General de la Nueva España* (that is, Aztec civilization before the arrival of the Spaniards).

In the second book he deals with "feasts and sacrifices."

> During the first of these festivities . . . the first month of the year . . . they killed many children, sacrificing them in many places on the peak of mountains, taking out their hearts in honor of the gods of the rain to get them to send abundant rain. The children they killed were dressed up as they carried them to their sacrifice on platforms adorned with feathers and flowers, on their shoulders. They went singing and dancing up front. As they took them to be killed, if the children cried and shed many tears, those who carried them were very pleased, because they took it as a good sign that they would have abundant water that year.[3]

Fray Bernardino is overcome by the unspeakable horror of the situation:

> I do not believe there can be a heart so hardened that, upon hearing of a cruelty so inhuman, and more than bestial and satanic, as the one described above, would not be moved to tears and feel shaken and horrified. It is indeed horrible and lamentable to see our human nature degraded to such low level and shame as to see parents persuaded by the devil to kill and eat their children (without thinking they were doing anything wrong), rather believing they were doing a great service to their gods.

3 Mexico, 1829. Beginning of the 2nd Book. My translation.

> The blame for such a cruel blindness as was executed on those unfortunate children, should not be laid so much on the cruelty of those parents, who actually felt the pain in their hearts and shed tears, but rather on the most cruel hatred of our most ancient enemy Satan, who, with most malicious cunning, persuaded them to do such an infernal thing. Oh, Lord, bring your justice to bear on this cruel enemy, which does and wishes to do so much damage to us! Take from him, Lord, the power to do damage.[4]

It is not only the horror of what they did to their own children. It is what they did to themselves. It is the system of which they are prisoners; it is, indeed, Satan, the absence of hope, the blindness: not just the death of the body, but of the soul as well:

> Do not fear those who kill the body but cannot kill the soul; rather, fear the one who can destroy both soul and body in hell. (Matt. 10:28)

It does not make any sense here to speak of blaming the victim. They are not accusing the children of anything. It is their god. It is Satan at the heart of their belief system. Anticipating the words of Lucretius, which we will examine in due course, *tantum potuit religio suadere malorum* "to such extremes of evil can human beings be persuaded by religion."

Christians believe that the crucified is the ultimate expression of a love that surpasses human understanding, but not irrational, not absurd. After all, God created us and made us different, each one of us, from any other creature; we carry God's image. But in Girard's theory, God has nothing to do, directly, with the emergence of the human out of the proto-human. As far as God's creativity is concerned, there is nothing special about humans. In Girard's anthropology, the idea of a divine love for humanity is "beyond understanding"; it is absurd, unmotivated, it does not make sense. It is not what they do to him that should hold our attention, but, once again, who he is. The gospel text of the synoptics is

4 Fray Bernardino de Sahagún, *Historia General de la Nueva España*, 100.

perfectly clear about it. Jesus wants to make sure the disciples understand who he is, before announcing to them the events of the Passion, Death and Resurrection:

> But who do you say that I am? Simon Peter replied, "You are the Christ, the Son of the living God." And Jesus answered him, "Blessed are you, Simon Bar-Jona! For flesh and blood has not revealed this to you, but my Father who is in heaven. And I tell you, you are Peter, and on this rock I will build my church, and the powers of death shall not prevail against it. I will give you the keys of the kingdom of heaven, and whatever you bind on earth shall be bound in heaven, and whatever you lose on earth shall be loosed in heaven." Then he strictly charged the disciples to tell no one that he was the Christ. From that time Jesus began to show his disciples that he must go to Jerusalem and suffer many things from the elders and chief priests and scribes, and be killed, and on the third day be raised. And Peter took him and began to rebuke him, saying, "God forbid, Lord! This shall never happen to you." But he turned and said to Peter, "Get behind me, Satan! You are a hindrance to me; for you are not on the side of God, but of men." (Matt. 16:15–23, Revised Standard Version)[5]

Does that mean that *Violence and the Sacred* was a mistake? We asked this question earlier in connection with the "transition from animal to man." And the answer, of course, is still no. The discovery of the scapegoat mechanism is an anthropological landmark. But, in addition to being such a scientific landmark, it also reveals in purely human terms the very structure of the Christian event, the coming of the Son of God to liberate humanity from its own violence. Same structure; two entirely different meanings. We have just discovered something that seems impossible: God's action in human history and Satan's action in human history are structurally identical. How can that be? We cannot hide the problem simply by saying that we are doing science and not theology. And it is certainly not an "attempt to demonstrate the

---

5 See also Mark 8:27–33, and Luke 9:18–22.

undemonstrable, the scientific truth of our religious faith."[6]

It is a question of hierarchy, a question that cannot be avoided: which of the two has pride of place? Which comes first? If we were trying "to demonstrate the scientific truth of our religious faith," we would be placing science above theology, examining God's action with a strictly human instrument. Of course, we do not want to do that. But we still have the hierarchical problem. A problem which only has one possible Christian answer: given the fact that whatever we know about God's action has been revealed by God, "not by the flesh," God's action must come first. God's action is already the solution to the problem of human violence, which, scientifically speaking, is solved by the scapegoat mechanism, the sacrifice of the human victim. Therefore, for the Christian believer, in the beginning, before "all ages," was the Crucified. In Him rests both the revelation of the problem, its definition, we might say, and its solution. If we change the order of precedence, we will not see the scapegoat victim as the work of God, but as a Satanic problem, which will be solved *a posteriori* by the late arrival of the Son of God (to which Girard's self-satire added God's apology for being tardy).

The hidden wisdom of God will be revealed at some point in the history of humanity. But that does not mean that the solution remains inactive "from before the ages," in anticipation of the revelation. Quite the contrary, as we can see in the parable of the yeast in the flour (Matt. 13:33).

In other words, when you are talking about the origin and the destiny of humanity, you are doing theology, whether you mean to or not. You are taking a position regarding the existence of God and his action or inaction in human history. The scientific rationality of the scapegoat mechanism knows nothing about that. It is an extraordinary achievement, because it can explain and make sense of an enormous body of mythical material in a way both incredibly simple

6 René Girard, *I See Satan Fall like Lightning*. Translated with a Foreword by James G. Williams (Orbis Books, 2001), 3.

and profound. And, as Girard was the first one to acknowledge, he could not have done it without the Judeo-Christian inspiration. But Christianity is not a myth, as he also said. And that changes everything. What was an extraordinarily revealing instrument when dealing with mythical material is not enough when we are reading Biblical text.

The wisdom of God, incarnate in the Crucified, of which Saint Paul speaks, is a mystery, but a Christian mystery; it is meant to be revealed. And it will be revealed "for our Glory," for our salvation. I believe these two things must go together, the revelation of that which was hidden, and our salvation. Which is exactly the opposite of what happens with the old sacred truth, as we will see in Virgil. For the Roman, "truth is wrapped in darkness," and is not meant to be revealed. Its revelation, such is the terror it inspires, would bring about an apocalyptic catastrophe, something before which the human mind would disintegrate. Such was the hold in which the forbidden sacred kept humanity.

Christ enters with an entirely new message: do not be afraid! Having conquered the ancestral sacred fear, something like Girard's strictly rational, scientific analysis becomes possible. Such analysis is not essential to maintain the new freedom from sacred fear, although it may be a welcome exercise. Girard knew this better than anybody I can think of. And yet, he insisted for a long time that what made it increasingly difficult for the mechanism to function properly was knowledge of the human violence that drives it. *Not Christ, but knowledge.* So we ended up with this characteristically Girardian situation of which we have been talking: Christ brought the knowledge that made it possible to talk about violence and the sacred, including the very "transition from animal to man," without even mentioning Christ or God the Father. Furthermore, since everything was made possible by Christ, the strictly scientific work itself could be considered an *apologia christiana.*

But this kind of silent complicity between Christ and human science does not work *ad majorem Dei gloriam*. It runs counter to the fundamental Christian message, which is one of hope (do not be afraid!); and it bypasses, or moves to the margins, central Christian concerns like the *Lamb of God* or the view of the Incarnation as God's reconciling humanity with Himself, or the immense suffering of Christ in Gethsemane. "For God made him who had no sin to be sin for us" (2 Cor. 5:21). I am not the only Girardian who disagrees with Girard's notion that Christ rejects the violence done to the victim. Father Schwager's disagreement was quite clear from the beginning:

> The sins of all the world were bunched up against the "beloved son" and were unloaded upon him. But he did not cast some sort of universal harm back upon the head of the many evildoers. Instead, he took this collective evil entirely upon himself and transformed it in his own body by his non-violent and forgiving love.... The worst act of violence in the world was not answered with a vengeful counterblow; instead, rivers of forgiving love flowed back.[7]

I think it is even more than that. Answering "the worst act of violence with forgiving love" does not quite rise to the level of the transformation that is happening here. In the words of Bernard Lonergan, a theologian who has been compared to Girard:[8]

> This is why the Son of God became man, suffered, died, and was raised again: because divine wisdom has ordained and divine goodness has willed, not to do away with evils of the human race through power, but to convert those same evils into a supreme good according to the just and mysterious law of the cross.... Sin and death in Adam are succeeded by resurrection and grace in Christ.... This succession is not a jump to something new but the transformation of death itself.[9]

7 Raymund Schwager, SJ, *Must There Be Scapegoats? Violence and Redemption in the Bible* (New York: Crossroad, 2000), 212–13.

8 See Grant Kaplan, "New Paths for a Girard/Lonergan Conversation," *Method: Journal of Lonergan Studies*, n.s. 4.1 (2013), 23–38.

9 Bernard Lonergan, *The Redemption*, vol. 9 of *Collected Works* (Toronto: University of Toronto Press, 2018), 197.

"Transformation": that is a key word which is absent from Girard's vocabulary at those crucial moments when it is most needed.[10] He sees the striking "symmetry" between the violent beginning and a Christian love that surpasses understanding. He sees the "tragic irony" of the situation. But there is nothing ironic about the power of God, because there is nothing human which is not ultimately of divine origin beyond the power of sin. There is irony when two opposite things look the same. But all oppositions disappear in the sight of God. There is nothing that a God cannot transform, who can "raise children of Abraham out of stones" (Matt. 3:9).

When the Messiah "before all ages" takes over the victimizing mechanism, the crucifixion, the whole event becomes something glorious, manifesting not only the radiant glory of God but the glory of man as well, "our glory." It is, in a sense, the defining moment for the Son of God, who is also the Son of Man. The curse of humanity, crushed, as it was, by the weight of its own unforgiven guilt, prostrate and trembling upon the ground, suddenly becomes a glorious manifestation of the love of God, who takes upon himself the whole weight of human guilt and lowers himself to the lowest level of his creature, while announcing to everything and everybody: your Savior is here, "do not be afraid."

All of that is lost if we look at the event, the historical passion and death of Jesus, the way Peter did when Jesus first told them. Is that not the way we would also be looking at it if our interpreter were the scientific rationality of mimetic theory, Girard's theory? Of one thing I am sure, however: that was not the way for the saintly man that I knew, for the Christian man who put all his trust in the way "God is taking care of it," not in his own theory, from which he was quite

---

10 In spite of its title, Wolfgang Palaver's book, *Transforming the Sacred into Saintliness. Reflecting on Violence and Religion with René Girard* (Cambridge: Cambridge University Press, 2020), which is an important contribution to Girardian studies, does not address the "transformation" in the sense in which I am trying to use it here, as defined by Lonergan. Only God can transform death into life.

capable of distancing himself. He never lost his noble sense of humor, just like Cervantes, who never lost his compassionate irony, his smile.

He insisted on the scientific character of his theory, which he defended against those who would dismiss it as a product of religious inspiration, "[which does not] even deserve to be refuted." So here we are facing a rather surprising paradox: the "madman" who dares to say that history has a meaning, and it is a religious meaning; the audacious intellectual who affirms "categorically" that biblical literature is superior to any other literature, appears to give it all up, in favor of a scientific discourse which, as a matter of principle, rejects the authority of religious texts. He denies that his theory is in need of any such authority. He appeals to no other authority but reason.

> It suffices to read my books with a minimum of attention to prove the falsity of this accusation. Mimetic theory renders an account of sacrifice and archaic religion in terms of a purely natural force, human hypermimeticism . . . there is not the slightest recourse to transcendence or to anything "irrational."[11]

Human hypermimeticism, "a purely natural force"? The paradigmatic example of human hypermimeticism is Don Quixote's madness. It was Girard who told us this. Hypermimeticism is anything but natural. It is what Girard called "metaphysical desire" exacerbated to a maddening degree; it is a "deviated transcendence," to use another Girardian term. It abandons Christ and turns the human other, whether in the flesh or in fiction (such a difference makes no difference) into a Quixotic Amadís, an idol. Unless God intervenes, hypermimeticism, Quixotic madness, would bring about what Cervantes called "the violence of the primeval discordant confusion," what Girard called original violence, blind, endless, except for the possibility of metamorphosing

11 René Girard, *Sacrifice*, trans. Matthew Patillo and David Dawson (East Lansing, MI: Michigan State University Press, 2011), 33.

into "the scapegoat mechanism." Girard thought the latter was a strictly human phenomenon, in spite of the fact that it is a clear anticipation of the sacrifice of Christ, without which we would not have modern anthropology—a human science that is supposed to stand on its own rationality without appealing to anything transcendental, that is to say, anything beyond rational understanding. If it is not a logical deduction from rationally evident principles, it is not scientifically true. The truth must give up its divinity in order to be scientifically acceptable.

Enter Girard, and we hear his joyful cry: Eureka! That is precisely what Christ did for us. He gave up his divine power, for our sake, and became a human victim like any other human victim since the foundation of the world, so that we could understand what we were doing. That is what the sacrifice of Christ is all about. Contrary to the mythical gods of the archaic sacred, who acquire their divinity, or have it confirmed, through the violence of the victimizing process, Christ is God from the beginning. It is a perfectly rational explanation. It should satisfy the scientific anthropologist as well as the Christian believer, because we are not trying to explain the divinity of Christ. All I'm saying—continues Girard—is that we owe to Christ the very historical possibility of talking about humanity without even mentioning Christ. Christ's revelation is unique; there is no other like it. But the content of the revelation is strictly human and fully rational.

> Human culture is fundamentally and originally religious rather than secondarily and supplementally. This hypermimeticism destroys the dominance patterns in animal societies, but it replaces them, in the paroxysm of violence it releases, with another natural restraint: the scapegoat mechanism, the founding murder that produces ritual sacrifice in its turn. In this genesis, there is not the slightest recourse to transcendence or to anything "irrational."[12]

---

12 *Sacrifice*, 33–34.

Yet how can the "scapegoat mechanism" be totally alien to any form of religious transcendence and still be the Christ's instrument of redemption, unless redemption itself is reduced to mere epistemology, a question of rational understanding?

How can you explain without reference to Christ what you would not know without Christ's revelation? How can we declare our scientific independence from Christ, when Christ, the Messiah, is the only thing we cannot explain scientifically? The fact of the matter is that if Christ is not (at) the center of our explanation, Satan will take his place; Satan will become the cornerstone.

If Christ's sacrifice is the very opposite of the original one, which is the only rational way to look at it, then, obviously, he has nothing to do with the formation of the scapegoat mechanism. He will simply "re-use it" when the time comes.

So great is the distance between the sacrifice of Christ in this sense and archaic sacrifice that a greater one cannot be imagined.[13]

> The Johannine *logos* is foreign to any kind of violence; it is therefore forever expelled, an absent *logos* that never had any direct, determining influence over human cultures. These cultures are based on the Heraclitan *logos*, the *logos* of expulsion, the *logos* of violence, which, *if it is not recognized*, can provide the foundation of culture. The Johannine *logos* discloses the truth of violence by having itself expelled. First and foremost, John's Prologue undoubtedly refers to the Passion.[14]

At the very foundation of Girard's anthropology are these two pillars in reference to which everything in between finds its meaning, yet they are radically inimical to each other: Christ, the *logos* of love, at one end, and the scapegoat mechanism at the other. They repel each other. Where one is the other cannot be. This mutual repulsion, this radical

13 René Girard, *The One by Whom Scandal Comes* (East Lansing, MI: Michigan State University Press, 2014), 41.

14 *Things Hidden*, 271. My emphasis.

incompatibility, is perhaps the most striking feature of Girardian theory. This is what motivated his initial attack on, and extremely harsh criticism of, the *Epistle to the Hebrews*, attributed to Saint Paul, which sees the pre-Christian or Mosaic sacrifice as an imperfect sacrifice, which is, nevertheless, an anticipation, a "shadow," of the perfect one, Christ's sacrifice, in which Christ is both High Priest or sacrificer as well as victim, the only perfect victim for a perfect sacrifice, which fully attains its goal and does not have to be repeated. It took the persistent effort of Father Schwager to soften Girard's rejection of the *Epistle*. He never really accepted the traditional sacrificial reading of Christ's Passion. But at least he accepted that it should be called sacrifice.

But as we saw already, the gospel text of the synoptics is perfectly clear about it. Jesus wants to make sure the disciples understand who he is, before announcing to them the events of the Passion, Death and Resurrection.

Simon Peter exemplifies here the two ways of looking at the person of Jesus: the one revealed to him by the Father, who says "you are the Christ, the Son of the living God," in sharp contrast with "men's way," exemplified by the horrified Peter, deeply scandalized by what he hears about the coming passion and death of Jesus, who is totally innocent of any form of evil. "No, no, my Lord. How can that ever happen to you? That can never be." Peter is scandalized and has become a "piedra de escándalo," a stumbling block, an obstacle, on Jesus's path. He is at that moment the embodiment of "the one by whom scandal comes," Satan. Every time we look at the death of Christ as "just murder," "a scapegoat killed to pacify a murderous crowd," we are treading on Peter's path. We forget what the Father revealed to Peter. We fail to see the only thing that is crucial for a Christian understanding of the event: the fact that the sacrificial victim, the only sacrificial victim, who will save us is the Christ, the Son of the living God. I do not think we can find a clearer warning against the kind of reading of the Passion and death of Jesus, which a purely scientific perspective would inevitably suggest. Nevertheless, let's be clear about it: what the Father reveals in no way denies or ignores the human perspective. Jesus was indeed falsely accused, mocked, tortured, and killed. The danger inherent in that kind of vision is the paralyzing outrage, the scandal against which you trip and fall; the danger is for the human to block the view and the way to the divine.

I did not know at the time how to react to Girard's ironic confidence. But his insistence on the strictly scientific character of his anthropology always struck me as unnecessary and a little devious. I knew the man; I knew he was anything but an atheist. On the other hand, it soon became clear to me that he was far less confident about the "atheism" of *Violence and the Sacred* than he let out. He mused about it frequently: "Maybe I should have written the book about Christianity first." I heard him.

As long as Christ's innocence is conceived of as a rejection, an absolute rejection, of violence, Christ's accusation against humanity is unavoidable, even if he pardons humanity. But Christ is not concerned with violence, human or otherwise, as a physical phenomenon, but in reference to salvation. Jesus is the one who is not governed by the fear of death. He is also the one who told us not to be afraid of those who can only kill the body, but to be afraid of him who can kill both your body and your soul (Matt. 10:28). The real danger in human violence is that it can kill you spiritually *because it is extremely contagious*. It was Girard who told us all about contagion. It is the spirit of violence that kills your soul. The spirit of violence is called scandal. And Christ is absolutely immune to such danger. He cannot be scandalized. He can descend into Hell, or break the doors of Hell because Hell has no power over him. With better justification than Dante's Beatrice, Christ is truly *the only one* who can say in the midst of Hell, *la vostra miseria non mi tange*. Nothing of what makes you miserable, hell-bound, guilty, "touches me." I can embrace it, because such a thing has no power over me. Or rather, I can embrace you, humans, because you cannot contaminate me with your disease, with your *miseria.* It doesn't matter how miserable, how sinful, you are. I can still embrace you. And my embrace will cure you, will clean you, if you accept it. Girard's totally rational and scientific Christ knows nothing about such an embrace.

The old sacred order accused the innocent victims, while Christ accuses the old accusers. We are still within the logic of expulsion and rejection. Satan is "the one who deceives men by making them believe that innocent victims are guilty."[15] But those victims are not innocent, they are like everybody else. They are part of the same persecuting group. The Satanic accusation against the victim is false because the victim is not uniquely guilty. Satan is a liar; the victim is not the only one. But Girard's Christ falls for it. He comes to save an innocent victim, whose innocence is determined by Satan's accusation. He comes to save what Satan condemns, because Satan condemns it. Perfect coordination. It's like a baseball game. Satan pitches the victim, and Christ bats it to Heaven. This is the result of the radical incompatibility between Girard's anthropologically conceived Christ and the scapegoat mechanism through which humanity exists.

We have reached a Girardian impasse. The discovery of the sacrificial origin of humanity, the scapegoat mechanism, is probably the most important anthropological discovery of our time. But I believe that Girard made a mistake by insisting on its scientific self-sufficiency; by imagining that something of such pivotal significance for an understanding of the human story on this planet could stand on its own rationality, without any religious reference. And he compounded the mistake, the self-deception, by imagining that it all happened with divine approval; by imagining a Christian God who stands back and lets Satan be in charge, manage the very survival of the race from the beginning. Occasionally this divine tolerance of evil is presented as God's way of respecting human

15 *The Scapegoat*, 207.

freedom. If that is the case, then human freedom rests entirely on Christ's benevolence. It is a gift from God. Sartre turned this declaration around: if human beings are free, there can be no God. I think Christ is far more believable than Sartre. There is no human freedom without the Crucified. There is no humanity without the Crucified. There is no scientific rationality, no scientific independence without the Crucified. If that is the case, as Girard himself told us repeatedly, whom are we fooling when we say that Christ gave us the possibility of a Christless, an atheistic, anthropology?

In Girard's anthropology the scapegoat mechanism is both what Christianity has in common with all other religions, as well as what makes the Judeo-Christian religious tradition, and especially Christianity, absolutely unique:

> The opposition between the scapegoat concealed in mythology and unconcealed in Judaism and Christianity illuminates not only archaic religions, not only many neglected features of the Gospels, but above all the relationship between the two, the unique truth of the Judeo-Christian tradition. Since all this knowledge comes from the Gospels, the present book can define itself as a defense of our Judaic and Christian tradition, as an *apology* of Christianity rooted in what amounts to a Gospel-inspired breakthrough in the field of social science, not of theology.[16]

But that is precisely the problem: yes, anthropology is one thing, theology another. They are different, but cannot lead to opposite results, or declare irrelevant for one what is fundamental for the other. "I am the truth," said Christ. That is the rock on which the believer builds his faith. That is irrelevant to the scientist, who is only interested in what Christ says, not in who he is. The Lamb of God who takes away the sins of the world, all of a sudden becomes the innocent victim unjustly killed by all of us. Humanity had gotten away with murder for too long. Not anymore.

16 *I See Satan Fall like Lightning*, 3.

The Gospel will reveal the bitter truth. And what about this notion that, through the sacrifice of Christ, God reconciled himself with humanity? How did it happen that the "blatant" evidence of our murder becomes the sign of our redemption? What kind of logic is that? Certainly not the logic of a scientific demonstration. But it is clearly the logic of sacrifice: the transformation of something horrible into something good. The most primitive human sacrifice becomes the eucharistic sacrament of today.

If the human violence that kills Christ does not become in some sense Christ-like, the Eucharistic feast is an empty symbol. If the Logos of love is infinitely distant from human violence, what is this whole business of the incarnation? *Cur deus homo*? Why couldn't God the Father send us a wise old sage instead of a son to be killed in the prime of life, so to speak?

CHAPTER 4

Epistemological Christianity

HAMLET'S "DULL REVENGE"

IF IT IS A QUESTION OF KNOWLEDGE, CAN WE FABRICATE our own sacred? Can we fake it, as Hamlet tried to do? I have no problem accepting the epistemological revelation that Girard sees in the Gospel text. I fully share Girard's sense of awe and amazement at the Gospel text in the context of his anthropology:

> The Passion accounts reveal a phenomenon that unbeknownst to us generates all human cultures and still warps our human vision in favor of all sorts of exclusions and scapegoating. If this analysis is true, the explanatory power of Jesus's death is much greater than we realize, and Paul's exalted idea of the Cross as the source of all knowledge is anthropologically sound.[1]

If the victim is the Christ, the Son of the Living God, through whom everything was made, to whom all authority has been given in heaven and on earth, in what sense can we say that he was "victimized" in the modern sense of the word? From a human standpoint he was clearly killed "without cause." There is no human reason for the killing. Humans have no right to kill Jesus. From a human perspective the killing is inexcusable. It is, indeed, murder. And yet, if we call it murder, if we see it as murder, we are wrong, dangerously wrong; we fail to see Jesus precisely as God the Father revealed to Peter, that is to say, as the Messiah, the Son of the Living God. If we call it murder, the death of Christ is no different from any other death, and Christ no different from any other victim. How could a mind like Girard's mind

---

1 *I See Satan Fall like Lightning*, 3.

fail to see that he was about to fall into Satan's trap? Who is to gain by seeing the death of Christ as murder plain and simple, an innocent man unjustly condemned? It's a perfectly rational way to look at it. Pilate himself realized what was happening on a strictly human level. He was just a political creature and a coward. And who would be delighted with a scientific discovery that says that nothing supernatural is needed to explain the victimizing mechanism, which is nothing less than the origin of humanity itself? I could see Screwtape, that famous civilized and British version of the old Devil, applauding such a magnificent discovery, in Hell. Fortunately, my friend's Christianity was never defined or restricted by his intellectual accomplishments, formidable though they were.

But there is, beyond all human comprehension, a divine reason. Ultimately, it is God, not Satan, who stands behind Christ's passion, death, and resurrection. And we must accept it, for that is a condition of entering the Kingdom of God. We must eat such bread and drink such wine. That's the message Christians get from Christ.

"God's way," we already know, is beyond scientific demonstration. "It was not the flesh" that revealed it to Peter, but "the Father who is in heaven." But "God's way" does not destroy scientific rationality, the strictly anthropological reading of the Gospel, which coincides with what was already known about sacrificial victimization before Christ. What it does in no uncertain terms is to warn against the notion that Christ's innocence is a transcendental revelation of *the* innocence of the human victim from the beginning.

Girard's anthropological reading of the Gospel, properly understood, should be welcomed by Christian believers. But it has also been welcomed by non-believers, who can see the "real" intellectual value of Christianity, free at last of all the theological mumbo-jumbo. Girard meant it as an *apologia christiana* in perfectly good faith. But that was not the way it was taken by many, also in good faith and with good reason.

The problem was brought up very early by Girard's main dialogue partner in *Things Hidden*, J.-M. Oughourlian:

> J.-M. O.: There is a paradox here. In a world that is secretly governed by the Gospel revolution and reflects the extraordinary concrete character of this revolution, as well as the desacralization it brings about and the way in which it brings to light the most hidden mechanisms of human culture, the type of experience you describe may indeed reproduce the immemorial process of religious conversion, but for the first time it need not rely on divine agency. . . . Such reliance will seem all the more unnecessary because there are already quite enough concrete results—both literary (like Proust) and non-literary—so that reference to any transcendence besides that of the knowledge being acquired will appear to be superfluous or even antithetical to the truth embodied in that knowledge.[2]

In my opinion, Girard never gave an adequate explanation for Oughourlian's "paradox." He continued to believe in the scientific independence of his anthropology, and in Christ as the ultimate silent and invisible guarantor of that same independence, in spite of his doubts. And the question persisted:

> I do not need Girard's hypothesis that the scientific project is a "byproduct" of the "subterranean" Revelation being wrought by the Holy Scriptures. My assumption is that many of Girard's original insights into human interaction and motivation are logically separate from such theological claims.[3]

Lucien Scubla:

> Our author affirms the transcendence of God . . . but nothing [in his theory] truly indicates that the "revelation" would require God to intervene in history, so that Christ could be mistaken for a sage come to teach men that they

2 Girard, *Things Hidden*, 401.

3 Paisley Livingston, *Models of Desire* (Baltimore, MD: Johns Hopkins University Press, 1992), xviii.

> have always been alone with their violence and that they must hasten towards reconciliation one with the other to avoid all being destroyed one by the other.[4]

This comes up again much later with Michel Treguer:

> I insist: why does your thesis require the hypothesis that God exists? I'm almost inclined to think that it weakens it.[5]

I do not agree with much of what these objectors were saying. But that is not my point here. I am simply pointing out that Girard's scientific "atheism," as well as its position chronologically ahead of the book on Christianity, opened the way for some serious doubts about the Christian character of Girardian theory.

The problem is not only that the "atheism" of the book can be taken quite literally. A more serious, and certainly more insidious, aspect of the problem is that its scientific rationality could actually determine Girard's interpretation of the Christian revelation itself, the subject of the second book. In other words, the problem was not only that "some people interpreted the first book in a Christian light," but the more dangerous one of reading the Christian revelation in the light of a scientific view of the sacred where faith in Christ, in the divinity of Christ, is irrelevant. Jean-Marie Domenach warned about this many years ago:

> To be sure, it is possible—the Fathers of the Church admitted it—to know the God of Jesus Christ through a rational operation. . . . But with René Girard, it is a question of much more than that. First because he derives from Christianity a precise anthropological hypothesis . . . next because he claims that this hypothesis is itself revelatory of the revelation, unveiling the meaning of divine intervention itself. An audacious enterprise and one which

4 "The Christianity of René Girard and the Nature of Religion," in *Violence and Truth*, ed. Paul Dumouchel (Stanford, CA: Stanford University Press, 1988), 170–71.

5 René Girard, *When These Things Begin*, trans. Trevor Cribben Merrill (East Lansing, MI: Michigan State University Press, 2014), 96.

> in other times—in other cultures—would have been judged sacrilegious.[6]

After all, if it can be proven that humans unknowingly, as a group, fabricated their own sacred by collectively expelling their own violence, whereby they were able to build complex civilizations lasting thousands of years, why could we not do the same thing? What difference does it make whether God exists or we invent it? Here is Michel Treguer again:

> What does it change that God exists and reveals himself—and not that Jesus invents him?

In order to answer this question Girard has to abandon his uncompromising scientism. Here is Girard:

> What does it change? It means that the entire sacrificial, moral, and religious history of humanity before Christianity is a holy history. It means that the pagan religions were a first path toward God, and that the practice of sacrifices was a way of keeping violence to a level that God didn't desire, but that he tolerated.[7]

Only from the perspective of religious faith can we say such a thing. How do we measure the level of God's tolerance? In fact, what is God's tolerance? Can anything exist without God's tolerance?

I can understand Charles K. Bellinger's recommendation: "Girard ought to drop the pretense of adhering to the methodological atheism of social science.... He ought to write straightforwardly as a Christian apologist and argue that a theological mode of knowing is required for real insight into human behavior."[8]

On the other hand, you do not have to be a Christian to believe that Christianity offers you a knowledge far superior

---

6 "Voyage to the End of the Sciences of Man," in *Violence and Truth*, ed. Dumouchel, 153.

7 *When These Things Begin*, 97.

8 Charles K. Bellinger, *The Genealogy of Violence. Reflections on Creation, Freedom, and Evil* (Oxford and New York: Oxford University Press, 2001), 88.

to that of any other religion. Dupuy defines himself as an "epistemological convert," "intellectually Christian":

> Note that I do not say I am a Christian intellectual, like Gabriel Marcel or G. K. Chesterton, who writes in the light of his faith. By "intellectually a Christian" I mean that I have come to believe that *Christianity constitutes a body of knowledge about the human world, one that is not only superior to all the human sciences combined, but that is also their principal source of inspiration.* And yet I do not belong to any of the denominations that compose Christianity. I might with equal justice say that I am also intellectually a Jew, to the extent that I believe Judaism made Christianity possible. It was my collaboration with thinkers such as Ivan Illich, and later René Girard, that led me to this epistemological conversion to Christianity.[9]

He asks a fundamental question about Girard's anthropology: "Is it not really a logic? Is it truly concerned with the laws of the human world, or is it not rather dealing with the principles of our understanding?"

> L'anthropologie que Girard a bâtie ne serait-elle pas en realité une *logique?* En d'autres termes, s'agit-il vraiment des lois du monde humain ou ne s'agit-il plutôt de principes de notre connaissance?[10]
>
> (The anthropology that Girard has built, would it not be in reality a logic? In other words, does it really deal with the laws of the human world or is it not rather dealing with the principles of our understanding?)

He knows, of course, that that is not the Christianity of René Girard. As we said, Christian believers believe in the historical flesh and blood person of Christ. That is the unavoidable, stubborn fact about the Christian faith: it all goes back to this one person, this human being, who lived in a very concrete space and time. He is the one who said

---

9 Dupuy, *Mark of the Sacred*, 93. My emphasis.

10 J.-P. Dupuy, "Mimésis et morphogénèse," in *René Girard et le problème du mal*, ed. Dupuy and Michel Deguy (Paris: Grasset, 1982), 277.

"I am the truth," together with many other things. He was killed, he died, and he resurrected. As Saint Paul said, if that didn't happen, our faith is nothing, and we are simply witnesses to the most colossal fraud ever performed on human beings. That is what Girard understood when he insisted on the historical, physical reality of the human violence that became the breeding ground of the human. He saw it in the light of Christ. It was not just knowledge. Faith has its own specificity. You do not have faith in Christ simply because you are convinced by the rationality of what he says. Faith is a gift. It is believing that Jesus is the Messiah, the Son of the Living God. And as Christ told Peter, "It was not the flesh that revealed that to you, but my Father who is in heaven." Scubla was right. If it is a question of knowledge, a sage can do the job. But Scubla's argument can be turned around: if it takes the body and the blood of Christ to be a Christian, to enter the Kingdom of God, then Christianity is much more than "a body of knowledge." Then human time is also God's time, both the beginning and the end, the alpha and the omega. The future is already in God's hands. And Girard was perfectly justified when he said "Yes, yes, God is taking care of it."

But that is not what Dupuy read in *Violence and the Sacred* and in *Things Hidden since the Foundation of the World.* What he read there is that humans have the power to create their own divinity, an outside or beyond, a transcendent realm, through which they manage to contain their own violence, which would otherwise destroy them completely. Threatened with imminent collapse, on the verge of being wiped off the face of the earth, they escape by channeling their violence through their victim to an outside, a sacred outside, which becomes the terrifying guardian of the group. And Dupuy is right. That is what Girard wrote, which is why he called it, half-jokingly, "atheistic."

Can Satan really expel Satan? As we will see, that is not what Christ said. If Satan could do that, who would need

Christ? If I understand Dupuy, we needed Christ, because without Christ we would not have had Girard, who got his inspiration directly from Christ in the Gospels, and Girard is quite unique:

> Only a madman or a crackpot, disregarding all the conventions of scholarship in the humanities and social sciences, could make the following outrageous claims today: that the history of humanity, considered in its entirety, and in spite—or rather because—of its sound and fury, has a meaning. That this meaning is accessible to us, and that although a science of mankind now exists, it is not mankind that has made it. That this science was given to mankind by divine revelation. That the truth of mankind is religious in nature. That of all religions, only one possesses full knowledge of the human world, and therefore encompasses the knowledge of all other religions. Finally, that this religion is Christianity, insofar as it is founded on the Gospels, which is to say on the accounts of the death and the resurrection of Jesus Christ.
>
> This madman is René Girard. The superiority of Christianity, he insists, may be seen above all in the light of its intellectual power.[11]

You may remember that that is exactly what I told Girard a lifetime ago: "People may think you are crazy." At any rate, "a science of mankind now exists." We may thank Christianity and Girard, and take it from there. In fact, we have no other choice but to take it from there, entirely on our own. For that is precisely what the new science of mankind revealed, for better or for worse. "Human beings, and human beings alone, will decide which."

Now we know what has saved humanity from self-annihilation: its capacity to expel its own violence, by sacralizing it. Expulsion and sacralization are the two sides of the same phenomenon. However, we have a problem that primitive humans did not have: according to Girard, sacralizing

11 Dupuy, *Mark of the Sacred*, 39.

doesn't work once you know what you are doing (knowing that you are dealing with your own violence). And if you cannot sacralize, you cannot expel. Dupuy disagrees. He thinks we can still expel and turn our violence into something transcendental, beyond us, in spite of the fact that we no longer believe in gods. For one thing, the very violence that threatens us today is impersonal. It has been de-humanized. We can kill millions without hatred. "Violence without hatred is so inhuman that it amounts to a kind of transcendence—perhaps the only transcendence yet left to us."

> Like the great moral catastrophes of the twentieth century, the apocalypse that looms before us will be less the result of our malignity, or even of our stupidity, than of our thoughtlessness. If it has the appearance of something fixed and ineluctable, this is not because it is fated to occur; it is because a multitude of decisions of all kinds, the product more of myopia than of malice or selfishness, bring forth a whole that hangs over its parts, as it were, and whose menace is generated by a process of self-exteriorization, or self-transcendence. This evil is neither moral nor natural. It is a third type, which I call systemic evil. Its form is identical with that of the sacred. Enlightened doomsaying urges us to seize the opportunity presented by our ability to recognize systemic evil. For this evil also has the same form as salvation—if it is not yet too late to save ourselves.[12]

Will this kind of self-transcendence, this "systemic evil," be able to do the job of the old divinities? The problem is that nobody is paying attention; nobody believes we are threatened by some superhuman power. There is nothing we can invent or discover that will substitute for the old sacred. The closest we can get to such a substitution would be through our capacity to imagine fictions. Apparently Dupuy agrees:

---

12 Dupuy, Jean-Pierre, *A Short Treatise on the Metaphysics of Tsunamis* (East Lansing, MI: Michigan State University Press, 2015), 58.

> Believing that [apocalyptic catastrophe] can be avoided, we do not believe that it really threatens us. It is this sophism that I have sought to demolish by applying the method of enlightened doomsaying—a ruse that consists in pretending we are the victims of fate, while keeping in mind that we are the sole cause of what happens to us . . . it is our very familiarity with literary fiction that makes this double game, the ruse of enlightened doomsaying, altogether natural. As we are reading a story, a part of us knows perfectly well that the author was free to end his tale as he pleased; and yet we experience the unfolding of events as though it were dictated by an implacable necessity that directly imposes itself on the author.[13]

In other words, "enlightened doomsaying" is something similar to the "suspension of disbelief" at work in our experience of literary fiction. After all, fiction-making, in narrative song or on the stage, was once a sacred art. Divine Homer's poetry was treated as some sort of sacred scripture among the Greeks; Athenian tragedy was always performed by the sacrificial altar; Livy tells us that Roman theater (*ludi scenici*) began as an imported sacrificial rite during a devastating epidemic, when traditional rites did not work (Livy 7, 2).

This is how Dupuy defined his new project of "enlightened doomsaying" in *A Short Treatise on the Metaphysics of Tsunamis*:

> Not a blueprint for political action [but] a metaphysical ruse, a piece of cunning by means of which the threat of systemic evil can be turned against itself. For want of access to genuine transcendence, the possibility of achieving self-transcendence, *even if it is the self-transcendence of evil*, allows us to step outside of ourselves and to see our predicament as it really is.[14]

I see the logic of this statement, and, perhaps, its profound sadness. But I think it needs some clarification. "Genuine transcendence" is inaccessible to us only in the sense that it is not of our own making. This is what faith is all about. The

13 *Mark of the Sacred*, 46.
14 Dupuy, *A Short Treatise*, 60. My emphasis.

only transcendence we can fabricate with any possibility of fooling us, no matter how briefly, into believing it is real, is an evil one.

"The threat of systemic evil can be turned against itself" simply means it can be fictionalized, turned into a fiction capable of "suspending our disbelief." That is to say, capable of generating the illusion that it is real. Genuine transcendence, the transcendence of the good, is, we might say, fiction-resistant. As Voltaire said, "our saints, who make so good a figure in our churches, make a very sorry one in our Epic Poems."[15] The devil will always be poetically much more interesting than the saint: Christ is not a literary hero. All attempts to make him look like one, and there were many, have failed. Therefore, I think it is self-contradictory to say that "the self-transcendence of evil allows us to step outside of ourselves to see our predicament as it really is." The transcendence of evil is not outside of ourselves. Such a transcendence can only reveal our own desperate need of transcendence, our emptiness, our shameful nudity, if you will. It is really a cover up. A literary fiction is a cover-up.

The time of heroes is gone, because the old sacred is gone. The archaic hero was the link between the human and the sacred. He was one of the forms which the saving victim could take. He was destined to die. He was unique, like the original tragic character, surrounded by the chorus. He was in touch with the absolute. That is no longer possible, because we no longer sacralize our victims. Instead of the unique and lonely hero, what we now have is—in the words of Franz Rosenzweig speaking of the tragic hero—"a multiplicity of characters."[16]

As I explained in *A Refuge of Lies*, the Homeric apparent disinterest in the truth, his complete absorption in the poetic

---

15 See Bandera, *The Sacred Game*, 9 ff.

16 Franz Rosenzweig, *The Star of Redemption* (University of Notre Dame Press, 1985), 211. See also Maria Stella Barberi, "Les trois règnes ou la crise de la représentation sacrificielle," in *La spirale mimétique* (Paris: Desclée de Brouwer, 2001), 90.

fabric he is creating, hides something else. The truth terrifies; not the truth that will be revealed, but the truth that cannot be known, the secret that cannot be revealed, terrifies. It is not that the ancient bard is indifferent to the truth; he does not want to face the dark truth. That is the radical difference between the Biblical text and the Homeric one that Auerbach tried to explain. The Biblical writer is passionately interested in the truth. The sacred muses on Helicon, on the other hand, "know how to speak many false things as though they were true." The poetic exemplar for the archaic sacred is a combination of the overwhelming violence of Achilles and the cunning, deceitful, master of disguise Odysseus. The archaic bard had no defense against the overwhelming sacred monster forever threatening, except to pretend that he was not there, wear a mask, fictionalize everything, look for a place to hide. Fiction was a question of survival, the only defense against an unbearable truth. Unbearable because, contrary to the hidden truth revealed by Christ because "there is nothing hidden, except to be made manifest; nor is anything secret, except to come to light" (Mark 4:21–22), the old truth is forever dark. The old truth is not in fact a truth, but an infinite absence of truth, an unfathomable abyss. When the truth reveals itself in the darkness, it is Christ.

In the light of Christ, all the sacred taboos surrounding the dark truth are broken, and what we see is just human violence in the nude. But, lo and behold! It does not frighten us. Quite the contrary, we are relieved it is *just our violence*. It is no transcendental monster. Actually, there is a Christian explanation for our unprecedented confidence in the face of our violence: it has been forgiven. The only question is, do we believe and accept God's forgiveness and act accordingly, or do we simply take advantage of our unprecedented non-threatening knowledge of the truth and try to do it our own way?

In our present situation, confronted by the ever-present danger of a thermonuclear conflagration, our problem is exactly the opposite of the one facing primitive man: how to keep awareness of the danger alive; how never to forget that the monster is out there; how to keep in mind that we are not really in full control of the monster; that the danger is constant and very real. In other words, our problem is not knowledge, our problem is hope, usually misunderstood in a selfish way, an illusory hope completely blind to its divine source. But whether genuine or stupidly blind and illusory, there is hope in our world, transcendental hope even in the face of what to human eyes appears to be hopeless. This is the real obstacle to Dupuy's "enlightened doomsaying" strategy: hope, but a hope inseparable from faith and charity.

HAMLET'S "DULL REVENGE"[17]

But let us imagine a world from which faith has disappeared, and with it the possibility of good transcendence. In such a situation the question must be, can we fake it? Or, to use Dupuy's word, can we trust a "simulacrum"? Since we are talking literary fiction, we should consult the experts, the literary masters. Shakespeare is particularly relevant in this regard. Our question is exactly Hamlet's question.

As you may remember, Hamlet's father, the king of Denmark has been murdered by his brother, Claudius, who is now the king, and has married the widow, Hamlet's mother. The ghost of his dead father roams the ramparts of the royal castle at night. It is the ghost who reveals the murder to Hamlet:

> GHOST: Revenge his foul and most unnatural murder.
> HAMLET: Murder!
> GHOST: Murder... most foul, strange and unnatural.
> HAMLET: Haste me to know it, that I, with wings as swift as meditation or the thought of love, may sweep to my revenge. (Act I, Scene v)

But Hamlet's spirit of revenge will prove to be far from swift. He procrastinates. Revenge is not something that occupies his mind to the exclusion of everything else, as he had promised to himself that it would do. He just does not feel

17 See Girard, *A Theater of Envy*, 271.

the urgency. His is a "dull revenge," as Girard noticed. His sacred obligation to avenge the murder is far from sacred. What a difference between Hamlet's attitude and that of the mythical Orestes, whose obligation to avenge the murder of his father, Agamemnon, is indeed sacred, as he is reminded by his companion, Pylades, putting an end to his hesitation about killing his own mother, Clytemnestra:

> What shall I do, Pylades? Dare I
> murder the Wife of my Father, my own Mother?
>
> PYLADES:
> Kill the killer of Agamemnon. Apollo
> has spoken. The gods guide you. Will
> you be hateful to the gods, as well as to man?[18]

To disobey Apollo's command would bring terrible consequences, as we hear from Orestes himself:

> If I falter
> and disobey this command, I shall die.
> Doom shall rise from the earth. The dead
> shall curse the coward...
> [...]
> My Father's Furies . . . will watch me,
> shake me, tear me, and drive me mad!

No such thing in Hamlet's case. Clearly the old sacred law of revenge has lost its power. Which is probably a very good thing:

> Let us imagine a contemporary Hamlet with his finger on a nuclear button. After forty years of procrastination he has not yet found the courage to push that button.[19]

Should we not encourage this kind of perennial procrastination to use the apocalyptic weaponry? Have we lost all hope in the desacralization of violence? Apparently, we have. Hence Dupuy's suggestion that we resacralize our violence,

---

18 *The Oresteia of Aeschylus*, trans. Robert Lowell (New York: Farrar, Strauss, Giroux, 1978), 84.
19 Girard, *Theater of Envy*, 287.

that we endow it with a transcendental dimension; that we make it look so monstrous and overpowering that it would look totally out of our hands, threatening us from an unreachable outside. That would scare us away from any temptation to push the nuclear button. And how are we planning to resacralize our violence? Hamlet himself will show us. The solution is in our poetic imagination, our capacity to create a fictional world. Fiction will be our savior. That is exactly what Hamlet did. The fictional solution came suddenly to his mind as he watched a famous actor representing queen Hecuba's lamentation, as she witnesses the savage killing of her husband, king Priam, at the hands of Pyrrhus:

> HAMLET:
> Now I am alone. O, what a rogue and peasant slave am I!
> Is it not monstrous that this player here,
> But in a fiction, in a dream of passion,
> Could force his soul so to his own conceit
> That from her working all his visage wann'd,
> Tears in his eyes, distraction in's aspect,
> A broken voice, and his whole function suiting
> With forms to his conceit? and all for nothing!
> For Hecuba!
> What's Hecuba to him, or he to Hecuba,
> That he should weep for her? What would he do,
> Had he the motive and the cue for passion
> That I have? He would drown the stage with tears
> And cleave the general ear with horrid speech,
> Make mad the guilty and appall the free,
> Confound the ignorant, and amaze indeed
> The very faculties of eyes and ears. (Act II, Scene ii)

The lesson is clear. If I do not really believe in the sacred character of revenge, if revenge is no longer a sacred duty, I will pretend. I will create such a convincing imitation of the old sacred duty that I will convince myself and I will amaze the world. A fake sacred, if properly performed, will be as good or better than a true one. "To be or not to be." There is a third possibility: to fake it.

But can he control such a powerful fiction? It is like riding on a tiger. Accidents happen. The final lesson of the play is that nobody predicted the senseless and tragic finale, with the death of Hamlet and all the main characters. The rehearsed drama went out of control. Unpredictable accidents happened that derailed the whole thing.

Yes, accidents happen, and they are unpredictable. The only thing that is not an accident is unpredictability itself. We fool ourselves if we think we can control a project such as Hamlet's project. More specifically, it is dangerous to play intellectual games with the sacred. Girard played such a game with the sacred, only to end up blaming historical Christianity for its failure. He started his game by imagining an absent Christ, just for methodological reasons—he thought—only to end up "discovering" that Christ had "really" left and we were on our own, utterly incapable of avoiding an apocalyptic, self-annihilating catastrophe. We will not reconcile with one another, "Eteocles and Polyneices will not reconcile." Our only hope is to realize that there is no hope. But it is too late for that, hope is killing us, because we have turned it into a fiction: the fiction of a universal reconciliation of all human beings motivated by the knowledge (revealed by Christ) that we are all equal. Christ, of course, never announced such a thing. He reconciled the world, the sinner, with God; and invited each one of us, by name, to repent because God has already forgiven each one of us.

We have put our hope, instead, in a satanic Antichrist, who promises perpetual peace. Can we still believe that we can pin our hope on an intellectually created sacred capable of scaring us into brotherly behavior? Will our intelligently created "evil transcendence" succeed where Christ failed? Will our thermonuclear monster move us to love one another better than Christ did? Can we substitute an intelligently manipulated strategy for a lack of faith? Do we hopelessly know too much for our own good?

CHAPTER 5

God of the Victims

WE FIND THE FOLLOWING PASSAGE IN *VIOLENCE AND THE Sacred*, as Girard analyzes Freud's *Totem and Taboo*:

> One passage in *Totem and Taboo* is of particular relevance to our inquiry. Freud is discussing tragedy, the tragic mode as it is practiced all over the world: "A company of individuals, named and dressed alike, surrounded a single figure, all hanging upon his words and deeds; they were the chorus and the impersonator of the hero. He was originally the only actor.... The hero of tragedy must suffer; to this day that remains the essence of a tragedy. He has to bear the burden of what was known as 'tragic guilt'.... But why had the hero of tragedy to suffer? And what was the meaning of this tragic 'guilt'? I will cut the discussion short and give you a quick reply. He had to suffer because he was the primal father, the Hero of the great primaeval tragedy which was being re-enacted with a tendentious twist; and the tragic guilt was the guilt which he had to take on himself in order to relieve the Chorus from theirs." According to Freud, the crowd of doubles stands in opposition to the absolute specificity of the hero. The hero monopolizes innocence, the mob monopolizes guilt. The flaw attributed to the hero is not his, but belongs exclusively to the crowd. The hero, then, is a victim pure and simple, charged with a crime he did not commit. This concept of a simple one-way projection of guilt seems to me inadequate. Sophocles is wiser; he makes it clear... *that the surrogate victim, even when falsely accused, may be as guilty as the others. For the traditional concept of the 'flaw' (perpetuated as 'sin' by theologically minded critics) should be substituted by that of violence . . . violence shared by all*.... The Freudian interpretation is thoroughly modern in its inversion of the mythical content. Thanks to the innocent victim, with whose fate one can easily identify, it becomes possible to inculpate all the false innocents.

> This is precisely what Voltaire did in his *Oedipe*, and what the contemporary antitheater is striving to do in an atmosphere of ever-increasing confusion and hysteria.... The Freudian approach is even more tendentious than tragedy because he shares the modern inclination to shift all blame for violence onto others.[1]

Girard's critique of Freud is in complete accord with the internal logic of the scapegoat mechanism. But he did not follow his own advice. He became, in accordance with his own criterion, "thoroughly modern in its inversion of the mythical content." This is what he wrote in *I See Satan Fall like Lightning*, as an interpretation of the following passage from Colossians:

> When you were dead in your sins and in the uncircumcision of your flesh, God made you alive with Christ. He forgave us all our sins, having canceled the charge of our legal indebtedness, which stood against us and condemned us; he has taken it away, nailing it to the cross. And having disarmed the powers and authorities, he made a public spectacle of them, triumphing over them by the cross (2:13–15).
>
> *The accusation against humankind is the accusation against the innocent victim* [my emphasis] that we find in the myths. To hold the principalities and powers responsible for it is the same thing as holding Satan himself responsible, in his role of public prosecutor that I have already mentioned.
>
> Before Christ and the Bible, the satanic accusation was always victorious by virtue of the violent contagion that imprisoned human beings within systems of myth and ritual. The Crucifixion reduces mythology to powerlessness by exposing violent contagion, which is so effective in the myths that it prevents communities from ever finding out the truth, namely, the innocence of their victims.[2]

"The accusation against humankind is the accusation against the innocent victim." What does that mean? There is no innocent victim in Saint Paul's letter. We were dead in

1 René Girard, *Violence and the Sacred*, trans. Patrick Gregory (Baltimore, MD: The Johns Hopkins University Press, 1977), 203–5.
2 Girard, *I See Satan*, 138.

our sin, which means we were sinful, not innocent. And our sin, our guilt, the legal charge against us, held us prisoners; we bore the burden of our guilt. We could not get rid of it. There was no possibility of repentance because there was no forgiveness. The victim was killed as the only way to unload the unbearable burden of our guilt.

The Cross has forgiven us, thereby declaring the accusation null and void. We are free. The door of our prison has been opened. Once again, we have been set free, not because we were innocent, but because despite being guilty, sinful, we have been forgiven. Forgiven does not mean innocent. Forgiven means that the death sentence pronounced against us will not be carried out. We can hear Christ's words to the woman caught in adultery: you are free now, go and sin no more. Only Christ is innocent. Therefore, he is the only one who could, in principle, throw the first stone. But he is precisely the one who forgives. Christ's unique innocence makes us free; Christ's innocence forgives us. But Christ's innocence is most definitely not a revelation of our innocence. It does not make any difference whether we are the one being stoned to death or the stone thrower. That kind of ritual sacrifice does not make anybody innocent. It is only a shadow of the one sacrifice which shows us in the light of a unique and transcendental innocence. We are only innocent when seen in that light, in the light of Christ. We might say that our innocence does not belong to us. It is given to us gratuitously by Christ. I think the theologians call it grace.

On the other hand, if we just look at the text of the Gospels as we would at any other text to be analyzed, what strikes us is the emphasis on the innocence of the man being accused. Clearly, he is being tortured and put to death "without cause." When we compare this with structurally similar killings, sacrificial killings, throughout the world from the earliest on record, we discover a fundamental difference between the Judeo-Christian text as a whole and all other mythical and sacred texts: in these non-Biblical texts the victim is sacrificed and nobody doubts that it is the right, indeed, the necessary, thing to do. In the Judeo-Christian tradition the victim seems always to be victimized without cause. The case of Jesus appears as the culmination of a multi-secular process. This is an epistemological fact, which we can interpret as we deem appropriate. But, as a matter of plain common sense, what could this insistence on the injustice done to the sacrificial victim mean but a condemnation of the sacrificial process itself? Certainly, we could not possibly imagine that Jesus, whose command was to love your enemy, would condone the sacrificial killing of the victim in any shape or form.

In Girard's reading, the Crucifixion "reduces to powerlessness" our Satanic cover-up, thus exposing our guilt and revealing the innocence of the victim killed unanimously. In Girard's reading, the revelation of the victim's innocence unavoidably carries with it the revelation of the guilt of those who kill the victim, that is to say, all of us, everybody. This Girardian revelation says absolutely nothing about forgiveness because he is not talking about any relationship with Christ. It is just us, killers, and the victim, in the hope that now that we know the victim is innocent, we will stop killing victims. But that is strictly our decision. There is no Satanic power, no evil transcendence, binding us to our guilt. It was just ignorance. Once we know the truth, "namely, the innocence of [our] victims," in a perfectly rational manner, it is entirely up to us. No terror, no hair-raising experience.

"Satan therefore is essentially the accuser," says Girard. But he is the accuser of humanity, not "the one who deceives men by making them believe that innocent victims are guilty."[3] Satan keeps human beings in his power, not by telling them false stories about intended victims, but by never allowing them to forget that they are guilty.

Guilty of what? Of the very violence that they have all discharged against the victim. That is to say, guilty of the very

3 René Girard, *The Scapegoat*, trans. Yvonne Freccero (Baltimore, MD: The Johns Hopkins University Press, 1989), 207.

same thing that will save them from utter annihilation. They must kill the victim and, at the same time, hide their violence. In Satan's system the accusation never ceases. Killing the victim will keep them alive, at least for the moment; alive, not forgiven. There is no liberation from guilt. The only way to find relief from the oppression of guilt, indistinguishable from the fear of death, is by passing it on to the victim. The guilt that humanity sees in the victim is the collective guilt under whose tyranny it lives.

"But when the Paraclete comes, whom I will send you from the Father, the Spirit of truth, who proceeds from the Father, he shall give testimony of me" (John 15:25–27).

The Paraclete will reveal the truth of who I am and of what I said. He is the Spirit of Truth, against Satan the accuser of the human race. But the Paraclete is not specifically "the chief defender of all innocent victims." Jesus does not say that the Paraclete "will reveal the meaning of my innocent death and of every innocent death, from the beginning."[4]

Returning the accusation against the accuser is not going to break the system. The inversion of the myth of which Girard speaks could be just as mythical. "Christianity sends back to human beings the violence that they have always projected onto their divinities [their sacralized victims]."[5] "Christ preferred to die rather than take part in violent sacrifices."[6] "The Passion is presented as a blatant piece of injustice. Far from taking the collective violence upon itself, the text places it squarely on those who are responsible for it."[7] "The victim's guilt is the mainspring of the victim mechanism. . . . Persecutors always believe in the excellence of their cause, but in reality, they hate without a cause. The absence of cause in the accusation (*ad causam*) is never seen by the persecutors. It is this illusion that must first be addressed if we are to release

4 Ibid., 212.
5 *When These Things Begin*, 92.
6 Ibid., 96.
7 *Things Hidden*, 170.

all the unfortunate from their invisible prison, from the dark underground in which they are stagnating but which they regard as the most magnificent of palaces."[8]

I do not know where Girard got this idea that the "unfortunate" human beings under Satan's power experience their "invisible prison," "their dark underground," as the most magnificent of palaces. In fact, they live in constant fear of the sacred. It terrorizes them. That is "the mainspring of the victim mechanism," as I have already explained.

Girard himself originally questioned such a view about the guilt of the victim, because this mechanism, he told us, had existed for thousands of years before any comprehension of something like individual guilt or responsibility could exist. This is what he said in *Violence and the Sacred*:

> When we require a direct link between guilt and punishment, we believe that we adhere to a fundamental truth that has somehow eluded the primitive mind. In fact, we are ignoring a problem that poses a very real threat to all primitive societies: escalating revenge, unleashed violence—a problem the seeming extravagances of their customs and the violence of their religious practices are specifically designed to meet.[9]

Originally, guilt and the sacred were the two sides of the same experience. Guilt was what threatened everybody. It was a collective guilt. It was ultimately the terror of the sacrificial crisis, of its endless violence. Their only option was to fictionalize it, to pretend it was not there, to hide from it. The original staging of tragedy shows the chorus gathered around the hero victim all wearing masks, hiding their identity.[10] And the hero is the victim, because of the hero's special, greater, association with violence. Which is also what makes the tragic hero different from everybody else. That is also the case with the epic hero, the reason why Achilles, as he himself knows, will not return

8 *The Scapegoat*, 103.
9 *Violence and the Sacred*, 27.
10 See *The Sacred Game*, 105.

home, will die. The hero embodies violence, and violence is what threatens the very existence of the group. And, of course, all these hiding or pretending strategies turn around the central sacred-making act, the killing of the victim. The archaic victim is not expelled or killed because he or she is guilty of some trumped-up charge. That is always a cover-up or a rationalization. Underneath the cover-up, there is always the original fear of the sacred. The victim bears the imprint of the sacred, has been contaminated by the sacred.

Historians of religion and anthropologists are familiar with these kinds of religious denials of the obvious. Plato blamed the poets for such inconsistencies next to the sacrificial altar. For example, mourning, bewailing, the fate of an incestuous parricide such as Oedipus, justly expelled from the city.[11] In some rituals the sacrificial knife is blamed for the killing. I remember reading about the bear hunting rituals of a Siberian tribe. The bear was a sacred animal to them, which was also hunted for a living. When the hunting party spots the animal, they carefully surround it, sometimes with spears turned, showing the blunt end, not the wounding tip, as if pretending not to be on the hunt. Eventually they kill the bear. But they leave the dead body on the spot and walk away. A short time later they return, and, lo and behold! a dead bear! Who could have killed it?—they ask. They blame the Russians for it. Then they take it home. Obviously, they know perfectly well what they are doing. But the hiding of the truth, the violent truth, in the presence of the sacred is a necessity. If some stranger showed up and told them that they could not hide the truth, that it was clearly they who did the killing, they would become, at the very least, extremely nervous, and fearful.

Truth is dangerous. It must be kept secret, hidden. Here is another example, taken from a study of the Lugbara, people living in Northwestern Uganda:

---

11 See *The Sacred Game*, "The *Poetics* and the Sacred," 105.

> The . . . truth is knowledge that is capable of changing and indeed of devastating all [social] categories and thus all relationships. It must therefore be carefully bounded and controlled. One aspect of this quality is that it cannot be spoken to ordinary people; indeed, it cannot be spoken at all in the sense that it is unspeakable, there is no language known to men that is capable of translating it.[12]

It is not, therefore, that the old victimizers did not know at all what they were doing; it is, rather, that the truth was unbearable. Early on, in *Violence and the Sacred*, Girard said something very close to what I am trying to say here:

> Because modern man clings to the belief that knowledge is in itself a "good thing," he grants little or no importance to a procedure, such as the one involving the surrogate victim, that only serves to conceal the existence of man's violent impulses. . . . Indeed, the formidable effectiveness of the process derives from its depriving men of knowledge: knowledge of the violence inherent in themselves with which they have never come to terms. . . . Men cannot confront the naked truth of their own violence without the risk of abandoning themselves to it entirely.[13]

I agree, but I would rephrase it. It is not a question of knowledge. What drives the victimizing procedure is not ignorance but terror. They were terrified by their own violence, which is another way of saying that they were terrified by their own guilt. It is not the innocence of the victim that they must hide, but their own violence, which is the infallible witness to their guilt. The victim is a decoy, and they know it. Its guilt or innocence is ultimately irrelevant. It is a diversion. They divert over to the victim the violence that threatens everybody, a threat that says that everybody is guilty. The violence that kills the victim turns the victim into a terrifying monster, from which they try to hide by

12 John Middleton, "Secrecy in Lugbara Religion," *History of Religions* 12.4 (May, 1973), 313.
13 *Violence and the Sacred*, 82.

pretending it wasn't they who did it. Their "comedy of innocence" keeps them alive for a while. But the whole ritual has to be repeated time and again, because they cannot get rid of the truth that accuses them. In short, they cannot get rid of their guilt. Blaming the victim for their own violence is still a ritual way of hiding their guilt; such blaming is usually followed by lamentations over the unavoidable fate that kills the victim. It is not the innocence of the victim that threatens them. They cannot see the innocence of the victim. The victim is always, by definition, a witness to the unbearable truth, the truth of their guilt. A truly innocent victim could only be recognized by them, could only be revealed to them, as a non-accuser, as a forgiver. Only forgiveness could rescue them from the horror that keeps them sacrificing victims and playing the ritual comedy of innocence.

The scapegoat mechanism is a sacred-producing mechanism. Perhaps it would be more accurate to say that it is the mechanism whereby the sacred is revealed to them, is recognized by them. Violence was sacred from the beginning. Original violence was sacred violence. But it did not have a name or a specific place. It involved everybody everywhere and, because of that, it could not be found anywhere in particular. Such violence has no history, it has no survivors. The scapegoat mechanism gives it a name and a place. Its signature is right there in the body of the victim unanimously killed, toward which all eyes converge now. And every ritual killing after that will be understood as a repetition of the original one. The original victim was killed and became sacred in a totally random way. Every other one after that was meant to be a reincarnation of the original regardless of what the mythical charges against them may have been. Ultimately, they have all been killed because they became sacred. In the old Roman law, the *lex sacrata*, the Pontifex or the judicial magistrate pronounced the death sentence touching the *reus*, the one found guilty, with the rod or *vindicta*, and the words: *sacer esto*, "be sacred." To be sacred is to be marked for death; and sacred is everything that threatens the survival of the group.

Terror, the sacred fear of death, is the force behind the unanimous killing of the victim. But a very different view of the sacred was being developed in the Biblical world. The idea of a God who sides with the victims against their persecutors is what Girard found repeatedly in the Old Testament. It is the basis of his reading of the Book of Job in *Job: The Victim of His People.*[14] It all began in *Things Hidden since the Foundation of the World*. There he would notice the striking contrast between the Bible and all other mythical texts, when it comes to the violent encounter between enemy brothers. The Bible always takes the side of the victim against those who plot against it. The prototypical Biblical encounter is that of Cain and Abel: Cain is a murderer, who slays his brother without cause; Abel is the innocent victim. This revelation of the innocence of the victim culminates with Christ. All previous victims, when seen in the light of Christ, are innocent of what they have been accused of, that is to say, of a collective violence in which they have all participated. The Passion of Christ becomes the revelation of the founding murder, or rather, the revelation of the original killing of the victim as murder, pure and simple, killing without a cause. Christ's mission will be seen as the denunciation of the scapegoat mechanism, an unjust and murderous enterprise.[15]

---

14 See below, pp. 131–34.

15 See Thomas Pietsch, "René Girard, anthropologist of the cross," *Lutheran Theological Journal*, 51.2 (August, 2017), 128: "Whether Girard rehabilitates orthodox theology has been the cause of some discussion. In an important sense, the issue is more with what Girard doesn't say, than with what he does. Strangely enough God is often absent from Girard's discussions and thus the vertical dimension of Christianity can be seen to be diminished, even as Girard strongly upholds the inspiration of the scriptures. At times it seems as if the redemptive goal of the cross was simply to inspire others to imitate Christ's solidarity with innocent victims against the scapegoating instincts of the world." This is really an understatement. The revelation of the innocence of the sacrificial victim is central to Girard's anthropology. Whether his anthropology "rehabilitates orthodox theology" is a different matter. I can fully understand the theologian's doubt. I think there are plenty of reasons for it.

This type of thinking either absolves the victim of any participation in the collective violence, or simply ignores it, and puts the blame entirely on the persecutors, a rather "modern" way of looking at it. The fact is that, to the best of my knowledge, beginning with *Things Hidden*, in every work, Girard's emphasis has been consistently on the innocence of the victim. In *The One by Whom Scandal Comes*:

> *Maria Stella Barberi*: It is clear from what you have said so far that mimetic theory is very well suited to interpreting the Incarnation and the Passion of Christ, respectively, as the demythologization of religion and the revelation of *the innocence of the victim*...
>
> *René Girard*: . . . not even two millennia have been enough for the influence of the Passion to really seep in, to penetrate men's minds to the point that this mechanism is disabled once and for all; for the non-guilt of the victim to be fully recognized, together with the illegitimacy of the persecution.[16]

Once again, the non-guilt, or the innocence, of the victim is a red herring. It diverts our attention from the real culprit, Satan, that is to say, the unforgiving horror of the system. This emphasis on the innocence of the victim and the guilt of everybody else provides the rationale for a view of Christianity in which "the person who suffers, the lost sheep of the flock is the only thing that counts. . . . Christianity acts as a lethal agent of disruption, a source of turmoil whose purpose and ultimate effect is to destroy all humanly constituted authority." Which is, of course, an exaggeration that ignores Christ's words: "Give to Caesar what is Caesar's and to God what is God's" (Mark 12:17).

But the point is that the lost sheep is not the innocent sheep. It is the guilty one, the one that went astray. And it is also the ritual one, the scapegoat, expelled into the desert carrying with it the sins of everybody. Neither is the prodigal son an example of innocence. But when the good shepherd

---

16 *The One by Whom Scandal Comes*, 67–68.

or the father finds the one that was lost, he is full of joy, and celebrates, and tells everybody; just like the woman who lost her coin and searched all over the house until she found it, and was overjoyed and went out and told her neighbors. Because "there will be more joy in heaven over one sinner who repents than over ninety-nine righteous persons who need no repentance" (Luke 15:7).

In mimetic anthropology's view of Christ as the anti-victimizing savior, the one who comes to reveal the innocence of the scapegoat, the situation seems to be the reverse: Christ comes in search of the innocent, who is defined as innocent for no other reason than that he or she has been declared guilty by everybody in compact unanimity, that is to say, by Satan. It looks as if Christ would have taken the bait offered by Satan: take your beloved victim, I will keep the rest. Except for Satan, is there any other reason for the divine intervention in Girard's mimetic anthropology? As we just said, if there is such a reason having nothing to do with Satan, I do not think we will find it within the logic of mimetic anthropology.

And yet, as far as I can tell, this view of Christ's revelation has been accepted by Girardians as practically self-evident. Sometimes, in addition to "innocence," weakness or marginality are considered necessary attributes of the victim. For example, Sean Salai, SJ:

> Girard focuses on the original sin of collective violence against the weak.... *Christ's death reveals the scandal that humankind collectively murders innocent victims*.... Although Girard agrees with Anselm that Christ atones for our sins, he thinks that Christ's atonement obliges us to take the victim's side.... *Jesus actually atones for atonement*...[17] (My emphasis)

So, there you are: not all sins are equal. To say that Christ atones for our sins is not enough, because that does not bring out what is central in Girard, the sin of sins, the victimization

17 "Anselm, Girard and Sacramental Theology," *Contagion* 18 (2011), 100–3.

of the victim. We need a second atonement to atone for the first. I wonder how my good friend might have reacted to such words.

Even those who may consider the revelation of the victim's innocence theologically insufficient, offer no objection. For example, Anthony R. Lusvardi, recently, in an otherwise excellent article in *Contagion*:

> What a theological perspective adds to Girard's anthropology is the belief that, *in identifying with innocent victims* [my emphasis], God is not only revealing to us a disturbing aspect of human nature, exposing the mimetic cycle of violence. He is at the same time . . . revealing the infinite self-giving love of the Trinity.[18]

The question is: is the revelation of "the infinite self-giving love of the Trinity" not enough? Should "innocent victims" be singled out for a special kind of love in the "infinite self-giving love of the Trinity"? Do we need a "second atonement," as the previous critic said?

Nobody questions the centrality of the innocent victim in Girard. This is also the case with Paolo Diego Bubbio: "Christ is the God of victims primarily in the sense that he shares their fate in its entirety."[19] However, as Bubbio points out, sharing the victims' fate does not mean agreeing to be a scapegoat. (Frankly, I do not know how you can accept being the victim, but refuse to be a scapegoat, since the victim is victimized because it is the scapegoat.) The logic of this distinction is far from clear. But Bubbio is right, logical or not, that that is really what Girard is trying to say: "Christ, in suffering a collective lynching but refusing the role of scapegoat, reveals the truth of mimetic violence."[20]

Clearly, Girard's anthropological Christ is not "the Lamb of God, who takes away the sins of the world." That is not

---

18 "Girard and the Sacrifice of the Mass," *Contagion* 24 (2017), 176.

19 Paolo Diego Bubbio, *Intellectual Sacrifice* (East Lansing, MI: Michigan State University Press, 2018), 8.

20 Ibid., 10.

his mission. His mission is the denunciation of the scapegoat mechanism:

> Jesus provides violence with the most perfect victim imaginable, the victim whom violence has the most reason to choose: the most innocent. Jesus, in effect, stands as the expiatory victim par excellence, the most arbitrary because the least violent.

If, on the contrary, Jesus accepts the fate of the victim willingly, out of love for humankind; if ultimately his mission is not to denounce the victimization mechanism, but to transform it into an instrument of redemption, then he is the least arbitrary victim, the only one who is not arbitrary at all, for "he was destined since the foundation of the world" for the job. Nobody else could bring about such a transformation.

The all-absorbing emphasis on the innocence of the human victim, and the "obligation to condemn their persecutors"[21] cannot fail to feed our anti-Christian modern victimism, the same victimism so many times condemned by Girard himself:

> The attempt by Nietzsche and Hitler to make humankind forget the concern for victims has ended in a failure that seems definitive, at least for the moment. But it is not Christianity that profits from the victory of the concern for victims in our world. It is rather what I think must be called the other totalitarianism, the most cunning and malicious of the two, the one with the greatest future, by all evidence. At present it does not oppose Judeo-Christian aspirations but claims them as its own and questions the concern for victims on the part of Christians (not without a certain semblance of reason at the level of concrete action, given the deficiencies of historical Christianity). The other totalitarianism does not openly oppose Christianity but outflanks it on its left wing.
>
> All through the twentieth century, the most powerful mimetic force was never Nazism and related ideologies, all

21 "[In order] to defend our victims it is obliged to condemn their persecutors, which is to say ourselves." *When These Things Begin*, 92.

those that openly opposed the concern for victims and that readily acknowledged the Judeo-Christian origin of that concern. The most powerful anti-Christian movement is the one that takes over and "radicalizes" the concern for victims in order to paganize it. The powers and principalities want to be "revolutionary" now, and they reproach Christianity for not defending victims with enough ardor. In Christian history they see nothing but persecutions, acts of oppression, inquisitions.

This other totalitarianism presents itself as the liberator of humanity. In trying to usurp the place of Christ, the powers imitate him in the way a mimetic rival imitates his model in order to defeat him. They denounce the Christian concern for victims as hypocritical and a pale imitation of the authentic crusade against oppression and persecution for which they would carry the banner themselves.

In the symbolic language of the New Testament, we would say that in our world Satan, trying to make a new start and gain new triumphs, borrows the language of victims. Satan imitates Christ better and better and pretends to surpass him. This imitation by the usurper has long been present in the Christianized world, but it has increased enormously in our time. The New Testament evokes this process in the language of the Antichrist.

The Antichrist boasts of bringing to human beings the peace and tolerance that Christianity promised but has failed to deliver. Actually, what the radicalization of contemporary victimology produces is a return to all sorts of pagan practices: abortion, euthanasia, sexual undifferentiation, Roman circus games galore but without real victims, etc.[22]

THE ANTICHRIST

The Antichrist is still the voice of the crowd. Vladimir Soloviev's *Short Story of the Antichrist*, published in 1899, a Girardian text *avant la lettre*, captures this aspect of the Antichrist perfectly. In contrast with Christ's personal image as a victim, degraded, mocked by people, crucified, in other words, the

22 *I See Satan Fall like Lightning*, 180–82.

very image of a loser in the eyes of the world, stands that of Superman, The Coming One, the Antichrist, radiant, the very image of triumph and success. He was dazzling when he appeared on the platform of the Congress of the United States of Europe, where he was unanimously elected by acclamation to the maximum power, that of Roman Emperor, in command of everything:

> When he appeared on the platform in all the glamour of young super-human beauty and power, and with inspired eloquence expounded his universal programme, the assembly was carried away by the spell of his personality, and in an outburst of enthusiasm decided, even without voting, to give him the highest honor, and to elect him Roman Emperor. The congress closed amidst general rejoicing, and the great elector published a manifesto, which began with the words: "Nations of the World! I give you my peace," and concluded, "Nations of the World! The promises have been fulfilled! An eternal universal peace has been secured. Every attempt to destroy it will meet with a determined and irresistible opposition, since a Power is now established on earth which is stronger than all the other powers, separately or conjointly." This unconquerable, all surmountable power belongs to me.[23]

"The Crowd Is Untruth," said Kierkegaard.[24] As we saw already in the passage about the adulterous woman, Jesus is the one who breaks the victimizing crowd. Let each victimizer look inside him/herself *in silence*. Christ's silence at that moment, in front of the victimizing crowd, speaks louder than words. In the midst of "war, confusion, and terror," Christ's silence is precious, and a constant invitation for each and every one of us to do the same. Christ speaks to us individually through this silence, at a distance from the victimizing crowd, from "the war, the confusion, and the

---

23 *Tale of the Antichrist. From Three Conversations* (HijezGlobal Press, 2017), 197–98.

24 *On the Dedication to "That Single Individual,"* by Søren Kierkegaard, translated by Charles K. Bellinger.

terror." I believe this is the "silence," "the withdrawal of God," which is only a concerned retreat, letting the other be in its alterity, of which Girard speaks in reference to Hölderlin's withdrawal.

In radical contrast, everything is public about Soloviev's Antichrist; everything is a public relations event. What is remarkable, in the Girardian context we are analyzing, is that at the center of the Antichrist's ideology, that which the Antichrist argues to be the reason for his coming, is the failure of Christ to bring about the general reconciliation of humanity, universal peace.[25] Soloviev's Antichrist wrote a masterpiece, which was universally praised and cleared the way for his absolute power. *The Open Way to Universal Peace and Wellbeing* explains his goals: being "agreeable" to everybody, so that nobody is ever excluded, no separation between the good and the bad. That was Christ's mistake. He was too judgmental, threatening humanity with a final judgement. Here is an extract from Soloviev's story:

> In a word, he considered himself to be what Christ in reality was.... At first, he had no ill-feeling towards Christ. He recognized His Messianic importance and

---

25 Remember Girard's change of heart regarding what he saw as the historical mission of the Christian Revelation: "My earlier faith in *the necessary reconciliation of men* [my emphasis] is what shocks me most today. I was a victim of it, in a way, and my book *Things Hidden since the Foundation of the World* expressed the confidence that universal knowledge of violence [as a consequence of Christ's Revelation] would suffice. I no longer believe that" (*Battling to the End*, 44). Giuseppe Fornari's observation may also help to situate historically the figure of the Antichrist: "'The history of the Antichrist follows the history of Christ like a shadow.' This statement is far from banal, not only for its consequences but also because Christianity as currently divulged typically denies that a figure like the Antichrist could be a cause for concern. When confronted with the Antichrist, with Satan in person, the current reaction of many Christians is one of 'dialogue.' That this may be interpreted, in terms of the doctrine of the Antichrist, as a sign of his proximity passes unnoticed among Christians of goodwill in this day and age. But the devil is never so near as when denied or when, following the dictates of what is 'politically correct,' we start negotiating with him under names that change to suit the occasion" ("Figures of Antichrist: The Apocalypse and its Restraints in Contemporary Political Thought," in *Contagion: Journal of Violence Mimesis and Culture* (2010) 17(1):53–85).

> value, but he was sincere in seeing Him only his own greatest precursor—the moral achievement of Christ and His uniqueness were beyond an intellect so completely clouded by self-love as his. He reasoned thus: "Christ came before me. I come second. But what in order of time appears later is in its essence of greater importance. I come last at the end of history for the very reason that I am most perfect. I am the final savior of the world.... As a moralist, Christ divided men by the notion of good and evil. *I shall unite them by benefits which are as much needed by good as by evil people. I shall be true representative of that God who maketh His sun to shine upon the good and the evil, and who maketh the rain fall upon the just and upon the unjust. Christ brought the sword; I shall bring peace. He threatened the earth with the Day of Judgement. But the last judge will be myself, and my judgement will be not only that of justice, but also that of mercy....*" Thus, this just but proud man waited for the sanction of the Most High to begin his saving of mankind; but he could see no signs of it. He had passed the age of thirty. Three more years passed by. A thought suddenly leaps into his mind and thrilled him to the core. "What," thought he, "what if by some accident it is not I, but the other one ... the Galilean. If He is not my annunciator but the true deliverer, the first and the last one?... What if he suddenly comes to me here, presently?... Shall I not be compelled to kneel down before Him as the very last silly Christian... It cannot be!" And here ... a sudden fear was born and grew in his heart, next followed by a burning envy, consuming all his being, and an ardent hatred that takes the very breath away.[26]

Clearly Soloviev would agree with Girard's view of totalitarianism, which is "not only alive but it also has a great future." To round up the picture of the Antichrist, and to see how close Soloviev's prediction comes to describing our own historical moment more than a hundred years later, we should know that

---

26 *War, Progress, and the End of History Including a Short Story of the Anti-Christ* (London: University of London Press, 1915), 191.

> The new lord of the world before everything else was a kind-hearted philanthropist, and not only a philanthropist, but even a *philozoist*. He was a vegetarian, prohibited vivisection, and instituted a strict supervision over slaughter-houses; whilst societies for protecting animals received from him every encouragement.[27]

IVAN KARAMAZOV'S CHRIST

And then there is Ivan Karamazov's Christ. We begin once more with the question of sanctity. Girard, as we know, was a firm believer in the need for "personal sanctity" as a response to the apocalyptic turmoil of our time. But is such an attitude possible today? Is it, in the opinion of many, even honest? In the face of so much violence, of so much suffering, as the world has witnessed, especially in the last hundred years, of so many millions of innocent helpless victims, is it even decent to retreat into silent interiority? Should we not all be outraged? Should we not all "remain with our unsatisfied indignation," in the words of Ivan Karamazov, lest we forget?

It may be argued that we have been sensitized to the victimization of the innocent to such a degree as to defeat the very purpose of the Cross. Can the sacrifice of Christ atone for the deliberate violence done to a child, for example, or the monstrous violence of a death camp? Is it possible to remain silent after the Holocaust? If Girard is right, if the sacrifice of Christ is meant to reveal the unjustified violence done to an innocent victim, he may have bought more than he bargained for. For the vision of such a violence, from a human point of view, may rob the sacrificial death of Christ itself of its efficacy. Christ may have exposed the kind of violence for which not even the atoning power of his death and resurrection would seem enough. Here are some examples:

> Christian theology has tended to be strenuously antitragic. At the beginning of history is a Fall that justifies suffering by interpreting it as a consequence of sin. At the end of history is the eschatological return to harmony.... It is the

27 Ibid., 199.

> neatness of this vision that disturbs me. It quells outrage over suffering by explaining it and, worse, by justifying it. I find myself in the company of Ivan Karamazov, who refuses to be comforted by any theodicy—purgation, punishment, vindication, harmony, retribution. None of these can make it all right that children are tortured by their parents or their governments.[28]

Or this other one:

> if religious theodicies now appear implausible or untenable, the most forceful reason for their failure seems to have been the evidence of suffering itself. The optimism with which history has been ingeniously fashioned to suit the logic of theodicy encountered an early setback with the Lisbon earthquake of 1775. This devastating event finally convinced Voltaire that belief in God's providence was really no more than "a cruel philosophy under a consoling name."[29] Affliction on this scale persuaded sceptics that religious rationalizations were morally objectionable in violating rather than redeeming a belief in truth, justice and human dignity by their sheer irrationality. A century later, Dostoevsky evokes similar sentiments in *The Brothers Karamazov*, where Alyosha refuses to accept a God who allows the torture and murder of innocent children to fulfil his higher purpose.[30]

Correction: Alyosha does not think that such a God exists. He believes in the Christian God, who does not allow "the torture and murder of innocent little children." Also, I do not think Voltaire's *Poème sur le désastre de Lisbonne* is in the same line of thinking as Ivan Karamazov. This is what worried Voltaire: Could evil spring from the author of all good? Are we still condemned to suffer under the tyrannical rule of the old sacred monsters, "black Typhon, the barbarous Arimane"?

---

28 Wendy Farley, *Tragic Vision and Divine Compassion: A Contemporary Theodicy* (Louisville, KY: Presbyterian Publishing Corporation, 1990), 12.
29 Theodore Besterman, *Voltaire* (New York: Harcourt, Brace, and World, 1969), 359.
30 David Morgan and Iain Wilkinson, "The Problem of Suffering and the Sociological Task of Theodicy," *European Journal of Social Theory* 4.2: 199–214.

De l'auteur de tout bien le mal est-il venu ?
Est-ce le noir Typhon, le barbare Arimane,
Dont la loi tyrannique à souffrir nous condamne ?
Mon esprit n'admet point ces monstres odieux
Dont le monde en tremblant fit autrefois des dieux.
Mais comment concevoir un Dieu, la bonté même,
Qui prodigua ses biens à ses enfants qu'il aime,
Et qui versa sur eux les maux à pleines mains ?
Quel œil peut pénétrer dans ses profonds desseins ?

(Could evil spring from the author of all good? Is it the black Typhon or barbarous Ahriman who condemns us to suffer under this tyrannical law? My mind rejects these heinous monsters the trembling world made into gods. How should we think of God, goodness itself, who lavishes gifts upon the children he loves, while he also pours abundant pain upon them? What eye may perceive the purpose of his designs?)

There is a mystery about evil. But there is clearly something which is new: hope. At some point Voltaire puts aside the philosophical argument against Leibniz or Pope, and points directly to the one thing that differentiates the new from the old, that is, hope; not optimism about variable circumstances, but hope beyond all circumstances, transcendent hope, regardless of what may happen circumstantially.

Des humains égarés partageant la faiblesse,
Dans une épaisse nuit cherchant à m'éclairer,
Je ne sais que souffrir, et non pas murmurer.
Un calife autrefois, à son heure dernière,
Au Dieu qu'il adorait dit pour toute prière :
"Je t'apporte, ô seul roi, seul être illimité,
Tout ce que tu n'as pas dans ton immensité,
Les défauts, les regrets, les maux, et l'ignorance."
Mais il pouvait encore ajouter *l'espérance.*[31]

(Sharing in the frailty of humanity, in the midst of the dark night, I seek clarity and know only suffering, but I won't

31 Voltaire, "Poème sur le désastre de Lisbonne," in *Œuvres Complètes* (Paris: Garnier, 1877), 9:470–79, 478.

> complain. Once a caliph, in his last hour, prayed to God, whom he worshipped: "I bring thee, O only and almighty king, that, which in your immensity, you lack —faults, regrets, pain, and ignorance." *He could have added hope.*)

The "rebellious"[32] spirit against a benevolent and forgiving Christian God, incapable of satisfying our "unsatisfied indignation," is a direct heir to Ivan Karamazov, Dostoevsky's character in *The Brothers Karamazov*, the crowning masterpiece of the Russian novelist,[33] another enthusiastic admirer of *Don Quixote.*

Is the survival of humanity worth the sacrifice of one single innocent victim? In the words of Ivan Karamazov:

> I want to forgive. I want to embrace. I don't want more suffering. And if the sufferings of children go to swell the sum of sufferings which was necessary to pay for truth, then I protest that the truth is not worth such a price. I don't want the mother to embrace the oppressor who threw her son to the dogs! She dare not forgive him! Let her forgive him for herself, if she will, let her forgive the torturer for the immeasurable suffering of her mother's heart. But the sufferings of her tortured child she has no right to forgive; she dare not forgive the torturer, even if the child were to forgive him! And if that is so, if they dare not forgive, what becomes of harmony? *Is there in the whole world a being who would have the right to forgive and could forgive?* I don't want harmony. From love for humanity I don't want it. I would rather be left with the unavenged suffering. I would rather remain with my unavenged suffering and unsatisfied indignation, even if I were wrong. (My emphasis)

To put it in the terms of mimetic anthropology, imagine the scapegoat victim to be a little child:

---

32 This is the word used by Alyosha to describe what Ivan is doing. *The Brothers Karamazov*, trans. Constance Garnett.

33 Needless to say, Dostoevsky is, together with Cervantes, Shakespeare, and a few others, a constant referent for Girard. See *Deceit, Desire, and the Novel* and *Resurrection from the Underground*, trans. James G. Williams (East Lansing, MI: Michigan State University Press, 2012).

> Imagine that you are creating a fabric of human destiny with the object of making men happy in the end, giving them peace and rest at last, but that it was essential and inevitable to torture to death only one tiny creature—that baby beating its breast with its fist, for instance—and to found that edifice on its unavenged tears, would you consent to be the architect on those conditions? Tell me, and tell the truth. "No, I wouldn't consent," said Alyosha softly. "And can you admit the idea that men for whom you are building it would agree to accept their happiness on the foundation of the unexpiated blood of a little victim? And accepting it would remain happy for ever?" "No, I can't admit it. Brother," said Alyosha suddenly, with flashing eyes, "you said just now, is there a being in the whole world *who would have the right to forgive and could forgive? But there is a Being and He can forgive everything, all and for all, because He gave His innocent blood for all and everything.* You have forgotten Him, and on Him is built the edifice, and it is to Him they cry aloud, 'Thou art just, O Lord, for Thy ways are revealed!'"

No, Ivan has not forgotten Christ. But the Christ of Ivan Karamazov is a mockery, a helpless creature, ultimately irrelevant, not the indignant God needed to put an end to indignant evil:

> "Ah! the One without sin and His blood! No, I have not forgotten Him; on the contrary I've been wondering all the time how it was you did not bring Him in before, for usually all arguments on your side put Him in the foreground. Do you know, Alyosha—don't—laugh—I made a poem about a year ago. If you can waste another ten minutes on me, I'll tell it to you."
>
> "You wrote a poem?"[34]

The "poem" is the famous story of the Grand Inquisitor. It is Ivan's response to Alyosha's remark about forgetting "the one Being who can forgive everything." It is, therefore, Ivan's story about Christ. The Grand Inquisitor, like the

34 *The Brothers Karamazov*. Amazon, 2022, 211.

Spanish Inquisition, is the stereotypical boogeyman of a certain historical hypocrisy. Karamazov's view of Sevilla and the *autos de fe* is mostly stereotypical nonsense. But we must pay attention to the Christ of the story, not to the historical nonsense. He comes on the scene, but does not say a word; he "only appears and passes on. Fifteen centuries have passed since He promised to come in His glory, fifteen centuries since His prophet wrote, 'Behold, I come quickly.'"[35]

> THE STORY OF THE GRAND INQUISITOR
>
> "My story is laid in Spain, in Seville, in the most terrible time of the Inquisition, when fires were lighted every day to the glory of God, and 'in the splendid auto da fe the wicked heretics were burnt'.... He visited His children only for a moment, and there where the flames were crackling round the heretics. In His infinite mercy He came once more among men in that human shape in which He walked among men for thirty-three years fifteen centuries ago. He came down to the 'hot pavements' of the southern town in which on the day before almost a hundred heretics had, *ad majorem gloriam Dei*, been burnt by the cardinal, in the presence of the king, the court, the knights, the cardinals, the most charming ladies of the court, and the whole population of Seville.
>
> "He came softly, unobserved, and yet, strange to say, everyone recognized Him. That might be one of the best passages in the poem. I mean, why they recognized Him. The people are irresistibly drawn to Him, they surround Him, they flock about Him, follow Him. He moves silently in their midst with a gentle smile of infinite compassion. The sun of love burns in His heart, and power shines from His eyes, and their radiance, shed on the people, stirs their hearts with responsive love.

(I cannot help but think of Soloviev's Antichrist, how "the assembly was carried away by the spell of his personality." Each in his own way is a crowd hero, each moves the masses with the radiant power of his personality.)

---

35 Ibid., 212.

> " . . . at that moment the cardinal himself, the Grand Inquisitor, passes by the cathedral. He is an old man, almost ninety, tall and erect, with a withered face and sunken eyes, in which there is still a gleam of light. He is not dressed in his gorgeous cardinal's robes, as he was the day before, when he was burning the enemies of the Roman Church—at this moment he is wearing his coarse, old, monk's cassock. At a distance behind him come his gloomy assistants and slaves and the 'holy guard.' He stops at the sight of the crowd and watches it from a distance. He sees everything. . . . He knits his thick grey brows and his eyes gleam with a sinister fire. He holds out his finger and bids the guards take Him. And such is his power, so completely are the people cowed into submission and trembling obedience to him, that the crowd immediately makes way for the guards, and in the midst of deathlike silence they lay hands on Him and lead him away. The crowd instantly bows down to the earth, like one man, before the old Inquisitor."[36]

That night the Grand Inquisitor will visit Christ in prison and will vigorously, passionately, explain to Him why He should have never returned; that He should be treated like a heretic; and also, that the freedom He brought to humanity is a danger to the people because they are too weak to be free, etc. This is not the place for an analysis of the Inquisitor's long speech. As is well known, *Christ remains perfectly silent*:

> "The old man longed for him to say something, however bitter and terrible. But He suddenly approached the old man in silence and softly kissed him on his bloodless aged lips. That was all his answer."[37]

"He came softly, unobserved, and yet, strange to say, everyone recognized Him. That might be one of the best passages in the poem." Indeed, this is a deliberate caricature of the Gospel narrative. The resurrected Jesus of the Gospels is not recognized by his own disciples, nor by Mary Magdalene at

---

36 Ibid., 213–14.
37 Ibid., 224.

the site of the open tomb, until he talks to them (John 20:4–16, and 21:4; Luke 24:16). His word reveals him as the Lord. Karamazov's Christ is, in Girardian terms, a romantic Christ, a figure of delicate yet beautifully passionate sensitivity. "He moves silently in their midst with a gentle smile of infinite compassion. The sun of love burns in His heart, and power shines from His eyes, and their radiance, shed on the people, stirs their hearts with responsive love." This is mockery. This Christ has nothing in common with the Gospel Christ on the *via dolorosa* or dying on the Cross.

"He came softly, unobserved," completely unannounced, no prophets here, no John the Baptist. But he is immediately recognized by everybody. He has some sort of magnetic power, "people are irresistibly drawn to Him," *en masse*. He has the magnetism of a crowd hero: "they surround Him, they flock about Him, follow Him." In Girardian terms, we may say that his attraction is profoundly mimetic. Which means it may turn into its opposite in the twinkling of an eye; as it actually does as soon as the Grand Inquisitor points his finger at Him to be sent to prison.

And all this brief and deeply emotional visit finally took place after "The tears of humanity rose up to Him as before . . . *And so many ages mankind had prayed* with faith and fervor, 'O Lord our God, hasten Thy coming'; *so many ages called upon Him*, that in His infinite mercy He deigned to come down to His servants. . . . And behold, He deigned to appear for a moment to the people, to the tortured, suffering people, sunk in iniquity, but loving Him like children. My story is laid in Spain, in Seville . . . "

It is a bitter, resentful, joke. While they are burning heretics at the stake, and people sink to the ground at the mere sight of the Grand Inquisitor, "He moves silently in their midst with a gentle smile of infinite compassion," and quickly disappears into the night as silently as he came. It does not change anything. Karamazov's Christ is there to prove that the tyrannical, insensitive, and cruel rule of the Grand Inquisitor is far more realistic than the "infinite compassion" of a Christ who is not human enough to talk with human beings. The desired of so many ages, "O Lord our God, hasten Thy coming," finally came and paraded his infinite compassion to soothe the suffering of his people, sunk in the iniquity of their sin.

Ivan Karamazov's world is unredeemable. He accepts God. But he has no faith, or hope, or love of God. To him, God is the creator of the world and in his infinite wisdom everything will make sense in the end, including the deliberately inflicted suffering of a child. In the great theater of the world everything and everybody has a role to play. Ivan Karamazov cannot accept that kind of overall "harmony" in which the suffering of the child makes sense ultimately. So, he "respectfully returns the ticket." He does not want the suffering of that child to make sense ever: "I would rather remain with my unavenged suffering and unsatisfied indignation."

What Ivan Karamazov does not know or does not want to know is that he would not think the way he does, nor would he feel the way he feels, except for Christ. It is amazing: he testifies to the truth with the very same gesture with which he indignantly rejects it. He chooses the child, the suffering of the child, as the ultimate bulwark of his resistance to accepting the atoning suffering of Christ on the Cross. And yet, he knew of Jesus's preference for children (Dostoevsky, too, felt such preference. The novel ends with the hope of the children in the Resurrection).

What is it that triggers Ivan's outrage about the suffering of the child in the outhouse beating his breast and praying "to dear, kind God"? What scandalizes him? Why is the innocence of the child different from that of the adult? The lack of outrage, I should say, that is the fundamental difference. The child suffers, but his suffering does not become a scandal to him. He may be sad, immensely sad and sorrowful, but not outraged. He suffers but does not stumble upon his suffering. That is what makes the suffering child Christ-like. To scandalize a child is to destroy his or her innocence:

> I say to you, unless you be converted, and become as little children, you shall not enter into the kingdom of heaven. Whosoever therefore shall humble himself as this little child, he is the greater in the kingdom of heaven. And he that shall receive one such little child in my name, receiveth me. But he that shall scandalize one of these little ones that believe in me, it were better for him that a millstone should be hanged about his neck, and that he should be drowned in the depth of the sea. (Matt. 18:3–6)

Girard places "scandal" at the very center of his reading of the New Testament.[38]

[Scandal is] a paradoxical obstacle that is almost impossible to avoid: the more this obstacle, or scandal, repels us, the more it attracts us. Those who are scandalized put all the more ardor in injuring themselves against it because they were injured there before.

Jesus reserves his most solemn warning for the adults who seduce children into the infernal prison of scandal. The more the imitation is innocent and trusting, the more the one who imitates is easily scandalized, and the more the seducer is guilty of abusing this innocence. Scandals are so formidable that to put us on guard against them, Jesus resorts to an uncharacteristic hyperbolic style: "If your hand scandalizes you, cut it off; if your eye scandalizes you, pull it out" (Matt. 18:8–9).[39]

Christ, the Lamb of God, is precisely the one who removes the scandal, who accepts the suffering out of love in a totally gratuitous manner. From a human perspective, there is nothing so Christ-like as the innocent suffering of the child. God's innocence shines on the innocence of the child. The Son of God, to whom all power has been given, willingly gives himself into human hands to be tortured and killed for our sake. Only his own scandalized indignation and outrage prevents

---

38 See Jeremiah Alberg, "Scandal," in *The Palgrave Handbook of Mimetic Theory and Religion*, ed. James Alison and Wolfgang Palaver (New York, NY: Palgrave Macmillan, 2017).

39 *I See Satan Fall Like Lightning*, 16–17.

Ivan Karamazov from seeing the innocence of Christ in the child and the innocence of the child in Christ. If there is a human image capable of expressing to some degree Christ's sorrow unto death praying to his Father in Gethsemane, it is probably that of the suffering child "praying to dear, kind God."

Yet Girardian anthropology, with its emphasis on the denunciation of the sacrificial violence that kills the scapegoat, inevitably runs the risk of feeding the very scandal it condemns. Girard is fully aware of this risk. In fact, he can parody his own theory on account of it, as we saw already, in God's apologizing for being late.[40]

The style of Girard's self-parody is not too far from that of Ivan Karamazov, without the latter's bitterness or cynicism. After all, they both complain about the absence of a supposedly benevolent God, who was not there when he was most needed. At least Girard's parodic God apologizes for having come too late to save all those millions of sacrificial victims. He would have saved them by revealing to us, humans, "the mechanisms of our violence"; by letting us know that our

---

40 There was always a distance between Girard and his own theory. It could take different forms, including self-satire, a classic way of doing it. A famous example is the one at the end of *A Theater of Envy*, his book on Shakespeare, in imitation of the English bard. It is the title of the last chapter, "Self-Satire in *The Tempest*," where he explains how "Shakespeare is ironically undermining himself." This is the last paragraph of the book: "If Shakespeare himself finally decided that enough is enough, what about his critic? Either my thesis became obvious ages ago or it never will. . . . It is too late for a graceful exit, but Shakespeare is not the kind of writer who would leave his friends in the lurch; he is beckoning to me; he has already suggested the most suitable conclusion for my enterprise, the inescapable ending for the study I have written. Miranda put to sleep by mimetic desire! With such a cue in front of me, the sole drift of my purpose doth extend not a line further." Girard is poking fun at his own single-minded pursuit of mimetic desire. It is a fairly mild and elegant way of distancing himself from himself. The parody we are examining now is far more serious. What is at stake is the very heart of Girardian anthropology. Nevertheless, behind Girardian theory, no matter how strongly or stubbornly defended, there is always the Girard whose ultimate allegiance is not to any kind of intellectual construct, but to the Truth itself, "the unique object of his desire, in the most traditional way" (Benoît Chantre, *Les derniers jours de René Girard* [Paris: Grasset, 2016]).

sacrificial violence was just murder plain and simple, in the hope, of course, that we would stop murdering them, once we knew the truth of what we were doing. Not only was he too late to save those millions of innocent victims, his tardiness also allowed humanity to get used to its sacrificial institutions, thus making it almost impossible to give them up in favor of the Christian solution. "We were never Christian enough."

In sum, if you read the Christian Revelation as a denunciation of the violence that kills the founding victim, you are automatically excluding Christ from the founding moment, from the very transition from animality to humanity. If, on the other hand, you see the Christian Revelation as the revelation of the Lamb of God, "which was slain since the foundation of the world" (Rev. 13:8), because "God chose him as your ransom long before the world began, but now in these last days he has been revealed for your sake" (1 Peter 1:20), in other words, if you see the origin, "the transition," from the perspective of the Faith, then it is perfectly possible to see Christ in the original founding victim. Hidden, unrecognized, or to use Girard's own word, "misrecognized," *méconnu*. Christ would be the true object of Girardian *méconnaissance*. But that would not be science, and Girard wanted to be scientific.

CHAPTER 6

Things Hidden since the Foundation of the World

Time
Is long but what is true
Will happen.
(Hölderlin, "Mnemosyne")

For there is nothing hid, which shall not be made manifest: neither was it made secret, but that it may come abroad. (Mark 4:22)

All this Jesus said to the crowds in parables; indeed, he said nothing to them without a parable. This was to fulfil what was spoken by the prophet: "I will open my mouth in parables, I will utter what has been hidden since the foundation of the world (*ereuxomai kekrummena apo kataboleis kosmou*)." (Matthew, 13:34–35)

THE VULGATE TRANSLATES THE GREEK *EREUXOMAI* AS *eructabo*: *eructabo abscondita a mundi constitutione*. "I will spew out [or 'exhale,' 'cast forth'] things hidden since the foundation of the world." *Eructabo* is a literal translation of *ereuxomai*, which—according to an old study of words in the New Testament—"means originally to belch, to disgorge. Homer uses it of the sea surging against the shore (*Iliad*, xvii., 265). Pindar of the eruption of Aetna (*Pyth*. I. 40)."[1] These are, therefore, the words of the prophet: "I will open my mouth in parables, and I will spew out with great force things hidden since the foundation of the world." The things ejected, spewed out, were not just things that had been hidden from public knowledge in some accidental or purely physical way. They were things hidden inside of Christ. He spews them out because he carried

1 Marvin R. Vincent, *Word Studies in the New Testament, Vol. 1* (New York: C. Scribner's Sons, 1887), 80.

them inside. Those things found refuge in him. They were not hidden anywhere else. He is the only carrier of those things. When he brings them out, he is bringing out something that belongs to him, a part of him. For nothing that is not a part of him can find shelter in him. In other words, he is revealing himself, for if he had in him something that was not him, he would not be the Son of God. Of course, this also means that Christ himself was hidden from the beginning of the world, as we also read in the first letter of Peter: "He was destined from the foundation of the world but was made manifest at the end of the times for your sake" (1:20).

The Gospel says that Christ always talked to the multitude of people that came to him, in parables. But Christ mentioned two radically different kinds of parables: his own, which, in a variety of narrative examples, always refer to one thing, and one thing only, the Kingdom of God; and then there are man-made parables. The difference between the two is that man-made parables are empty words, narratives without true referent; they do not connect with anything real, they are fictions.

Mimetic anthropology should understand that. Because, in strictly human terms, the only transcendence that the scapegoat mechanism can generate is illusory, a sacralized projection of collective violence, and that is the symbolic level that makes human language possible. Christ confirms that, when he tells the disciples that he has given them the key to all parables, which is to say, to human language in general; the key is the Kingdom of God. The "parables," the words, of those who do not have the key, are nothing but parables, words lacking any true referent. If God is not behind the words, their meaning is nothing but an illusion, a mirage.

> And when he was alone, those who were about him with the Twelve asked him concerning the parables. And he said to them, "To you has been given the secret of the kingdom of God, but for those outside everything is in parables; so that they may indeed see but not perceive,

> and may indeed hear but not understand; lest they should turn again, and be forgiven." And he said to them, "Do you not understand this parable [of the sower]? How then will you understand all the parables?" (Mark 4:10–13)

It is a strange text. Matthew makes it easier to understand:

> Then the disciples came and said to him, "Why do you speak to them in parables?" And he answered them, "To you it has been given the secrets of the kingdom of heaven, but to them it has not been given. . . . This is why I speak to them in parables, because seeing they do not see, and hearing they do not hear, nor do they understand. With them indeed is fulfilled the prophecy of Isaiah which says:
>
> > You shall indeed hear but never understand,
> > and you shall indeed see but never perceive.
> > For these people's heart has grown dull,
> > and their ears are heavy of hearing,
> > and their eyes they have closed.
> > Lest they should perceive with their eyes,
> > and hear with their ears,
> > and understand with their heart,
> > and turn for me to heal them." (Matt. 13:10–16)

To those "who have been given the secrets of the kingdom of heaven," to them have also been given the key to all of Christ's parables. We should keep this in mind: once you have the secret of the Kingdom, you can understand all of Christ's parables. *It is the Kingdom of God that gives meaning to the parable, not the other way around.* But when Christ addresses those outside, those who do not have the secret of the Kingdom, the situation is the reverse one: all they have is parables, words without ultimate meaning, mere appearances. That is all they see or hear or understand. Christ speaks to them in parables, which is the only language they understand, in order to reveal to them the secret of the Kingdom, without which they do not have the possibility of converting and being healed. Or rather, they should not be allowed to convert and be healed without hearing first the word of the Kingdom, without which any conversion would be meaningless. Thus, once again, it is the Kingdom of God that gives meaning to the conversion, and not the other way around. The message is not, "convert and then be admitted to the Kingdom," but rather "hear the word of the Kingdom of God and then, on the basis of such understanding of the word, your conversion will be meaningful and real."

Outside the Kingdom of God there is no forgiveness and, therefore, no meaningful repentance. Outside is the world of sin, and it is in the nature of sin not to allow the sinner to see the reality of what they see, or hear the reality of what they hear. A world which is not sustained by the word of God is a world of mere appearances, deceptive appearances. They see everything, but they do not really see the reality behind it. They hear everything, but they do not hear the only thing that they should hear, so they do not understand. Which can be a perfectly good definition of those living under the overwhelming power of the archaic man-made sacred. For there is no such thing as forgiveness in the realm of the old sacred, and, therefore, no such thing as repentance. And without repentance, which is simply accepting the forgiveness offered by Christ, we are still living under the old regime.

If we look at the world through the mystery of the Kingdom it appears to us as an immense parable, a narrative open to that mysterious reality that gives light and meaning to everything. Otherwise, although we see the world out there, we do not see the reality behind it. We see but do not really see; we speak about it, but our words are nothing but words; they do not reveal anything that is true. If we are not open to the mystery that sustains all things, we live in a world of shadows. We keep on talking even though we have nothing to say. Life becomes, in the words of Shakespeare's Macbeth, "A tale told by an idiot, full of sound and fury, signifying nothing" (*Macbeth* V, v), or, "a walking shadow." Or as Calderón would say, "[a] shadow, a delirium, a fiction."[2]

---

2 *Life is a Dream and Other Classics*, ed. Eric Bentley, trans. Roy Campbell (New York: Applause, 1989), 268.

The "things hidden since the foundation of the world" must be things that concern the Kingdom of God. Hidden things that give meaning to the words of the parable that precedes them in the Gospel text: "The kingdom of heaven is like leaven which a woman took and hid in three measures of meal, till it was all leavened" (Matt. 13:33). Or the one before, the parable of the mustard seeds, "which is the smallest of all seeds, but when it has grown it is the greatest of shrubs." In other words, things hidden but very active, either fermenting the very thing that hides them, or growing to be the best, the most visible. The things hidden are not simply things unknown, they are living things. They grow and are intimately connected with everything around them. These are the things that come out of the mouth of Jesus with great force and testify to who he is and to his mission.

And he said to them, "Is a lamp brought in to be put under a bushel, or under a bed, and not on a stand? For there is nothing hidden, except to be made manifest; nor is anything secret, except to come to light" (Mark 4:21–22).

Everything hidden will be revealed. That includes man's most guarded inner thoughts, as well as things hidden since the foundation of the world. Everything will be revealed in the light of the revelation itself, the light that was brought to be put on a stand, not hidden under a bushel. Christ is the light that was brought into the world. So, everything will be seen, will make sense, in the light of Christ, the light that is Christ. He did not come to reveal things alien to him, human reasons to hide the truth. The reasons that were hidden in him were Christ's reasons. They were hidden in order to be revealed as Christ would reveal himself. Even when hidden they were already an integral part of the light that was Christ. Christ did not come to reveal Satan's things, Satan's ugliness, he came to reveal himself. He is the light that makes sense of everything.

All of which means that he was the light at the center of the darkness created by the victimizing mechanism. When the light eventually conquers the darkness, the mechanism will reveal its own inner truth, Christ. With Christ the dark hiddenness vanishes. There is no longer any reason to hide anything because it has been revealed, not as a human thing, but as a divine thing. It was always a divine thing from the beginning. This is the truth that comes out in parables from the mouth of Christ.

In mimetic theory, however, there is no distinction between Christ's parables of the Kingdom and the parables of all those "who are outside." A parable is simply "an indirect discourse that can, but need not, include narrative elements. . . . The essential factor in the Gospel use of parable is Jesus's willingness to be imprisoned within the representation of persecution from the persecutors' standpoint, and to do so for the sake of his listeners who cannot understand any other viewpoint, since they are prisoners of it themselves."[3] Thus, basically, a parable is, like all human language, rooted in the foundational killing of the victim. To speak in parables about the Kingdom is to speak indirectly about it, taking an old sacrificial detour, so to speak, in order to make the truth of the Kingdom accessible to a persecuting humanity.[4] Girard seems to remain deaf to Christ's explanation to his disciples: "You have the key to all parables, because I have revealed to you the secrets of the Kingdom." Those who are outside do not have the key. Therefore, they have nothing but empty words, parables "taken literally," to use Girard's words. Obviously for Girard the parable is an imperfect way to explain the Kingdom, given the fact that it is strictly human and, therefore, of Satanic origin in the scapegoat mechanism. This human language does not share in the light of the revelation. It is, in fact, the opposite. Given its persecutory origin, it actually darkens the light. Christ is willing to become "imprisoned" in it for the sake of the persecutors. Parables are as alien to Christ as the scapegoat mechanism itself, in Girard's theory. He is willing to submit to it, but it is definitely not his thing,

3 *The Scapegoat*, 186.
4 See *When These Things Begin*, 116.

if you will allow the expression. He uses it because he has no other way of communicating with the human creature who became human in a horrible satanic way.

Which, once again, raises the question of what it is that Christ saw in this creature—a product of random evolutionary processes and of its own violence—which merited such an extraordinary sacrifice of the Son of God. Girard, the sincere Catholic believer, knows the answer to that, which is the traditional one based on the love of God for the creature that he made in his own image. But within the context of mimetic anthropology, that will forever remain a mystery; not a mystery of faith, of course, but a purely epistemological one. Mimetic theory never explored such a problem. It was obviously not within the purview of its "purely scientific" explanation of the transition from animal to man, "without the slightest recourse to transcendence, or anything irrational," of which we have already spoken. And yet Girard's whole enterprise was meant to provide a rational explanation of Christ's sacrifice. As we have said repeatedly, in Girard's "scientific" thinking Christ is never mentioned, but it is always assumed.

The parable of the leaven hidden in the flour, or that of the mustard seed, are clear indications that the "things hidden since the foundation of the world" are not the circumstances attending to the foundational murder of the victim, the workings of the scapegoat mechanism, the hiding of which was essential, according to mimetic theory, for the proper functioning of the mechanism. Quite the contrary, the "things hidden" were the seed of redemption at the very center of the violence; the hidden presence of Christ himself; the hand of God which prevented the maddening ambivalence of sacralized human violence from destroying human society at its birth, and created the conditions for the eventual shedding off of the Satanic cover up. Satan's rule over the kingdoms of the world was the reflection of a humanity which had forgotten the true God, and was not ready yet to receive its savior in the flesh.

CHAPTER 7

Can Satan Expel Satan?

THIS IS THE GOSPEL PASSAGE:

> All the crowds were amazed and said, "Can this be the Son of David?" But when the Pharisees heard it, they said, "It is only by Beelzebub, the ruler of the demons, that this fellow casts out the demons." He knew what they were thinking and said to them, "Every kingdom divided against itself is laid waste, and no city or house divided against itself will stand. *If Satan casts out Satan, he is divided against himself; how then will his kingdom stand?* If I cast out demons by Beelzebub, by whom do your own exorcists cast them out? Therefore, they will be your judges. But if it is by the Spirit of God that I cast out demons, then the kingdom of God has come to you." (Matthew 12)

"How then will his kingdom stand?" It is a rhetorical question. The answer is perfectly clear: if a kingdom divided against itself cannot stand, if a city or house divided against itself cannot stand, how can you expect Satan's kingdom divided against itself to stand? "You cannot" is the obvious answer. Which is the answer in Mark, 3:26: "And if Satan is risen up against himself and is divided, he cannot stand, but is coming to an end."

These gospel words are at the very center of Girard's mimetic anthropology. "Satan casts out Satan" is the very definition of the "scapegoat mechanism." Violence expelling violence. Of course, Girard was aware of the rhetorical character of Jesus's question. But he saw it as an integral part of the announcement that "the kingdom of God has come upon you." Christ reveals both the arrival of the Kingdom of God and the fatal weakness of Satan simultaneously. They belong together. In a sense, they are the two sides of the same revelation. The kingdom of Satan is revealing its weakness, is coming to an end, because the Kingdom of God has arrived:

> Jesus does not deny that Satan expels Satan. He has been Satan for a long time. But he says he is not going to do it for long because his kingdom is at an end. The Kingdom of Satan exists and can be a kingdom only because Satan can expel Satan. The Kingdom of Satan is founded on negative imitation. If this bad mimesis did not expel itself, did not moderate itself, did not repress itself, there would be no kingdom of Satan. There would quickly be nothing at all.[1]

So God must make an exception to the general rule that a house divided against itself will not stand:

> What is true of every kingdom, city, and house must be true of the kingdom of Satan. But the kingdom of Satan is not one among others. The Gospels state explicitly that Satan is the principle of every kingdom. How is that possible? By being the principle of violent expulsion and the deceit it produces. The kingdom of Satan is none other than the violence that casts itself out in all the rites and exorcisms alluded to by the Pharisees, and even before that in the original, hidden deed that serves as a model for all these rites, the unanimous and spontaneous murder of a scapegoat.[2]

God must make an exception in the case of the kingdom of Satan, because "the kingdom of Satan is not one among others." Indeed, "if this bad mimesis [rivalrous violence] did not expel itself, did not moderate itself, did not repress itself, there would be no kingdom of Satan. There would quickly be nothing at all."

This is an amazing declaration. If Satan did not expel Satan, "there would quickly be nothing at all," humanity would have disappeared from the face of the earth. If this is true, if Satan has the power to keep humanity in existence by "moderating, or repressing, or expelling himself," who needs Christ? If Satan, by expelling Satan, can become "the cornerstone," who needs Christ?

---

1 David Cayley, *The Ideas of Rene Girard: An Anthropology of Religion and Violence*, 47.

2 *The Scapegoat*, 186–87. My emphasis.

"But if it is by the spirit of God that I cast out demons, then the Kingdom of God has come to you." The Kingdom of God has arrived. The Kingdom of God is the truth, which is being revealed in their sight, even though they do not see it, which can only mean they are deceived by Satan, who is a liar, and the father of lies.

Is it really true that Satan cast out Satan? Where was the truth that has now arrived? Was it kept in suspension while humanity was built on a lie? While thousands upon thousands of years of human culture and civilization spread throughout the planet on a lie? Are we the children of Satan? Is that the truth that Christ came to reveal to us as a price or a prologue to forgiveness? But, if we are God's children, where was He?

It is not good enough to say that we are reading anthropology and not theology. The truth is one and not two, as Girard knew and argued throughout his life. I knew, as I have already indicated, and as he always admitted, that he worried about the connection between his science and his religious understanding. Perhaps he should have been more explicit about it. Perhaps he should have stopped when he became—in his words—"convinced that [he could] demonstrate the transition from animal to man" without even mentioning Christ; because at that very moment he either was deluded regarding the power of his "demonstration," or his "atheism" was more than a joke. This second possibility must be discarded immediately by anybody who knew the man. But his "demonstration" must be reexamined.

At the root of the problem, once again, lies Girard's unwavering view of a radical incompatibility between Christ and human violence, of which we have already spoken (see pp. 36–37 above), and which I find a constant source of amazement. Is it not amazing that this absolutely unpolluted person, this divine omnipotence infinitely removed from, and absolutely incompatible with, violence, chooses the bloody Cross as a symbol of his presence, and tells us that he is the Paschal Lamb, whose flesh we must eat and whose blood we must drink if we want to live *in aeternum*? Whatever the unfathomable reason may be for such a divine act, it doesn't seem it would support the notion of a radical incompatibility between Christ and human violence. Human violence must be redeemable, or neither the Crucified or the Eucharist would make any sense.

This is a matter of common sense. I am not a theologian nor do I have any interest in theological debate. What I am trying to say is that the original foundational violence postulated by Girardian anthropology cannot stand on its own on purely rational grounds, From a Christian perspective one cannot accept the idea that humanity was built on a lie. The origin of humanity and, simultaneously, that of the archaic sacred, cannot be fully explained without the least reference to the Christian faith.

It is not a question of choosing one explanation or the other, anthropological or theological. There is no purely anthropological explanation. Girard was wrong, he could not explain "the transition from animal to man," even though he thought he did. He discovered and explained everything convincingly except the final "sacred" step. "[Man] is the only creature on earth which God willed for itself."[3]

Christ, not Satan, is "the stone that the builders rejected." This is what Christ will reveal about himself, in accordance with the prophetic announcement. This is a revelation of what has always been the case. If the scapegoat mechanism, Girard's extraordinary discovery, is indeed the anthropological structure underpinning every sacrificial rite everywhere at any time, as he says and as I believe, then Christ was also there, everywhere, from the beginning. That is what was hidden since the beginning "in order to be revealed." We know now, because it has been revealed, what those early humans could not possibly know.[4]

---

3 *Gaudium et Spes*, 24.

4 See Charles Journet, *The Meaning of Grace*, trans. A. V. Littledale (New York: Scepter Publishers, 1996). "Immediately after the Fall the mediation of Christ began. It worked in a very hidden manner, by anticipation. This was the age of the expectation of Christ. It was possible for men to be saved by him without

To reiterate what I said in the previous chapter, Christ reveals himself; the truth that he reveals is not the ugly truth hidden by Satan the liar, the deceiver, but Christ's own truth, the truth that does not deceive. What Girard calls the expulsion of Satan by Satan is the transformation of violence into something good, the power of destruction into something constructive. What could this transformation be but an anticipation of what lies at the center of the Christian revelation, the transformation of death into life?[5]

---

knowing of his future coming, except in a very obscure and very imperfect manner.... No sooner had man fallen than God, from the height of heaven, poured down grace and forgiveness.... But all grace before Christ was given only in view of his future coming; it was Christian grace by anticipation.... St. Thomas calls this age the age of the natural law. Why? Because grace came into men's hearts by adapting itself to the movements of nature" (94–95). In the words of Romano Guardini: "Ultimately it is difficult to understand how [human beings] could survive the moment of rebellion, the Fall. The fact that they did not succumb to the ripping apart undergone by their very essence at that moment, and have been able to continue making history, could only be possible because God sustained them and led them toward their salvation, which would arrive one day." (This is the author's translation from Romano Guardini, *El comienzo de todas las cosas* [Bilbao: Desclée de Brouwer, 2013], itself a translation from Guardini, *Der Anfang Aller Dinge*, 1987.) See also Gil Bailie's *God's Gamble. The Gravitational Power of Crucified Love* (New York, NY: Angelico Press, 2016), "The First Victim," 95 ff.

5 What we might call a side effect of the incongruous belief in the absolute incompatibility between Christ and death is to interpret the undeniable relationship between the two in a poetic or "creative" way. Since death has no power over Christ, he can treat his own death in whichever way he wants to serve his own purpose, which, according to James Alison, includes demonstrating to us, human beings, what it means to live a life free from the fear of death; to show us that death is powerless (as long as you follow Christ, I should imagine; as long as "Christ lives in you and you in Christ"). This is how Alison explains it: "There is a deliberate element in the way in which Jesus goes to his death, and this deliberate element has nothing to do with any masochism or death wish. Quite the contrary. It is the attitude of someone who is so entirely free of being involved in death that he manages to mount, to stage, a show, a mime, in such a way that other people will be able to learn to live as if death were not. That is the difference between dying and redeeming death. Someone who is totally and utterly free with respect to his death is capable of making of his death a sort of 'show' which takes the sting out of death's tail, detoxifying the reality of death, revealing it to be without power, and doing this forever.... [God's] project was, if you'll excuse the inappropriate language, to organize a sort of stage death—a real death but transformed into theater—from which he would rise, so as to reveal the impotence of death, and with it the impotence of all the

CHAPTER 8

"God created humankind in his own image"

THE POWER OF THE CROWD AND THE DISAPPEARANCE OF THE OBJECT

LET US RECAPITULATE SOME OF THE BASICS. IMITATION becomes human imitation as the imitator's attention shifts from the object or the action to the subject or agent, that is to say, the human other. Traditional Christian doctrine can account for this shift from object to human subject within the framework of the Christian belief that God is the ultimate object of human desire, and every human being is a bearer of God's image. Even though everything has been created by God, there is nothing in the whole of creation quite like a human being, as Adam found out when he received Eve as his proper companion. It is the doctrine of the Church that God paid special attention to the creation of man. He intervened directly. "[Man] is the only creature on earth which God willed for itself."[1] In the Bible "the *imago Dei* constitutes almost a definition of man: the mystery of man cannot be grasped apart from the

1 *Gaudium et Spes*, 24.

mechanisms of violence which dominate our lives" (*Raising Abel. The Recovery of the Eschatological Imagination* [New York: Crossroad, 1996], 58–59). It is hard for me to imagine that Alison would summarize the message of Christ's demonstration of his triumph over death as something like this: "You see, there is nothing to it, all your fears were for nothing." That would make Christ's beyond-the-human anguish meaningless. All that sweating of blood for something that was really nothing? I know that is not likely to be what Alison means. "The impotence of death"? Only because of Christ, and only because we have been forgiven. Take Christ, the uniqueness of Christ, out of the picture, and there is nothing but death, all-powerful death.

mystery of God."[2] However, the very same thing that was an expression of the love of God, became the occasion for something bad, envious desire. That is how it all began in the history of Fallen Man, the only human history open to rational investigation.

The reason for the Fall, as originally described by Girard, is hidden in the Devil's deceitful words to Eve: "you will become like God," yes, you will become like God in each other's eyes. The story of Cain and Abel is the story of Cain's envy because he sees Abel as God's favorite, as a God-like creature.

Another example of this transformation of something inherently good into the occasion for something bad is the Biblical story of the mark of Cain and its historical interpretation. After Yahweh had condemned Cain to be "a fugitive and a wanderer over the earth," Cain said to Yahweh, "My punishment is greater than I can bear. See! Today you drive me from this ground, I must hide from you and be a fugitive and a wanderer over the earth. Why, whoever comes upon me will kill me!" "Very well, then," Yahweh replied, "If anyone kills Cain sevenfold vengeance shall be taken for him." So, Yahweh put a mark on Cain, to prevent whoever might come across him from striking him down (*Genesis* 3–4).

The sign was supposed to protect Cain, to stop the cycle of vengeance, by showing to everybody that Cain was God's creature, his property, so to speak. Cain was under his protection. As it turned out, God's sign produced the opposite effect. Instead of stopping the violence, it started an endless violence covering the whole earth, until the earth became "corrupt in God's sight, and the earth [was] filled with violence" (6:11). So "the Lord was sorry that he had made man on the earth, and it grieved him to his heart" (6:6).

---

2 *Human Persons Created in the Image of God*, International Theological Commission of the Catholic Church. https://www.vatican.va/roman_curia/congregations/cfaith/cti_documents/rc_con_cfaith_doc_20040723_communion-stewardship_en.html. Accessed February 16, 2024.

God will flood the whole earth. However, one must wonder, in terms of the destruction of the human race, what is the difference between the mythical flood which covers the whole earth, and the human violence which "has filled the earth"? It looks like the human race would have destroyed itself without any help from God. Ruth Mellinkoff says that "both in Jewish and Christian thought [the mark of Cain] came to be overwhelmingly understood as a badge of punishment,"[3] a stigma, a sign pointing to the guilty one.

It should be noted also that the mark of Cain is by no means unique in its association of the sacred with punishment, and ultimately with the sacrificial victim. As we saw already, in ancient Roman law, the magistrate pronounced the death sentence by touching the convict with his staff while pronouncing the words: *sacer esto*, "be sacred." In other words, he put the sacred sign of the gods on the man, thereby rendering him sacred, untouchable, the one that must be sacrificed. Or the very opposite: declaring a person to be sacred could also mean that the law could not sentence him to death, but if anybody killed him, the killer would not be prosecuted. *Sacer esto* is also the title of a poem by Victor Hugo, a political attack on somebody who deserves something worse than a death sentence, like being forever a fugitive rejected by everybody. The connection with both the biblical Cain and the Roman law is perfectly explicit. He is just attaching the Roman label to biblical Cain.

The Power of the Crowd

In Girard's "scientific" explanation of the emergence of the human, the attraction of the image of God in man disappears from view but is replaced by its degraded and evil product: the overwhelming power of a crowd solidly held together in a violent hypermimetic way of all against one, the victim, on whom this power is collectively projected and sacralized. This

3 Ruth Mellinkoff, *The Mark of Cain* (Berkeley and Los Angeles: University of California Press, 1981), 51.

God-like power of the crowd is something like the hypermimetic attraction of the crowd infinitely magnified, a Satanic imitation of the true God.

But we do not really know. This manner of talking, these rhetorical images are simply attempts to describe a historical reality, something called sacred, which ruled humanity everywhere on planet earth for thousands of years by sheer terror, as Voltaire put it, *monstres odieux dont le monde en tremblant fit autrefois des dieux* (hateful monsters of which the trembling world once made gods). We do not know, but we cannot ignore it or minimize it. And, I am afraid, Girard never paid enough attention to this monstrosity. It remained mostly invisible behind the brilliant rationality of the explanation.

This tremendous power seems to emanate from the cadaver of the victim. It is an illusory transcendence, of course, a collectively created mirage, but everything will be seen through it. Which means that everything will be seen through the crowd. The human phenomenon which Shakespeare or Lucretius described as desiring "through another's eye" or "by hearsay," enormously multiplied, will be the iron rule of the newly created human community.[4]

---

4 James Alison's description of the originary scene, the "transition from animal to human," is probably one of the best in keeping with what Girard intended. I quote from it: "Imitation among simians clearly contributes to group cohesion and certainly makes much faster learning possible. But this very same positive dimension of imitation is always poised to turn into a negative one: Imitation can, and very easily does, flip into rivalry. Thus, as a group becomes better and better at imitation, so also does the risk grow that the potential for rivalry implicit in ever-better imitation is able to overcome whatever instinctual braking mechanisms and dominance patterns the group has. And, this can quickly threaten the group's survival. The question then arises: What was it, or is it, that prevents the growing equality among ever more efficient imitators from leading them to destroy one other? Between the 'all together' of imitation and the 'all against all' of rivalry. . . . The 'Scapegoat Mechanism,' Girard's answer to this question, is well known: the movement from all against all to all against one, commonly referred to as the scapegoat mechanism . . . it can happen, in the midst of the growing (and terrifying) frenzy of the all against all that, without anyone being aware of how or why, attention comes to be drawn toward one or other member of the group. This happens in such a way that the group begins to coalesce round that member, who is thrown out, most probably killed. In finding themselves caught up in this together, those involved are also brought together to a place of sudden

It must be difficult for us to imagine the power of the crowd gathered around the victim in the originary scene proposed or suggested by mimetic anthropology. It would be wrong to imagine it as a unanimous agreement. An agreement is not an agreement if there is no consent involved. Here every individual sees and feels what everybody else sees and feels, directly, immediately. The crowd weighs with overwhelming force on everybody, eliminating the slightest possibility of dissent in the expulsion of the victim. The only possible singularity, the only individual difference that counts, is that of the victim. Nevertheless, this is no longer a herd. If the result is going to be a human society, the power of the crowd cannot be a blind force, purely instinctive. Unanimity must become significant. It has to be more than a physical agglomeration. Everybody must be aware that everybody is doing the same thing. It is not enough for everybody to be doing the same thing, like a herd, for that could be a meaningless accident. In order for unanimity as such to be the decisive factor that the theory requires, everybody must know that everybody is doing the same thing. Everybody must feel the anxious and overwhelming need to conform. Unanimity as such must exert an irresistible attraction.[5] We must remember that this is the matrix of the archaic

unanimity, and therefore of shared peace, in the presence of a cadaver. This is a unique and new form of shared attention in which the now absent one, present as cadaver, comes to acquire an importance as having apparently produced the peace which the group is now enjoying. Eventually, this can lead to the victim being deified. For it is perceived as having caused, as only a 'god' could, both the violence that led to its murder, and the peace which befell the group thereafter. Girard's thesis is that 'the peoples of the world do not invent their gods. They deify their victims.'"

5 Girard has insisted on the "monolithic" character of archaic unanimity. See *Violence Renounced*, ed. Willard M. Swartley, "Response by René Girard" (Telford, PA: Pandora Press, 2000), 309. See also Eric Gans, *The Origin of Language. A Formal Theory of Representation* (Berkeley and Los Angeles: University of California Press, 1981): "Let us assume with Girard that the community contemplates the body of its victim as a 'transcendental signifier' of the whole process of crisis and resolution . . . this sign could only have a collective significance within the presence of the community to itself. That is, not only would each member contemplate the victim, he would be aware of his fellow participants in the same act of contemplation. Awareness of presence and awareness of the cadaver are two elements of the same movement" (19).

sacred. The attraction of which we are talking is already the attraction of the sacred, a sacred attraction.

But the question is not whether the hypermimetic attraction of crowd violence can do the job assigned to the powerful attraction of the image of God in man. In truth, it cannot. Satan cannot possibly do Christ's work. The question is rather whether the attraction of the victimizing crowd can do the job assigned to it by mimetic anthropology. In Girardian terms, the question is this: can the scapegoat mechanism do the job that it claims as its own?

We must begin with the human crowd, the formidable power of the originary human crowd. First of all, the crowd constitutes itself as such in the presence of the victim that has been killed. In the beginning was the victimizing crowd. The human individual becomes self-aware, or self-conscious, as member of the crowd, not just any crowd, but the crowd gathered around the victim that has been killed. That is what it means for Girard to say that the sacrificial victim is the originary symbol, the ur-symbol:

> [In] order for the symbolic level to be reached . . . it isn't sufficient to have an adequate brain size. One needs a *center of signification*, and the *scapegoated victim* provides this center. . . . In the repetition of the event . . . a form of "staging" in the shape of a killing of a surrogate victim had to be set in place. This victim . . . is a *symbol* of the proto-event, *it is the first symbolic sign* ever invented by these hominids. It is the first moment in which something *stands* for *something else.* It is the ur-symbol.[6]

Clearly the killing of the surrogate victim, which stands for the original one, is indeed symbolic, but the dead body of the original victim was already symbolic. It meant something beyond its sheer physical presence:

> Because of the victim, in so far as it seems to emerge from the community and the community seems to emerge from

6 Rocha and de Castro, *Evolution and Conversion*, 76–77.

> it, for the first time there can be something like an inside and an outside, a before and an after, a community and the sacred. We have already seen that *the victim appears to be simultaneously good and evil, peaceable and violent*. . . . Every possible significant element seems to have its outline in the sacred and at the same time to be transcended by it. In this sense, the victim does seem to constitute a universal signifier.[7]

The human creature that emerges through the scapegoat mechanism sees everything through the crowd, or rather through the sacralized victim which has been invested with the power of the crowd, which owns the crowd. The force of the evidence, the clarity with which they see what they see, is in direct proportion to the collective solidity of their unanimous vision. No rational, no scientific evidence can go beyond such obviousness, because, according to the theory, that initial vision is not only the ground of the sacred; it is also the ground from which rationality itself will evolve. According to theory, the most compelling, clearest, evidence that human rationality can produce, cannot go beyond that which is evident to everybody minus one. That one, the victim, will forever maintain a minimum of uncertainty even in the clearest possible rational evidence. That is the kind of unanimity required to sacralize the victim in the absence of God. Let us also keep in mind that, in Girard's theory, it took the divine power of Christ to break the power of the crowd, so strong was it.

On the other hand, the sacred power of the victim is, according to theory, a collective hallucination, a mirage. The new human creature does not see the reality of the world out there, but only a deceiving image of it, a false image, filtered through the crowd, through the violent sacred. The new human lives in some sort of ontological vacuum. The reality of the object remains invisible.[8]

---

7 *Things Hidden*, 102.

8 Compare Paul Dumouchel, "A Theory of Everything," in *The Palgrave Handbook of Mimetic Theory and Religion*: "The sacred, according to mimetic theory, has been the teacher of humanity, it taught us how to think, and

THE DISAPPEARANCE OF THE OBJECT

Girard was questioned about this matter in *Evolution and Conversion*:

> Going back to the . . . role of the object in your theory, how do you respond [to those] who claim that you are doing away with the object and in some sense, you are scapegoating it?
>
> *Girard*: [My] realism is essential and pervasive in my approach to cultural phenomena. In my view, the object disappears only during the peak of the escalation of the mimetic crisis; otherwise, it is always there.[9]

I have no doubt at all about Girard's realism, his belief in the reality of the world guaranteed by God:

> Regarding the so-called important questions, I still operate within a traditional epistemology, which considers things as real and sees God as the guarantor of that reality.[10]

The problem is that it is precisely at the moment when "the object disappears during the peak of the escalation of the mimetic crisis" that the victim is killed and immediately becomes a profoundly ambivalent object of fear and fascination. It is at that moment that sacred symbolism becomes possible.

The battle ground of the original violence must have been strewn with corpses, none of which made any significant

---

it made us human. Yet what is the sacred? It is violence of course, but it is also more than just violence, and something other than violence. It is violence's capacity to end before it has completely exterminated everyone in a situation where each act of violence is a motivation for further violence. Each act of violence except one: the unanimous violent convergence against a single opponent. What is the sacred then? The referent of the sacred is not a thing. Nor is its referent a person—the unfortunate victim—but an abstract mechanism, an event that is misunderstood and misrepresented by those who experienced it. *It is nothing, a mistake, but this mistake, according to Girard, is at the origin of symbolic thought and culture.*" I think Dumouchel is right. I also think he knows that is not what Girard would say. For Girard the sacred generated by the scapegoat mechanism is indeed a mistake, but it is not nothing. It is a Satanic misuse or usurpation of the real thing.

9 *Evolution and Conversion*, 104.

10 Ibid., 105.

difference, because none of them became the unique center of solidly unanimous attention. The victim made unique by the violent unanimity of the crowd is the origin of the sacred. The archaic sacred is born, not out of the physical disappearance of the visible object, of course, but rather the disappearance of its ontological status, its reality as guaranteed by God, and, therefore, its truth. *The violence of the crisis alone would create a human mind radically incapable of seeing the truth of the world out there, incapable of seeing anything beyond the crowd. The reality of the entire world beyond the crowd, independent from it, vanishes. There is no such thing as objectivity. Everything points back to the only god there is at the moment, the crowd turned god; or the victim directly, as embodiment of the violence of the crowd. The violent crowd presides over a world of mere appearances, a delusional world. That is the original emptiness, the breeding ground for all manner of madness.* And always on the brink of catastrophic violence.[11]

Henri Grivois, who is familiar with Girard's work, places psychosis at the very origin: "la folie [est un] tribut payé à l'hominisation."[12] Which means that psychosis is universal: "la psychose est la folie universelle, celle qui n'épargne aucune culture, aucune société" (Madness is a tribute paid to the

---

11 In the words of J.-P. Dupuy, "un monde dans lequel les hommes ne sont plus séparés et réunis tout à la fois par un monde commun d'objets est un monde dans lequel la violence peut se répandre comme un virus dans une population dépourvue de défenses immunitaires." (A world in which men are no longer separated and united at the same time by a common world of objects is a world in which violence can expand like a virus in a population without immunity defenses.) *La Jalousie. Une géométrie du désir* (Paris: Éditions du Seuil, 2016), 52.

12 *Tu ne sera pas schizophrène* (Paris: Le Seuil, 2001), 177. In this work we also find the following: "Seules les attitudes expriment au début la violence et l'ampleur des pressentiments. Le sentiment d'être happé de tous bords et de tous côtés alterne avec celui d'être abandonné. Communion avec la multitude, destin inconnu, messianique ou diabolique. Chasse à l'homme, triomphe et extermination, divinisation et anéantissement" (63). (In the beginning only attitudes express the violence and the scope of presentiments. The feeling of being trapped from all sides alternates with that of being abandoned. Identification with the crowd, unknown destiny, messianic or diabolical. Manhunt, triumph and extermination, divinization and annihilation.)

process of becoming human . . . psychosis is the universal madness which does not spare any culture, any society). What he calls "nascent psychosis" is a common denominator of all kinds of mental illnesses in their initial stage, "before they enter into one or another chronic form of mental illness."[13] At this initial stage "He [Grivois] found that every patient had experienced the same type of event, an event whose unchanging structure can be characterized by three points: a feeling of being at the center of the totality of others: *unanimity*, surprise, and astonishment at occupying this position all alone: *absolute singularity*, initial inability to attribute a meaning to this situation: *Why?*... As Grivois comments, 'the isomorphism of the central crisis in nascent psychosis and of the sacrificial crisis in Girardian anthropology cannot be in doubt.' The comparison between the two is all the more compelling insofar as the psychotics often resort to religious language or imagery in their efforts to come to grips with a situation that has no parallel in normal experience."[14]

"Only the mad can see firsthand that momentous phenomenon Girard helps us understand: the origin of divinity in unanimity minus one."[15]

The mad, therefore, are exceptional witnesses to the original, spontaneous, operation of the scapegoat mechanism. Or more precisely, they are witnesses to a scapegoat mechanism frustrated, without any social purpose. The failure of the mechanism leaves the individual unprotected in the midst of a human society disintegrated; a collectivity which has failed to coalesce around the scapegoat victim. We might say that the madman is a failed god, a human god (or a human victim) without a job, surrounded by everybody for nothing.

But this failure of the collective, social, mechanism, which leaves the individual isolated before all the others, also

13 Mark R. Anspach, *Vengeance in Reverse. The Tangled Loops of Violence, Myth, and Madness* (East Lansing, MI: Michigan State University Press, 2017), 59.

14 Anspach, *Vengeance in Reverse*, 60.

15 Ibid., 70.

damages the relationship of the individual with the world out there. He becomes doubly isolated: from the others and from the physical environment.

We must keep in mind that the world human creatures see is no longer the world animals see. The physical world out there acquires a meaning which extends beyond the purely physical presence, in the eyes of a human being. The new creature, the human, not only knows that things are there, he is a self-conscious creature, he also knows that he knows that things are there. He discovers himself in what he sees. A human being is born with the mind of an artist. Their first language was poetic.[16] In the world out there the thing known and the knowing meet, but neither one disappears into the other; they remain distinct. If they do not, the human identity of the individual is in crisis.[17]

In the Biblical story, Adam and Eve, human beings before the Fall, see the world through God; everything testifies to the presence of their creator. After the Fall, expelled from Paradise, to which they will never return, the human situation changes radically. Scientific anthropology knows nothing about prelapsarian humans. The history of humanity begins after the Fall. But to the extent that man is a symbolic animal, everything in his world points to something beyond the world, a universal mediator or universal signifier.

---

16 "We find that the principle of these origins both of languages and of letters lies in the fact that the first gentile peoples, by a demonstrated necessity of nature, were poets who spoke in poetic characters. This discovery, which is the master key of this Science, has cost us the persistent research of almost all our literary life, because with our civilized natures we [moderns] cannot at all imagine and can understand only by great toil the poetic nature of these first men." Giambattista Vico, *The New Science*, trans. Thomas Goddard Bergin and Max Harold Fisch (Ithaca, NY: Cornell University Press, 2016), 20–21.

17 Santiago Zúñiga, "Psycose et restructuration du corps vécu: L'analyse de Blankenburg et Pankov à la lumière du transcendental," *Acta Universitatis Carolinae*, 1–2 (2016), 194–211. "Selon Blankenburg, chez les psychotiques le problème de la réalité est en cause, là où effectivement l'identité ne va pas de soi." (According to Blankenburg, the problem of reality is at stake for psychotics just at the point where identity cannot be taken for granted.)

The Biblical story says that Adam and Eve saw everything as the work of God, the creator of everything. Mimetic anthropology says that the victim of the scapegoat mechanism is the universal signifier:

> We have already noticed that the victim appears to be simultaneously good and evil, peaceful and violent, a life that brings death and a death that guarantees life. Every possible significant element seems to have its outline in the sacred and at the same time to be transcended by it. In this sense the victim does seem to constitute a universal signifier. . . . I am not saying that we have found the *true* transcendental signifier. So far we have only discovered what functions in that capacity for human beings. . . . The signifier is the victim. The signified constitutes all actual and potential meaning the community confers on to the victim and, through its intermediacy, on all things.
>
> The sign is the reconciliatory victim. Since we understand that human beings want to remain reconciled after the conclusion of the crisis, we can also understand their penchant for reproducing the sign. . . . There is no difficulty in explaining why ritual is repeated. Driven by sacred terror and wishing to continue life under the reconciliatory victim, men attempt to reproduce and represent this sign.[18]

The victim, or rather the cadaver, direct witness to a terrifying violence, is the universal signifier. And it appears to be good and bad simultaneously. But what does "good" or "bad" mean at that originary moment? I suggest it could only mean distant, not immediately threatening, or the opposite, close by, menacing, hostile. Good and bad simultaneously simply meant radically unpredictable, and totally beyond our control.

In the beginning was the scapegoat mechanism, which produced the victim, which became a symbol, signaling the birth of a new species, the human. In this sense, it could be said that humanity emerged from the body of the victim, which became the universal signifier, that which everything

18 *Things Hidden*, 102–3.

ultimately signifies, the universal giver of meaning, a god, which can be described as follows: 1. Extremely violent. It can destroy everything. 2. Good when he is not violently destroying, but his violence (or his goodness) is unpredictable. 3. Entirely beyond our control. 4. There is nothing like it. It is unique, which also means it transcends everything, which, in the violent language of the humans, means everything is under its dominion.

Let us try to imagine a human world dominated by such a violent and sacred power which is definitely not friendly, and is unpredictable. To make matters even worse for those early humans, they had blood on their hands. For human violence is first and foremost, at its birth, the violence that kills the victim. That is what defines the violence as human in a circular, self-justifying, process: the victim is the victim (reaches the symbolic level) because it is the object of everybody's violence, and it is the object of everybody's violence because it is not just any meaningless object, but the object of everybody's violence.

What this circularity means is that the same violent process that sacralizes the victim turns it into a god, sacralizes the human violence that kills it. The sacralization moves the violence away; it allows the human group to function, but it will also reveal the violence as human. In other words, from its sacred transcendence the man-made god will forever know who killed the victim; will forever know that humans are guilty; in fact, they are human because they are guilty.

From a Christian perspective, we might say that humanity, by sinning against (disobeying) the true God, turned their sin into a god before which humans will always be guilty.

Girard spoke repeatedly about the arbitrary blaming of the victim by the crowd of hominids that kills it. We should also be talking about how the very idol they had fabricated by putting the blame on the victim, will terrorize them by returning the accusation, by crushing them with the weight of their guilt, the very guilt that they placed on the victim.

We can understand in this context why Christ's mission was understood as reconciling humanity with God. But does that mean that God and humanity were ever enemies? I believe that Girard, properly understood, can be a great help here. God and man did not meet to come to an agreement. The reconciliation was entirely God's initiative, and it was inseparable from God's forgiveness. It was humanity who fabricated a Satanic god who could not possibly forgive because it was the stuff of human guilt, human guilt sacralized.

"The sign is the reconciliatory victim," says Girard. But there is nothing reconciliatory about the old sacred victim. The old victim-turned-God, the owner of everything—because everything is seen in its light—does not rule by consensus, but by fear, by frightening all humans, victim killers, out of their senses. It may be true, of course, that "men want peace." But the peace they want or need is not the peace they get from the scapegoat mechanism alone, which is unavoidably tied to the ultimate, the sacred, source of terror. They cannot get one without facing the other. It would have to be a peace haunted by a terror they cannot control.[19]

I do not think that either Girard, or we, Girardians, have properly meditated on the horror of the "transition from animal to man" when there is nothing to account for it but "hypermimeticism." It is truly a Satanic beginning, a hellish one. Girard has likened it to the Fall, the expulsion from Paradise: humans fallen from grace and expelled by a righteous God. But this unhappy situation would fall far short of the horror of the Godless "transition." Perhaps the God of the

---

19 The terror of the sacred is what is usually missing in Girard's description of the original ambivalence. For example: "In archaic communities … self-deception must have been so monolithic that it produced not one but two illusions in quick succession. First the scapegoat phenomenon properly speaking, turned the victim into [a] dangerous malefactor. … Then came the reconciliation, so sudden and so miraculous, it seemed, that the beneficiaries apprehended it not as their own doing but as the work of the scapegoat once again. … The result was the 'ambivalent' notion of the sacred and its divinities." *Violence Renounced*, ed. Willard M. Swartley, "Response by René Girard" (Telford, PA: Pandora Press, 2000), 309.

Flood, who "repented" of having created the human race, together with the Flood itself, would be a closer approximation, if we imagine God at that moment to be truly disgusted ("touched with sorrow at the heart") by the state of generalized evil covering the earth.

The newly emerged human creature of mimetic anthropology formally stands in relation to the archaic violent and ambivalent sacred as Adam stood in relation to God, the Creator, before the Fall. But that is where the formal similarity ends. Behind the *Genesis* story we can only imagine the new vision, the unprecedented human perception of the world, the new human world, as an incredible opening up of a new horizon, a glorious and amazing new world. As Raymund Schwager put it,

> The "fulguration" or the emergence by which they arose out of the animal realm (speaking scientifically), or the self-transcendence by which they became human through the creative action of God (speaking theologically), would have led to opening up in them an utterly new feeling of immeasurable vastness with intense emotional clarity.[20]

Or, in the words of Romano Guardini,

> What we call "world" in the full sense of the word is something constantly formed on the basis of man's encounter with what is out there. It is enough for us to imagine such a human being as he has just been created by God: full of life, free, joyful, and complete.... He is fully open to God, in full agreement with the creator of the world.... If this is the man who encounters the things, what world will emerge from his vision, from his feeling, from his action? Paradise! "Paradise" is the world as it realizes itself, breathes and develops around that human being who is an image of God and strives to realize such an image better and better every time.[21]

---

20 *Banished from Eden*, 52.

21 This is the author's translation from Romano Guardini, *El comienzo de todas las cosas* (Bilbao: Desclée de Brouwer, 2013), itself a translation from Guardini, *Der Anfang Aller Dinge*, 1987.

This is the view that the new human creature would have of a world created by God: "an opening up in them [of] an utterly new feeling of immeasurable vastness with intense emotional clarity." Paradise, "the world as it realizes itself, breathes and develops around that human being who is an image of God." This would be the first time that a new creature, a product of this world, sees it as true and real, sees the spiritual dimension of the physical world out there. Truth is not an accident of the world; it belongs to its very essence.

On the other hand, it is impossible to imagine the humanity produced by the scapegoat mechanism as anything like that. But we can see that Girard, consciously or not, is influenced by this traditional image of humanity's original experience of the sacred, in the following passage, in response to a question by Oughourlian. The question concerns the sacred role of the victim as the hypermimetic creatures involved in the violent crisis unanimously turn their attention on it: "Would this already be a sacred victim?" asks Oughourlian. Let us hear Girard's answer again:

> R. G.: To the extent that the new type of attention is awakened, the victim will be imbued with the emotions provoked by the crisis and its resolution.... As weak as it might be, *the 'consciousness' the participants have of the victim is linked structurally to the prodigious effects produced from its passage from life to death, by the spectacular and liberating reversal that has occurred at that instant*.... One would have to answer your question by saying that once the victim has appeared, however dimly, the process leading toward the sacred has begun, although concepts and representations are not yet part of it.[22]

So, the satanic sacred, human violence sacralized, "is linked structurally to the prodigious effects produced from [the victim's] passage from life to death, by the spectacular and liberating reversal that has occurred at that instant."

"Prodigious," "spectacular," "liberating"? How is that

22 *Things Hidden*, 100.

possible? These hypermimetic creatures have just emerged from a paroxysmal state of violence, where reality has disappeared in the midst of monstrous hallucinations. They are terrified as they see in the victim the very image of everything that has just happened. They see in the victim a terrifying, "an immense invisible power." They cannot possibly be amazed spectators of something "spectacular." The last thing they could possibly feel is "liberated." In the presence of such immense and violent power, they can only be terrified by what they did, by their own violence. The immensely powerful violence of which the dead victim is a symbol, the first symbolic thing, totally unprecedented, could not produce the liberating "utterly new feeling of immeasurable vastness" of which Schwager speaks with regard to human beings before the Fall.

Quite the contrary, the world in which the sacred signifier produced by the scapegoat mechanism places the human being, is inherently ambivalent, inherently unstable. It can only be the very breeding ground of madness. It seems to me that if our original ancestors became human in such an environment, they would have gone mad rather quickly. Existentially speaking, a radically ambivalent sacred, which is supposed to be the ground of everything human, is no ground at all, it oscillates permanently in a vacuum; it is neither here nor there, or in both places at the same time. And so is the meaning that emerges from it. The scapegoat mechanism cannot possibly be a substitute for God, the creator of heaven and earth. It can only turn existing reality into a hallucinatory nightmare. Furthermore, this maddening situation must be envisaged as being particularly intense because it happens at the very origin. If Father Schwager is correct, even the smaller size of the human brain at the moment of the original violent encounter with the sacred could have contributed to such an existential intensity.[23] If

23 *Banished from Eden*, 51. In this book Father Schwager is trying to fit Girard's view of the transition from animal to man through the scapegoat

Christ was not already there at the beginning, what we have is the situation parodied in Girard's self-satire at the beginning of his last book, in which "Christian revelation [is] a kind of divine expiation in which God through his Son could be seen as asking for forgiveness from humans for having revealed the mechanisms of their violence so late." In other words, permitting so many millions of victims to be sacrificed. *Christ is not only the avowed reason why Girard was able to discover, in a fully rational way, the existence of the scapegoat mechanism; Christ is also the reason why the scapegoat mechanism worked and saved humanity from extinction.* Christ tilted the balance in favor of the reconciliatory side of the maddening ambiguity of the sacred. The scapegoat mechanism without Christ is an entirely closed system driven by the unanimous violence that kills the victim, thereby automatically establishing a safe distance between the crowd and its own violence. But the safety thus created is perpetually at risk of disappearing, in need, therefore, of more and more victims. The terrifying threat of imminent destruction does not seem to support the possibility of creating a stable functioning society. A "reconciliatory dimension" is, indeed, needed, but it will not come about mechanically. *What Girard discovered through Christ cannot work without Christ.*

mechanism within a larger theological framework that safeguards the creative power of God as the decisive factor. I agree with Father Schwager, but I am trying to analyze the scapegoat mechanism in its scientific isolation from theology (which is the way Girard presented it) in order to prove that, all by itself, it would not work.

CHAPTER 9

What Is the Sacred?

THE QUESTION HAS BEEN ASKED SO MANY TIMES AND IN so many ways that I cannot but hesitate. Nevertheless, I do not see how it can be avoided when talking about Girardian theory. For Girard there is Christ, preceded by a long Judeo-Christian tradition, and there is the sacred, non-biblical, archaic. Christ is the truth, the archaic sacred is a lie. And yet, this lie holds the key to the very "transition from animal to man." Why is it a lie? Because it calls "god" what in truth is nothing but a collective violent projection; hypermimetic human violence externalized, turned into an illusory transcendence. In Girardian theory the sacred as such has no ultimate specificity, it can always be reduced to human violence, although human violence carried to the extreme. Anthropologically speaking, everything human begins in violence. In this sense, we can say that human violence is unique, just as a human being is unique; no other form of animal violence is like it. Human violence is unique in its capacity to generate, to become, an illusory transcendence.[1] Which is, indeed, a strange qualification: something unique and unreal. Can there be such a thing? Can the sacred be something truly unique and also unreal? There is a mystery

1 Paul Dumouchel's view of Girard's sacred can be of help here: "The sacred, according to mimetic theory, has been the teacher of humanity, it taught us how to think, and it made us human. Yet what is the sacred? It is violence of course, but it is also more than just violence, and something other than violence. It is violence's capacity to end before it has completely exterminated everyone in a situation where each act of violence is a motivation for further violence. Each act of violence except one: the unanimous violent convergence against a single opponent. What is the sacred then? The referent of the sacred is not a thing. Nor is its referent a person—the unfortunate victim—but an abstract mechanism, an event that is misunderstood and misrepresented by those who experienced it. *It is nothing, a mistake, but this mistake, according to Girard, is at the origin of symbolic thought and culture*" ("A Theory of Everything," in *The Palgrave Handbook of Mimetic Theory and Religion*).

demanding a theological attention beyond my limits.

Dupuy carries this lack of substantive specificity much further. The sacred cannot be reduced to anything empirically real, not even human violence. The sacred is just a formal possibility, a name given historically to our incapacity or inability to control the ultimate consequences of our actions. We, as humans, can set in motion irreversible processes which can turn against us and threaten our very existence. When that happens, we may interpret this evil independence (or independence of evil) as "sacred":

> I owe to Ivan Illich . . . the insight that humanity has always had to be on its guard against three types of threat, and not simply the two that immediately come to mind: the brute force of nature and the brutality of human beings—the earthquakes that reduce glorious cities to rubble and the barbarism that massacres, mutilates, and rapes their inhabitants in time of war. . . . But there is a third front on which it is much more difficult to fight, for here the enemy is ourselves. We do not recognize this enemy, though it has our own features. Sometimes we suppose it to be the agent of a malign and treacherous Nature, sometimes of a malevolent and vengeful Nemesis. Yet the evil that besieges us from this direction is a consequence of our own faculty of action, which is to say our ability to irreversibly set in motion processes that are liable to turn against us, with lethal effect. . . .
>
> It is from the primordial experience of action acquiring autonomy in relation to the intentions of actors that not only the idea of the sacred, but also religion, tragic drama, and politics—so many real and symbolic systems that serve to set limits to the capacity to act—were born.[2]

Here the word "sacred" is just a word inherited from the past without any specific existential referent. It is a form of ignorance or incapacity. We may or may not be aware of it, but there is no such thing as an encounter with the sacred. We have no idea what it would feel like, what the existential

2 *Mark of the Sacred*, 22.

content of such an encounter might be. The sacred is not an experience. It is a formal category of our understanding, which can be applied to any number of collective experiences.

For Girard, as we said already, the sacred refers specifically to human violence. It is nothing but human violence "sacralized." That is to say, perceived or presented as something divine, pertaining to some mythical superhuman power. For example, in the Book of Job, the three friends in dialogue with Job, "under our very eyes . . . sacralize the violence. The insults and meanness are metamorphosed into the grandiose accomplishments of a supernatural mission."[3] At any rate, both Girard and Dupuy agree that the sacred, the old sacred, can be explained. In fact, we owe this explanation to Christ, we are told. Christ's Passion reveals the sacred, that is, the sacrificial killing of the victim, as murder, arbitrary, unjustified, human violence. In other words, in Girard's theory, Christ reveals the old sacred as pure idolatry, a completely false image of the true God, literally a cover-up for murder. Human guilt, original sin—we might say—is revealed in all its unmitigated ugliness.

However, among the ruins of the old sacred, religious historians have been able to find credible testimonies of what it was to be in the presence of the sacred as a human experience. I think that Girard should have paid more attention to studies such as those of Rudolf Otto, Lucien Lévy-Bruhl, or Mircea Eliade. He dismissed them too quickly.

What Rudolf Otto called the "numinous" relates to a *numinous* state of mind:

> This mental state is perfectly *sui generis* and irreducible to any other; and therefore, like every absolutely primary and elementary datum, while it admits of being discussed, it cannot be strictly defined.[4]

In his introduction to *The Sacred and the Profane*, this is what Eliade said of Otto's book:

---

3 *Job: The Victim of His People*, 27.
4 *The Idea of the Holy*.

> In his book, Rudolf Otto tries to recognize the features of an experience both terrifying and irrational. He discovers a feeling of terror in the face of the sacred, before this *mysterium tremendum*, this *majestas* which exhibits an overwhelming superiority of power; the religious fear before the *mysterium fascinans*, where the perfect plenitude of being opens up.... Specifically the *numinous* is "*ganz andere*," that is, radically and totally different; it does not resemble anything human or cosmic.[5]

Otto's view of the sacred as "totally other," in the presence of which the human mind freezes in a state of profound stupor, seems to me to fit perfectly Virgil's description of such a state of mind in Aeneas, when he encounters the sacred.

In the *Aeneid* the sacred is a dark reality, "truth wrapped in darkness," *obscuris vera involvens*, like the "horrendous enigmas" chanted by the Sibyl. The sacred is the guardian of a truth that terrifies; a truth which, if revealed, would bring an apocalyptic catastrophe, complete annihilation. When its presence is felt the human freezes in horror, loses his mind, his voice gets stuck in his throat, etc. Here are some poetic examples from Virgil's poem: "A cold shudder shakes my limbs, and my chilled blood freezes with terror," at the tomb of Polydorus in Book III; or describing Aeneas's reaction to Mercury's presence, when this messenger from Jupiter appeared to remind him of his mission and reproach him for staying too long with Dido:

> Indeed, Aeneas, stunned [*amens*] at the sight, was struck dumb; his hair stood up in terror and the voice clave to his throat. (IV: 279–80)

This mythical language to describe the encounter with the sacred has a long tradition behind it. It appears in *Job*, to describe the vision of Eliphaz of Teman, one of Job's "comforters":

5 "Dans son livre, Rudolf Otto s'efforce à reconnaître les caractères de cette expérience terrifiante et irationnelle. Il découvre le sentiment d'effroi devant le sacré, devant ce *mysterium tremendum*, devant cette *majestas* qui dégage une écrasante supériorité de puissance; il découvre la crainte religieuse devant le *mysterium fascinans*, ou s'épanouit la parfaite plénitude de l'être."

> Now a word was brought to me stealthily, my ear received the whisper of it . . . dread came upon me, and trembling, which made all my bones shake. A spirit glided past my face: and hair of my flesh stood up. It stood still, but I could not discern its appearance. A form was before my eyes: there was silence, then I heard a voice. (Job 4:12–16)

These mythical images repeated for so long in so vastly different environments—to use Shakespeare's language again—"More witnesseth than fancy's images/ And grows to something of great constancy/ But, howsoever, strange and admirable" (*A Midsummer-Night's Dream*, Act V, sc. 1).

They may be all wrong in their interpretation of what they claim to experience. But how do they invent such an experience? Are they all lying everywhere, universally, through the ages, when they say they experience what they say they experience? Are they just hallucinating? How could "airy nothing" acquire such constancy, such universality? I think we should pay attention to Otto and his description of that which cannot be explained, the sacred as that which is radically other, irreducible to anything else. However, the "numinous" has a history. It used to be, but no longer is, terrifying. We owe such a monumental change to Christ. We, as Christians, should be careful about explaining the old sacred, or we may run the risk of leaving Christ without a job.

FEAR OF THE SACRED AND GUILT

We read the following in Lucretius:

> When the parched earth rocks with the appalling thunder stroke and rattlings run through the great heaven [or] again when the whole earth rocks under their feet and cities tumble with the shock or doubtfully threaten to fall. . . . Do not peoples and nations quake, and proud monarchs shrink into themselves smitten with fear of the gods, lest [they be found guilty]? (*De rerum natura*, V, 1218 ff.)

This is truly amazing. In the midst of an "appalling thunder" storm or an earthquake that makes "cities tumble," people do not simply run for safety in fear for their lives, they "cower in terror," or "shrink with fear" that they will be found guilty. Guilty of what? They do not know. It could be anything, "any foul transgression or overweening word."

This seems to be the logic underlying this fear: no threat, no evil, happens accidentally. If it is evil and does harm to you, if it threatens you, believe it, it is meant for you. It is a punishment, and it is the will of some sacred Omnipotence which owes no explanation to you. This is a radical and very primitive manifestation of something which will leave deep psychological marks in the human psyche, as observed by our literary masters. Calderón's text is particularly rich in this regard. It may happen in the form of a rhetorical question: "Quién no da crédito al daño?" (who is there does not believe an evil fate?) says King Basilio in *La vida es sueño*. And a little further on, in the words of Astolfo:

> ¡Qué buen astrólogo fuera [el hado]
> Si siempre casos crueles
> Anunciara; pues no hay duda
> Que ellos fueran verdad siempre. (jornada II)

> (What a great astrologer would be the one who foretold nothing but harms, since there is no doubt at all they would always turn out to be true.)

The old sacred reading sees the will of the gods behind the evil prediction. This is why it is seen as a punishment meant for you. You are always found guilty in the eyes of the gods.

There is no such thing as human innocence when facing the old sacred. Which means guilty and sacred; guilty as the sacrificial victim is guilty. There is no other guilt under the old sacred regime. The same mechanism that spares the group by killing the one, testifies against the group, against everybody. The sacrificial victim saves and accuses at the same time. You hide behind the ritual, which is intended to be a smokescreen, a saving lie, which says that it wasn't you who killed the victim. The ritual lie (obligatory "comedy of innocence") will spare you for the moment, but it will not make you innocent, because you know you are lying, because you know the truth will kill you. There is no such thing as innocence under the old sacred.

It is an error to think that the uniqueness of the old victim washes off the guilt from everybody else, or somehow everybody's guilt is transferred onto the victim, thereby liberating everybody from guilt. There is no such liberation under the old sacred. The killing of the victim, ritually lamented, will spare you for the moment, but it will not be forgiven or forgotten. The truth that must be kept hidden, tabooed, unspeakable, will not make you free. It will haunt the group; it will be the ground on which an indelible sense of guilt will be rooted. The very uniqueness of the victim will forever testify to the collective violence that made it so. It was not ignorance of the violence, as Girard said, that kept human beings chained to the old sacrificial mechanism. It was fear, sheer terror: the terror of an evil that attaches to your very self in the form of guilt without the possibility of repentance, for there is no repentance where there is no forgiveness.

Repentance is the key. Jesus is quite clear about it, as we see in the case of the blind man from birth, or the eighteen people killed accidentally when the tower of Siloe fell on them:

> Jesus saw a man who had been blind since birth. His disciples asked him, "Rabbi, who sinned, this man or his parents, that he was born blind?" Jesus replied: "Neither this man nor his parents sinned . . . but this happened so that the works of God might be displayed in him." (John 9:1–12)

> As he went along, he saw a man who had been blind from birth. His disciples asked him, "Rabbi, who sinned, this man or his parents, that he was born blind?" Jesus replied, "Neither he nor his parents sinned. He was born blind so that the works of God might be revealed in him." (Luke 9:1–3)

> "Or those eighteen upon whom the tower fell in Siloe and slew them: think you that they also were debtors above all the men that dwelt in Jerusalem? No, I say to you: but except you do penance, you shall all likewise perish." (Luke 13:4–5)

Christ broke the power of the accusation; guilt is no longer sacred, it does not define our relationship with God. It has been forgiven. So, we are now free, or rather, it is entirely up to us to take advantage of our new God-given freedom, by repenting. The old tyrant, the horrible deity, is no longer threatening. Which means that now repentance becomes possible. In fact, we may go too far in the opposite direction. For now, "when the earth rocks and cities tumble," we may quickly forget that God is also dying with us, for us. We feel forsaken. Where is God? Our guilt has been forgiven, why are we being punished? That was Voltaire's question.

Lucretius's description of the state of human life under the old *religio* is quite appropriate: "human life to view lay foully prostrate upon earth crushed down under the weight of religion, who showed her head from the quarters of heaven with hideous aspect lowering upon mortals" (*De Rerum Natura*, I. 62–65).

Is it any wonder "there is no atheism in the ancient world," as Girard pointed out?[6] There were different opinions regarding "the nature of the gods," as we learn in Cicero's dialogue by that name (*De natura deorum*), including some who thought they were basically poetic inventions. What nobody doubted for a moment was the existence and the human experience of something sacred, what Lucretius called *religio*. Whatever the gods might be in theory, nobody doubted that, in the human mind, they are unavoidably associated with the sacred, the awesome power of *religio*: "So constantly does some hidden power trample on human grandeur and is seen to tread under its heel and make sport for itself of the renowned rods and cruel axes,"[7] the symbol of authority, the power of the law. In other words, there is a power much greater than the power of human authority, a power above the law, that makes even the most terrible and powerful tyrant tremble. The whole purpose of the scientific endeavor, the study of the physical origin

6 *Evolution and Conversion*, 183.

7 *De Rerum Natura*, V. 1233–35.

of things (*De rerum natura*) is to maintain "an unperturbed mind" in the face of such a lawless and terrifying power.

In the face of a devastating catastrophe, nobody in the ancient world would dare to ask our most common question, "where is God?" You do not ask such a question when you sense the presence of the sacred next to you and you are trying desperately to avert your eyes, to pretend you are not there. We have no idea how terrifying such a question would be in the context of the old sacred, because it is a question about guilt; and guilt is precisely what brings you, who are nothing, to the horrifying accusatory presence of a God who is totally unpredictable and can reduce you to nothing in the blinking of an eye. "Who shall stand when he appeareth?" These words of the prophet Malachi (3:2) are still an echo of the old sacred terror.

Once again, Lucretius was right, human life lay foully prostrate upon earth crushed down under the weight of religion." But if there is a society where this crushing weight was particularly vicious, that would be, in the opinion of the greatest expert on the subject, Fray Bernardino de Sahagún, the Aztec society before the arrival of the Spanish:

> Regarding the religion and cult of their gods, I don't think there have ever been in the world idol worshipers with greater reverence for their idols and at a greater human cost than these here in New Spain; neither the Jews nor any other nation ever had to wear such a heavy burden and perform so many sacred ceremonies as these natives had for so many years.
>
> (En lo que toca a la religión y cultura de sus dioses, no creo ha habido en el mundo idólatras tan reverenciadores de sus dioses, ni tan a su costa, como éstos de esta Nueva España; ni los judíos, ni ninguna otra nación tuvo yugo tan pesado y de tantas ceremonias como le han tenido estos naturales por espacio de muchos años.)[8]

The Aztec equivalent of Jupiter was called Tezcatlipoca. "[He] was invisible and moved everywhere in heaven and on

8 *Historia general de las cosas de la Nueva España. Prólogo.*

earth, as well as in hell. They believed he was the only one in charge of managing everything in the world. He alone gave prosperities and riches, and he alone took them away whenever he felt like it. That is why they feared and revered him, because he had the power to raise you up or bring you down." In other words, he was omnipotent, omnipresent, and totally unpredictable.

There is no divine covenant between God and his people in the domain of the old sacred. Everything is in the hands of an unpredictable deity, with whom you can only communicate ceremoniously, that is to say, sacrificially. Outside these collective ceremonies the world is a huge question mark, the breeding ground for all kinds of omens or signs. To quote Calderón again, "the sky is nothing but omens, and the whole world is a prodigy."

Omen readers, augurs: Fray Bernardino calls them "*agoreros*." They are essential to the old sacred society. They not only interpret the omens, but their interpretation is also a constant reminder that whatever happens to you, to any member of the group, is ultimately in the hands of a divinity who cannot be questioned. The implicit message in this interpretation is meant to keep the peace: do not blame anybody or anything; accept the fact that there is nothing that you can do about it. Here is an example in which Fray Bernardino paraphrases the standard answer given by the "agoreros" when they are consulted about the first omen, "when somebody heard the roaring of a wild beast in the mountains, or some buzzing sound." It was taken as a bad omen. Then this person would go to the "agorero" for an explanation. This is what the "agorero" would say:

> The meaning of this omen is bad and difficult to bear; not because I say so, but because that is what our ancestors said and wrote; therefore, the meaning of your omen is that you will be in poverty and trials, or that you will die. Maybe he, by whom we live, is angry with you, and does not want you to live any longer. Keep your courage

> in anticipation of what is coming to you, because that is how it is written in the books that we use to explain these things to those to whom they happen; it is not I who terrifies and alarms you, it is the Lord God himself who wanted this to happen to you, and you should not blame the animal, which does not know what he does, since he lacks understanding and reason; and you, poor thing, should not blame anybody, because the sign in which you were born brings these risks with it; the evil of the sign in which you were born has just been verified.

The *agoreros* played a crucial role in the fall of the Aztec empire. It appears that there is no other known case in which the fate of an entire society and civilization depended so much on its art of reading the sacred signs of the future.

Octavio Paz, a Nobel laureate in literature, and arguably the most profound analyst of the fall of the Aztec Empire, wrote the following in *El laberinto de la soledad*:

> Why did Moctezuma surrender? Why is he so strangely fascinated by the Spaniards, experiencing before them a kind of vertigo which can be properly called sacred—the lucid vertigo of the suicide before the abyss? The gods have abandoned him. The great betrayal which marks the beginning of the history of Mexico, is not that of the *tlaxcaltecas*, or that of Moctezuma and his group, it was the betrayal of the gods. No other nation has felt so totally abandoned as the Aztec nation felt before the warnings, prophecies, and signs announcing its fall.[9]

"Nothing else can explain the Conquest of Mexico." Not the political genius of Cortés, or the technical superiority of the Spaniards, which did not exist in battles as decisive as that of Otumba, nor the defection of vassals and allied. None of that would have caused the ruin of the Aztec Empire if the Empire itself had not felt suddenly "a fainting, an intimate doubt which made it hesitate and yield."

---

9 Octavio Paz, *El Laberinto de la Soledad* (Mexico City: Fondo de Cultura Económica, 1999), 102–3. My translation.

In those primitive battles, it is not the contenders who win or lose, but their gods. The gods of Moctezuma knew they were no match for the gods of the Spaniards. What Octavio Paz is really saying is that it was the Cross, rather than the sword, that won the battle against the Aztec empire. Satan simply yielded in the presence of Christ. The people who knew about this victory were those missionaries, like Fray Bernardino, who clearly understood they were not fighting against a nation of incredibly cruel people, but against the tyrannical power of Satan. We already saw an example in the sacrificial killing of so many children to pray for abundant rain, whose tears were seen as a good omen.

Let us listen again to Fray Bernardino's horrified reaction:

> I do not believe there can be a heart so hardened that, upon hearing of a cruelty so inhuman, and more than bestial and satanic, as the one described above, would not be moved to tears and feel shaken and horrified. It is indeed horrible and lamentable to see our human nature degraded to such a low level and to such shame as to see parents persuaded by the devil to kill and eat their children (without thinking they were doing anything wrong), rather believing they were doing a great service to their gods. The blame for such a cruel blindness as was executed on those unfortunate children, should not be laid so much on the cruelty of those parents, who actually felt the pain in their hearts and shed tears, but rather on the most cruel hatred of our most ancient enemy Satan, who, with most malicious cunning, persuaded them to do such an infernal thing. Oh, Lord, bring your justice to bear on this cruel enemy, which does and wishes to do so much damage to us! Take from him, Lord, the power to do damage. (My translation)

In these circumstances, does it make any sense to speak of the victim's guilt? Did those parents, who sacrificed their children, believe their children were guilty in any sense? Apparently, they did what they did "con gran dolor de sus corazones" (with great sorrow in their hearts). It was not the parents' cruelty, says Fr. Bernardino, but the cruelty of Satan.

The point that Lucretius and Fry Bernardino are trying to make concerns the amazing, the unbelievable, power of "persuasion" or "suggestion," that *religio*, Satan, had over humanity.

The picture that emerges from Fr. Bernardino's extensive and detailed historical account is that of a society totally mediated by their experience of the sacred. There does not seem to be anything the meaning of which is not determined by the way it relates to the sacred. There are no purely human winners or losers, the battle is always decided by sacred whim. It all depends on whether or not you win the favor of the gods. This is not only the case with Moctezuma and the fate of the Aztec empire. This is also the case with Homer and the Trojan war. Let me repeat here what I said in *A Refuge of Lies* about the *Iliad*:[10]

> The subject of the *Iliad* is not the Trojan war, of which a relatively small portion is narrated. . . . The subject is not the glorious exploits of the old heroes either. . . . It is not even the glorification, in a modern sense, of its central hero, Achilles, who is most definitely not presented as a model of behavior to be followed. The subject of the *Iliad* is clearly stated in a couple of verses right at the very beginning of the poem: "Sing, O goddess, the anger of Achilles son of Peleus, that brought countless ills upon the Achaeans. Many a brave soul did it send hurrying down to Hades, and many a hero did it yield a prey to dogs and vultures, for so was the will of Zeus fulfilled."

The anger of Achilles, which sent so many Achaeans to their death, whereby the sacred will of Zeus was fulfilled. That is the subject of the Homeric poem. How is that possible? Achilles never lifted a finger against the Achaeans. It was Hector and the Trojans who sent so many of their war enemies to their death. But it does not really matter who does the actual killing. In the final analysis what caused such a devastation among the Greeks was this terrible thing called

10 Cesáreo Bandera, *A Refuge of Lies: Reflections on Faith and Fiction* (East Lansing, MI: Michigan State University Press, 2013), 63.

"the anger of Achilles," which is the sacred instrument of the gods. It will eventually kill Achilles himself. Through it "the will of Zeus is fulfilled." When Zeus thunders from mount Ida people are "stunned, and pale terror takes hold of all of them" (VIII, 77).

As soon as the sacred appears, in whatever form, nothing else makes any difference. In its sacred form the devastating violence becomes independent from the violent contenders. It can go against either side with perfect equanimity. There is never a question of who is to blame. After the death of Patroclus, his dear friend and comrade in arms, at the hands of Hector and the Trojans, the anger of Achilles, the power of the sacred, is turned the other way and the fate of Troy and the Trojans is sealed. Homer deals with the death and devastation of the Trojans with the same compassionate attitude which he had previously showed for the Greeks. Simone Weil saw in this Homeric compassion, which makes no distinction between the two contending parties, an anticipation of Christ. I think she was mistaken. It was not Christian but ritual compassion, a mixture of sacrificial reverence and fear. He will speak in exactly the same way about the twelve frightened, trembling, Trojan youths captured by Achilles to be sacrificed at the funeral of Patroclus. Where the sacred is you step back, and keep your distance. Greeks or Trojans, it doesn't make any difference, they are equal in death. They all deserve the same ritual lamentation. And there is never a question of who is to blame, whose fault it is. When the sacred strikes, you do not ask questions, least of all any involving why, or who. Everything is taken in stride and an unwavering sense of inevitability. It is all decided at a sacred level for or against this or that contender, and there is no appeal.

THE BOOK OF JOB

You do not want to appear in the presence of the old God, in the presence of the one who reveals your guilt. To such a God does Job elevates his protest:

> So, tell me, [God] what are my misdeeds, my sin? Why do you hide your face and look on me as your enemy? Would you intimidate a wind-blown leaf, would you pursue a dry straw, you who lay bitter allegations against me and tax me with faults of my youth?[11]

These are Job's words. The Book of Job is, to my knowledge, the most extensive and direct denunciation of this general accusation against humanity. What happened to Job, the richest and most powerful man in the land, his downfall, in which he lost absolutely everything, including his physical wellbeing—he was covered from head to toe with "malignant ulcers"—was meant to be a test. It was allowed by the Lord, but it was all engineered by Satan. "Strech out your hand and lay a finger on [his possessions and his person] and he will curse you to your face," said Satan. So, the Lord allowed Satan to do as he pleased with Job, short of killing him. Thus, it could be argued that what is at stake in this Divine test is not only Job's righteousness and integrity, but the Satanic system as well, which as Girard brilliantly demonstrated is "the ancient trail of the wicked," or, in Girard's theory, the scapegoat mechanism.[12]

The results of the test were as follows: Job not only did not curse the Lord, but, instead, what he did was to reveal and denounce the fundamental injustice of the Satanic system, which completely ignored the difference between the innocent and the guilty:

> Though I am innocent, my own mouth would condemn me. Though I am blameless, he would prove me perverse. (Job, 9:20)

---

11 *The New Revised Jerusalem Bible*, 881–87.

12 The connection between Job, "the victim of his people," and Christ is the subject of Girard's book by that title, *Job: The Victim of His People*, a translation of *La route antique des hommes pervers* (1985). But that does not mean that "The God of the Gospels is clearly a candidate for the God of the victims. The Father sends his Son into the world to defend the victims, the poor and the disinherited" (154 ff.). As Girard knew perfectly well, the Father sends his Son to save the sinners, to forgive their sins so that they may convert and be saved. The adulterous woman was a sinner, the prodigal son was a sinner, the lost lamb was lost, alone, not with all the others entrusted to Christ's care.

The divinity being addressed here looks very much like the one spreading terror, capable of "persuading" people to do horrible things to their neighbors, even to their own children, as described by Lucretius. It is the spirit of the archaic sacred as defined explicitly or implied by mimetic anthropology, the spirit that inhabits "the ancient trail of the wicked."

But how can that be compatible with the God of Abraham, of Isaac, of Jacob, God Almighty, Creator of Heaven and Earth? How can my God, who created me, "look on me as [his] enemy"? Why would he terrorize me? What am I next to him, "a wind-blown leaf," "a dry straw"?

> Is it right for you to attack me, to despise the work of your hands. . . . You gave me life and steadfast love, and in your care watched over my every breath. Yet all the while you had a secret plan—I know that this was your plan: if I should sin you would be watching me and would not acquit me of my faults. Woe to me, if I am guilty; if I am righteous, I dare not lift up my head, overwhelmed with shame, drunk with pain as I am! (Job 10:3, 12–15)

And yet, somehow, the very fact that he is able to defend himself before God is already a hopeful sign:

> I will defend my ways to his face. And this will be my salvation, for the wicked would not dare to come before him. (Job 13:15–16)

This is not yet the God of Love ready to die for our sake. But it is clearly a prophetic announcement of his coming, a *figura Christi*, which will become more explicit further on:

> For I know that my Redeemer lives, and in the last day I shall rise out of the earth. And I shall be clothed again with my skin, and in my flesh I shall see my God. (Job 19:25–27)

What interests me here, however, is what the Book of Job reveals about the archaic sacred as a whole, and not only about the fate of the victim. Because the fate of the victim weighs heavily on everybody without exception. As he tells his "comforters,"

> How would you fare if he examined you? Can he be duped like human beings? He would inflict a harsh rebuke on you if in secret you are biased. Does his majesty not frighten you? Does not dread of him overcome you? (Job 13:9–11)

Nobody is innocent in the eyes of this tyrannical God. The fate of the victim is a constant reminder of what could happen to anybody. The guilt of the victim is the guilt of everybody. There is no significant individuality other than that of the victim, the one made unique by everybody else, when it is expelled or killed unanimously. Nobody wants to be "himself" or "herself." Everybody wants to be what everybody is. Individuality, isolation, stand-out difference, this is all a source of danger and panic. It will take the uniqueness of God himself in the place of the victim to eliminate such danger, and either restore or create the possibility of a meaningful or transcendent individuality, an individuality supported by God himself.

LUCRETIUS

But the classical text that deals explicitly with the human experience of the sacred, and tries to explain its origin, is that of Lucretius, *De rerum natura* (On the nature, birth, origin, of things). Lucretius himself gives precedence to his revered master Epicurus, revered as a god:

> For if we must speak as the acknowledged grandeur of the things itself demands, a god he was, a god, most noble Memmius, who first found out that plan of life which is now termed wisdom, and who by trained skill rescued life from such great billows and such thick darkness and moored it in so perfect a calm and in so brilliant a light. (V:1–12)

The "great billows and thick darkness" from which Epicurus rescued human life, were those brought about by *religio*, that is, the sacred.

> When human life to view lay foully prostrate upon earth crushed down under the weight of religion, who showed her head from the quarters of heaven with hideous aspect

> lowering upon mortals, a man of Greece dared first to lift up his mortal eyes to her face and first to withstand her to her face. Him neither story of gods nor thunderbolts nor heaven with threatening roar could quell: they only chafed the more the eager courage of his soul, filling him with desire to be the first to burst the fast bars of nature's portals. (I:62–72)

Epicurus himself had said in his letter to Pythocles: "We must understand that no other end is served by the study of celestial phenomena... than mental composure and a sturdy self-reliance, just as in the case of the other disciplines.... [For] we have no use now for [vain opinions]...[but] to live the unperturbed life."[13]

Clearly, Epicurus was not an atheist. He was simply the first to find a way to avoid being crushed by the terrible power of the sacred; or so he thought. But finding a rational explanation for things in place of the old mythical or sacred stories did not mean there was nothing sacred; it simply meant keeping the sacred and the human separate. It meant recognizing that the mixing of the human and the divine was the ultimate source of evil and misfortune for humanity. You couldn't say that the sacred was nothing without implying that human evil and misfortune were ultimately imaginary, self-generated hallucinations without any real basis. As Girard told us, it was not human reason that killed the old sacred, it was Christ.

Epicurean gods were thought and meant to be real. But they do not intervene in human affairs at all. They live a life of perfect bliss and perpetual undisturbed happiness. Humans who, originally, could see them both in dreams and while awake, and saw their beauty, their effortless movement, their unchanging youth, etc., began by attributing to them superhuman powers: the power to move the world, the changing of seasons and all natural phenomena for which human beings had no rational understanding. But they also attributed to

13 See Bandera, *The Sacred Game*, 96.

them things that are strictly human, like wrath. All the fables of the gods and mythical places are just fantasies, things, that do not and cannot exist. However, all those things happening in places that do not exist, are a reflection of what does happen here in our lives. For example:

> There is no wretched Tantalus, as the story goes, fearing the great rock that hangs over him in the air and frozen with vain terror: rather it is in this life that the fear of gods oppresses mortals without cause, and the fall they fear is any that chance may bring. (*De rerum natura*, III:981–83)

All those terrible things narrated in mythical stories are fictional. There is no "Tartarus belching horrible fires from his throat" (III:1011).

> Yet the guilty conscience, terrified before anything can come to pass, applies the goad and scorches itself with whips, and meanwhile does not see where can be the end of its miseries or the final limit to its punishment, and fears that these same afflictions may become heavier after death. The fool's life finally becomes a Hell on earth. (III:1018–23)

"Terrified before anything can happen." Shakespeare could not say it any more clearly. This is the fear of a sinful soul, as we already heard from Hamlet's mother, the Queen.

Human life on earth changed radically for the worse when human beings first attributed their misfortunes to the gods. They multiplied and enlarged their misfortunes immensely:

> O unhappy race of mankind, to ascribe such doings to the gods and to attribute to them bitter wrath as well! What groans did they then create for themselves, what wounds for us, what tears for generations to come! *It is no piety to show oneself often with covered head, turning towards a stone and approaching every altar, none to fall prostrate upon the ground and to spread open the palms before shrines of the gods, none to sprinkle altars with the blood of beasts in showers and to link vow to vow; but rather to be able to survey all things with tranquil mind.* (V:1194–1203; my emphasis)

Reading these words of Lucretius, how can we not think of strikingly similar words in the Book of the Prophet Isaiah?

> What to me is the multitude of your sacrifices? says the Lord.
> [...] I do not delight in the blood of bulls, or the lambs, or the he-goats.
> [...] Bring no more vain offerings; incense is an abomination to me.
> [...] When you spread forth your hands, I will hide my eyes from you;
> even though you make many prayers, I will not listen;
> your hands are full of blood.
> Wash yourselves; make yourselves clean;
> remove the evil of your doings from before my eyes; cease to do evil, learn to do good. (Isaiah 1:11–17)

The Lord, God of Abraham, does not want sacrifices or vain offerings. What he wants is a clean soul. Lucretius is also condemning a religion based on external signs of worship, which attributes to the gods desires unworthy of their holy divinity. When you do that, their divinity, corrupted, brought down to your level, will harm you. There is nothing worse than the corruption of the best.

> Unless you . . . put far from you thoughts unworthy of the gods and alien to their peace, their holy divinity, impaired by you, will often do you harm; not that the supreme power of the gods is open to insult, so that it should in wrath thirst to inflict sharp vengeance, but because you yourself will imagine that they, who are quiet in their placid peace, are rolling great billows of wrath. (VI:68–74)

Remember what we said about the pagan experience of the sacred: the paralyzing, hair-raising, fear, the "blood-freezing" terror, the shrinking of the mind and every member of the body, the maddening. That is what happens when you approach the gods with "unworthy thoughts." You will turn "their peace, their holy divinity" into a monster that will terrorize you. Your "guilty conscience" will take possession of you, and make your life a living hell. This is also what will transform true reverence and piety into the kind of religion that will "persuade" human beings to do such abominable things as the sacrifice of Iphigenia.[14]

This is why we must not only find a rational, physical, scientific explanation for everything around us, and stop assigning their existence or operation to the gods, but must also abandon all vanity and ambition, that is, all those things that make our life miserable; for that will inevitably lead to sacred terror, and plunge us into a hopeless state of gloom and despair. Lucretian rationality is an island surrounded by an ocean of dark and threatening irrationality:

> Pleasant it is when over a great sea the winds trouble the waters, to gaze from shore upon another's great tribulation: not because any man's troubles are a delectable joy, but because to perceive what ills you are free from is pleasant. Pleasant is it also to behold great encounters of warfare . . . with no part of yours in the peril. But nothing is more delightful than to possess lofty sanctuaries serene, well fortified by the teachings of the wise, whence you may look down upon others and behold them all astray. . . . O pitiable minds of men . . . in what gloom of life, in how great perils is passed all your poor span of time! (II:1–16)

Attributing our misfortune and the troubles of our mind to the gods is to divinize or sacralize an evil of our own making. On the surface, Lucretius's view of sacralized human evil

14 This antisacrificial stand on the part of Lucretius has been frequently misinterpreted, read from a modern perspective which is not that of the Roman poet. "Of the three claims which he makes to immortality"—said classical scholar William Young Sellar more than a century ago—"the importance of his subject, his desire to liberate the mind from the bonds of superstition and the charm and lucidity of his poetry, that which he regarded as supreme was the second. The main idea of the poem is the irreconcilable opposition between the truth of the laws of nature and the falsehood of the old superstitions" (in *Lucretius*, Delphi Classics, trans. H. A. J. Munro). Sellar's assessment regarding "the main idea of the poem" is somewhat misleading, though. Lucretius was not particularly concerned with "the falsehood of the old superstitions," but with their terrifying character. He wants to liberate the mind from fear and anxiety, not primarily from error.

appears to be very similar to Girard's view of the old sacred as nothing but human violence hypostatized. But that can be misleading. In Lucretius, human evil sacralized, deified, is more than just human evil grown bigger, or given an illusory transcendence. It is a qualitative jump into something beyond the human, into something divine, which is perverted, corrupted, as it is taken over, usurped, by a corrupt human conscience. The gods remain untouched by this corruption. They have nothing to do with it. It was all a human affair, the work of an envious desire forever fixed on what is at the top, attempting to bring it down to its own level. This is not the idea of a god becoming human, but the human seeing itself as god, or enviously bringing the divine down to human level.

The human and the divine cannot be mixed without terrible consequences for the human. For Lucretius, therefore, the idea of a god's becoming human would be far worse than just absurd. It would probably be some kind of unimaginable monstrosity, the annihilation of the human race. In a sense, that is precisely the kind of hair-raising monstrosity, the fear of which could "persuade" humanity to carry out such horrible crimes as the killing of your own children.

The monster that terrorizes a guilty conscience is an unbearable mixture of the human and the divine. We already know that Lucretius's scientific defense against sacred irrationality will not work. There is credible testimony that in the end he committed suicide. But historically, the testimony of his life and work is precious. About fifty years after his death, Jesus of Nazareth was born in Bethlehem of Judea. The Christian solution became flesh, and it pointed directly to the problem as defined by Lucretius: the monstrous joining of the human and the divine. Miraculously, where the problem was God found the solution: Christ, true God and true man, two natures in one person.

Not only did the Christian faith address Lucretius's problem, it also explained why human beings were inherently inclined to mix the human and the divine. There is something divine already in every human being, an image of God. Human beings are meant to participate in the divine nature.

It is a remarkable coincidence, which cannot be overlooked: a pagan explanation of the origin of a religion that oppresses humankind with implacable cruelty, demanding human sacrifice, keeping humanity in the prison of its own guilt, under constant threat of total annihilation. All of which humanity brought upon itself by imagining the gods were behind it as accusers and making sure that humans would never forget that they were guilty. It was at this point that a savior was needed, which, for Lucretius, could only be Epicurus. For Christians, of course, the savior is Christ. At first sight, it seems grotesque to attempt any kind of comparison between them. Yet their avowed purpose appears to be the same: to liberate human beings from the prison of their own guilt. The means to achieve such a liberation, is, in the case of the Epicureans, rational knowledge, *scientia*. For Christians, the instrument of their liberation is Christ himself, who is also the victim of a sacrifice that will make all other sacrifices irrelevant, useless, incapable of achieving reconciliation.

Girard's anthropology (not Girard the devout Christian) stands somewhere between Lucretius and Christ: the liberator is, of course, Christ, in his role as sacrificial victim. But in Girard's theory Christ liberates us by giving us knowledge of what we actually do when we sacrifice. He reveals and denounces the sacrificial cover-up, our way of dealing with our own violence. Originally, Girard thought that by the evangelical revelation of the truth of our own violence behind the sacred cover-up, we would stop blaming and killing the victim and become reconciled with one another. Later on, he realized that would never happen, finally realizing that the Gospel revelation had failed. We will say more about this failure further on.

At this point, however, Lucretius can still be a great help to us. First of all, there is the obvious fact that the world did not have to wait for the coming of Christ to know that the sacrificial victim may be completely innocent. We just heard Lucretius cry out in horror at the traditional image of the sacrifice of Iphigenia by her own father. *Tantum potuit religio suadere malorum* (I:101), "to such extremes of evil can human beings be persuaded by religion." When one hears of horrible sacrificial practices, children burnt alive, or left on a mountain peak to freeze, or hundreds of slaves in one single celebration being cut open to take and eat their hearts, as the Aztecs, for example, used to do, we must think of the kind of sacred monster who persuaded people to do such things.

The sacrificial killing of victims is a consequence of this horrendous sacred monstrosity, before which archaic communities trembled in complete submission. Absolutely nothing is gained by proclaiming the innocence of the victim while the monster is up and about. Lucretius and Virgil knew everything it was humanly possible to know about the sacrificial victim and its fate. But all that knowledge did nothing to change the victim's fate. While the monster is around, humans feel hopeless:

> Who is there, whose mind does not shrink into itself with fear of the gods, whose limbs do not cower in terror, when the parched earth rocks with the appalling thunder stroke and rattlings run through the great heaven? Do not peoples and nations quake, and proud monarchs shrink into themselves smitten with fear of the gods, lest for any foul transgression or overweening word the heavy time of reckoning has arrived at its fulness? . . . So constantly does some hidden power trample on human grandeur and is seen to tread under its heel and make sport for itself of the renowned rods and cruel axes. Again, when the whole earth rocks under their feet and cities tumble with the shock or doubtfully threaten to fall, what wonder that mortal men feel contempt for themselves while seeing in the gods high prerogatives and marvelous powers, sufficient to govern all things? (V:1218–1240)

It is not the gods who are to blame, but the "unhappy race of mankind" who attributed to the gods, on the one hand, an immense, unlimited power to move the entire universe, and, on the other, "bitter wrath as well."

These spurious gods, the misguided creation of "unhappy mankind," these immensely powerful and heartless tyrants, are the ones "keeping human life shamefully lying on the ground for all to see, heavily oppressed under religion, which showed its head from the regions of heaven, with horrible aspect hovering over mortals" (*De rerum natura*, I:62–65). Voltaire understood what Lucretius was talking about, the power of those "heinous monsters the trembling world made into gods," as we read in his poem on the Lisbon earthquake. Is it any wonder that there were no atheists in the ancient world?[15]

A catalog of sacrificial practices across the ages would most probably be too horrible, too much to bear for most people today. And yet, in spite of its dangers, such a reading might deepen our Christian understanding of Christ on the Cross, that is to say, our understanding of the immensely powerful hold that the old sacred had on humanity, which only the power of the non-violent God, the equally immense non-power of love, could break. It was so much more than a question of knowledge, or of mythical accusations against a victim. Of what were those millions of victims accused? Ultimately, there was just one universal accusation and one universal accuser.

HIROSHIMA AND NAGASAKI, A TWENTIETH-CENTURY EXAMPLE

In *A Short Treatise on the Metaphysics of Tsunamis*, Jean-Pierre Dupuy reports an amazing observation:

> In 1958 the German philosopher Günther Anders traveled to Hiroshima and Nagasaki to take part in the Fourth World Conference against Atomic and Hydrogen Bombs. After many conversations with survivors of the catastrophe, he noted in his diary: "*Their steadfast resolve not to speak of those who were to blame, not to say that their event had been caused by human beings*, even though they were the victims

15 See *Evolution and Conversion*, 183.

> of the greatest of crimes—this really is too much for me, it passes all understanding." And he added: "They constantly speak of the catastrophe as if it were an earthquake or a tidal wave. They use the Japanese word, *tsunami.*"[16]

Dupuy sees this as an example of our human incapacity to comprehend the causes of evil when evil "becomes disproportionately enlarged in relation to the human condition. In that case evil acquires a power that is independent of the intentions of those who commit it. Both Anders and Arendt probed a scandalous paradox, namely, that immense harm may be caused without the least malevolence."[17]

This is clearly inadequate. It does not explain what is most striking and amazing about the attitude of the Japanese victims: they are terrified; thirteen years after the event, they are terrified. They refuse to talk about guilt. They steadfastly resist any talk about blame. The perfectly rational question of who is responsible and why makes them visibly anxious; they run away from such a topic. They might as well cover their ears. They do not want to hear. Anders speak of "the fear with which their memories were recounted." If their "steadfast resolve" is a measure of their fear, they were terrified. And they are ashamed. In fact, their shame appears to be quite contagious, like a smile, says Anders.[18] It is occasionally the kind of shame that, in the eyes of the Western observer, rises to the level of "virtue," probably because it may appear in the eyes of the western observer as humility, as in the case of two young women in the Nagasaki hospital:

16 *A Short Treatise*, 63 (my emphasis). Dupuy wrote the preface to the French edition of *Hiroshima est partout* (Paris: Éditions du Seuil, 2008) in which Anders's diary is included with the title "L'Homme sur le pont. Journal d'Hiroshima et de Nagasaki."

17 *A Short Treatise*, 63. This is basically what Anders called *décalage prométhéen* (Promethean displacement). See Édouard Jolly, *Nihilisme et technique. Étude sur Günther Anders* (Toulouse: EuroPhilosophie Éditions, 2017). "L'auteur définit synthétiquement ce concept comme étant 'l'a-synchronicité chaque jour croissante entre l'homme et le monde qu'il a produit.'" "The author defines this concept synthetically as 'The asynchronicity which increases every day between man and the world which he has produced.'"

18 Anders, *Hiroshima est partout* (Paris: Seuil, 2008), 207.

> [The] two young women seemed to embody none other than this kind of shame: shame of being fragile, shame of having to die; shame of being honored by a visitor.... They could not understand a single word of what I said, but it is impossible to imagine that they could not understand the tone in which I spoke to them. This being so, I have never been able to understand why their faces showed an expression of fear. I had no awareness of having made any mistake in that regard.[19]

Their shame has nothing to do with Christian humility. It is the shame that attaches to the primitive fear of the sacred. Just as their steadfast refusal to talk about who was responsible for the devastation had nothing to do with Christian-inspired love of your enemy, as Anders made clear:

> That each member of this group of victims chosen at random which was facing us this evening be a genius of love, indulgence, or wisdom, that is ultimately unthinkable. So, what is going on here? What is there behind it?[20]

It is amazing, so close and yet so far. It does not occur to the philosopher that he may be in the presence of the old sacred.

Their attitude in view of the devastation is still basically the one described by Lucretius, which we should remember once more:

> When the parched earth rocks with the appalling thunder stroke and rattlings run through the great heaven [or] again when the whole earth rocks under their feet and cities tumble with the shock or doubtfully threaten to fall.... Do not peoples and nations quake, and proud monarchs shrink into themselves smitten with fear of the gods, lest [they be found guilty]? (*De rerum natura*, V:1218 ff.)

Substitute this unknown thing in the history of mankind, an atomic explosion, for the old earthquake and you will

---

19 Ibid.

20 "Que chaque membre de ce groupe des victimes pris au hasard qui était face à nous ce soir-là soit un génie de l'amour, de l'indulgence ou de la sagesse, voilà qui est finalement impensable. Que se passe-t-il ici? Qu'y a-t-il là derrière?" Anders, *Hiroshima est partout*, 168.

get the same reaction from a population still attached to the old rituals. It is an attitude of total submission, no questions asked, literally. When Zeus thunders nothing human dares to respond (we may remember in this regard the radical novelty of Job). The manifestation of the old sacred obliterates everything else; in its presence nothing else makes any difference. They know about the Americans and the planes. But that is irrelevant. That is not what frightens them thirteen years after the event, nor were the two women at the Nagasaki hospital afraid of the courteous Western visitor, except for the fact that the visit itself was linked to the sacred. The Western philosopher wants to find a rational explanation. But he is dealing with something beyond the rational: the presence of the old sacred mentality among the survivors. If we had any doubts, what Anders observed on the morning of August 9, the anniversary of the catastrophe, will dispel them.

He attended a celebration which took place on a hill overlooking the city of Nagasaki. This was his reaction:

> In short: I was indignant, scandalized. Because this feast had been a *Baal* feast. To repeat: it was an idolatrous cult; the first in which I have taken part, and the last, I hope, in which I will participate. Idolatrous, not only because it unfolded at the foot of a god of stone, but even in its honor exclusively. It is not that the stone is dressed up in honor of the god, the stone itself was the god. It was this stone deified, which was invoked; they prostrate themselves unto it.[21]

This god of stone, this "Memorial Statue," deserves special attention. Anders's comments are particularly relevant when read in a Girardian context. First of all, "[It] is something

21 "Bref: j'étais indigné, j'étais scandalisé. Car cette fête avait été une fête de *Baal*. . . . Encore une fois: ce fut un culte idolâtre; le premier auquel j'aie prit part; le dernier, je l'espère, auquel je participe. Idolâtrie, car non seulement la fête . . . s'est déroulée au pied du dieu de pierre, mais encore en son honneur et en son honneur exclusif. Ce n'est pas en l'honneur du dieu que se dresser la pierre, mais c'est elle-même qui était le dieu. Et c'est cette pierre déifiée que l'on invoquait; c'est à elle qu'allaient les prosternations." *Hiroshima est Partout*, 214–15.

horrific," a colossal statue on a granite base, "which is supposed to represent the god of peace, but, in reality, it is a perfect image, an idol, of the most blind and irrational violence.... What is supposed to be a warning against violence turns out to be the typical image of that against which it is supposed to warn."[22]

If somebody, said Anders, had asked him what it represented, he would have responded without hesitation: "a colossal Baal." The name is not important. It could go by any other mythical god's name. What is fundamental to any archaic divinity is this ambivalence: only that will save you, which can also destroy you. The archaic god is always double-faced. It could be Baal or any other primitive idol, any image of the archaic sacred. What I believe Anders failed to realize is that it was indeed the spirit of "Baal," or rather its horror, that still governed the response of the Japanese survivors to the horror of the atomic attack.

Anders's report of his encounter with the Japanese survivors opens for us an exceptional window on to a human world, which in some fundamental way is radically different from our own as well as from Anders's. We get a glimpse of a world where the place of the victim is the place of shame; where being crushed by overwhelming force is the ultimate proof, the irrefutable evidence that you have been found guilty before the absolute power of the god of the thunderbolt. The old god is manifested in your guilt. Human beings were the slaves of their own guilt. Guilt was sacred. Nobody could question the terrifying existence of the sacred or of your guilt. The fact that you were crushed, facing annihilation, was a double manifestation: your guilt and the power of God. Nothing but a loving God in the place of the victim could put an end to the power of the old sacred.

This is the point where Girard's theory must be recalibrated, so to speak. As we said from the beginning, Christ did not come to reveal *the innocence of the human victim but*

---

22 *Hiroshima est Partout*, 211.

the innocence of God, which separates God from our guilt. The unbreakable, the sacred, link between the two is broken. We are no longer the terrified slaves of our own guilt, or rather, of the Satanic god we had built with the stuff of our own guilt. The passion of Christ reveals our guilt and, at the same time, liberates us from its tyrannical power. Now we can repent.

But something both strange and logical is happening now in our desacralized, secular, world. Our liberated scientific and technological progress has reached the point where we can actually destroy humanity and its environment over the entire planet. How do we prevent this apocalyptic devastation? Can we resacralize this enormous power that we have? Can we resurrect the old tyrant? We know we cannot do it completely; the old gods are gone forever. But can we do it just a little? Just enough to "suspend our disbelief," to pretend, to fool ourselves into believing that the monster is still out there? Dupuy thinks it may be possible. He calls such a possibility "enlightened doomsaying." Anders believed that the vacuum of a purely negative, inhuman, absence of hostility or hatred can be humanized, turned into, filled with, love. To a Christian, I would imagine, such a vacuum can only be filled by Christ.

CHAPTER 10

"The revelation failed"

LET'S RECALL VOLTAIRE'S *POEM* :

> Un calife autrefois, à son heure dernière,
> Au Dieu qu'il' adorait dit pour toute prière :
> "Je t'apporte, ô seul roi, seul être illimité,
> Tout ce que tu n'as pas dans ton immensité,
> Les défauts, les regrets, les maux, et l'ignorance."
> Mais il pouvait encore ajouter *l'espérance.*

> (Once a caliph, in his last hour, prayed to God, whom he worshipped: "I bring thee, O only and almighty king, that, which in your immensity, you lack—faults, regrets, pain, and ignorance." *He could have added hope.*)[1]

Hope in the midst of "a dark night." Hope despite "the faults and the ignorance." That was Voltaire in his famous poem on the Lisbon earthquake. Girard, the man of faith striving for sanctity, could say the same thing. But that is not the conclusion of his mimetic anthropology.

Intended to be a scientific display of the hermeneutic power of the Christian revelation at its deepest level, Girardian anthropology, to the surprise and disbelief of most Girardians, ended up declaring in his last book, *Achever Clausewitz* (*Battling to the End)*, that the revelation has failed, "it has not been heard."

> Did Christianity predict its apocalyptic failure? A reasonable argument can be made that it did. This failure is simply the same thing as the end of the world. From this point of view, one could argue that the verse "when the Son of Man comes, will he find faith on earth?" is still too full of hope.[2]

---

1 Voltaire, "Poème sur le désastre de Lisbonne," in *Œuvres Complètes* (Paris: Garnier, 1877), 9:470–79, 478.

2 *Battling to the End*, 47. This is the full quotation from Luke 18. It comes at the end of the parable of the widow and the unrighteous judge: "Hear

> The relevance of the apocalyptic texts is therefore absolutely striking.... They say paradoxically that Christ will only return when there is no hope that evangelical revelation will be able to eliminate violence, once humanity realizes that it [i.e., the evangelical revelation] has failed. Christians say that Christ will return to transform the failure into eternal life.... The positivity of history should not be eliminated, but shifted. The rationality that mimetic theory seeks to promote is based entirely on the shift. Saying that chaos is near is not incompatible with hope, quite the contrary. However, hope has to be seen in relation to an alternative that leaves only the choice between total destruction and the realization of the Kingdom.[3]

No wonder he is convinced "that history has meaning, and that its meaning is terrifying."[4] "From this point of view," he says. What point of view is that which offers such a dismal vision? At a certain moment Benoît Chantre asks the following question:

> BC: You are leaning toward the worst.... Why do you think that the "epiphany of identity" [of all men] necessarily has to take an apocalyptic turn?
>
> RG: Because the Gospels say so and because the fact has become so obvious ...[5]

Let us leave aside the question of whether or not it is so obvious. It is true that the Gospels announce a terrible apocalyptic situation of unparalleled violence:

> For nation will rise against nation, and kingdom against kingdom, and there will be famines and earthquakes in various places: all this is but the beginning of the sufferings.... For there shall be then great tribulation, such as

---

what the unrighteous judge says. And will not God vindicate his elect, who cry to him day and night? Will he delay long over them? I tell you, he will vindicate them speedily. Nevertheless, when the Son of man comes, will he find faith on earth?" (Luke 18:6–8). Clearly this quotation does not warrant the kind of pessimism expressed by Girard.

3 *Battling to the End*, 119.

4 Ibid., xvii.

5 Ibid., 48.

> has not been from the beginning of the world until now, neither shall be. (Matthew 24:7–21)

But these are the words of Christ, and there is a reason why he is telling these things to his disciples: he wants to prepare them, to tell them that it is possible to maintain the faith through the devastation: "he who endures to the end, will be saved" (Matthew 24:13). He wants them and the world to remember that these were his words, so that "when these things begin to come to pass, look up and lift up your heads, because your redemption is at hand" (Luke 21:28). And the words of Christ in John the Apostle:

> I will not leave you orphans: I will come to you. Yet a little while and the world sees me no more. But you see me: because I live, and you shall live. (John 14:18)

> These things have I spoken to you that you may not be scandalized. They will put you out of the synagogues: yea, the hour comes, that whosoever kills you will think that he does a service to God. And these things will they do to you; because they have not known the Father nor me. But these things I have told you, that when the hour shall come, you may remember that I told you of them. (John 16:1)

So, yes, "the Gospels say so." But why does he leave out the hope that Christ attaches to his own words? Let me repeat the question I formulated a moment ago: "What point of view is that which offers such a dismal vision?" Clearly, one that focuses on the inevitability of what is going to happen to humanity, and ignores the voice that announces it—thus separating the message from the messenger, in order to define the Apocalypse in strictly human terms, because apocalyptic violence is not God's violence, "it is all on our side." It is the hypermimetic violence, about which he has been talking from the beginning, the backbone of a theory without "the slightest recourse to transcendence." A theory that converts a divine message into a strictly human one. Thereby eliminating all hope. Thus, as we move ineluctably toward the end we are simultaneously regressing toward the origin, the foundational violence, except that now violence can no longer be the foundation of anything:

> BC: On one hand, we would have the escalation to extremes [the inexorable worsening of our reciprocal violence], and on the other a return to origins . . . toward what you call the founding murder. The two movements would be linked: the closer we get to the end, the further back we go. The more history tends toward the worst, the less we will be able to hide the need for a clear discussion of archaic religion.
>
> RG: Exactly. It is now time for that discussion. This is why mimetic theory does nothing but analyze archaic religion. . . . It is now clear that the further we progress in history, the further we regress back to that Alpha point. Historical Christianity and what we are obliged to call its "failure" is nothing but the accelerated bridging of the beginning and end of time.[6]

Within the logic of the theory, this regress toward the origin follows the failure of the Christian Revelation and the concurrent absence of Christ. For in the beginning there was nothing but the hypermimeticism of the crowd and the blind automatism of the scapegoat mechanism, which is the "scientific" Girardian way of talking about "original sin." The problem is that scapegoating, which appeared to work well all by itself in the beginning, no longer works, so reconciliation, a new beginning, cannot happen either. We are, according to theory, back at the origin engaged in a state of desacralized violence beyond our control, because we have no sacrificial way to stop it, and Christ is no longer with us. It is a complete dead end. Humanity is trapped. There is no escape. Complete annihilation is imminent. At that moment, what does it mean to say that "Christ will only return when there is no hope that evangelical revelation will be able to eliminate violence, once humanity realizes that it [i.e., the evangelical revelation] has failed"? Does that mean that Christ wants to teach humanity

6 Ibid., 79.

a lesson, let humanity learn the hard way, through horror and despair: see what happens when the evangelical revelation does not work? Will Christ return in glory to tell us, "I told you, why did you not believe in me?" Will "God's patience" be satisfied now? Will he accept our panicky repentance out of despair as a proper reparation for not believing in his Son? Will he believe in our sincerity when we receive his returning Son proclaiming, "Blessed is he who comes in the name of the Lord"? For this will be, according to Christ, what he will hear upon his return.

This is obviously absurd. My point is that Girard's anthropological hope out of complete hopelessness, hope in the face of "an alternative that leaves only the choice between total destruction and the realization of the Kingdom" is not Christian hope at all, but despair. And my point is also that this unbelievable apocalypse is the only one available within the scientific parameters of mimetic anthropology; an anthropology which can discover and explain the scapegoat mechanism and how it works, from a human perspective, which is no small feat. But that is all it can do. Hope, Christian hope, which is inconceivable without divine forgiveness, as Girard knew perfectly well, is beyond its purview.

But he forgot. As he reads Clausewitz's *On War* and meditates on the future of Europe and the world, he realizes Clausewitz is really talking about the ultimate mimetic structure and dynamics of human violence, about its inherent open-ended character. It is ultimately the old duel between enemy brothers in a world-wide dimension. It is the destruction of Europe and the rest of the world. It is the apocalypse. And it is all predicted in the Gospels. It is Christ himself who told us. Yes, I have no problem with that.

But he goes further. What he sees in the Gospels, he thinks, can be explained much better, from a human perspective, by mimetic anthropology. At which point he pays no attention to the explicit expressions of hope and support in Christ's words. As a result, he drives himself into a hopeless dead end.

He becomes a victim of his own logic: if you concentrate on the predicted facts alone, as a scientific approach seems to demand, and put aside the predicter, i.e., Christ, who happens to be the only reason for hope, of course you will end up in a hopeless situation. To make matters even worse, the factual hopelessness of the scientific view now becomes, in turn, the proof that Christ is no longer there: and the epistemological circle is complete. All hope has been blocked out. But Girard is a Christian man, he knows that such a dead end is not Christian. There must be hope still. Yes, as long as we realize that we have reached a dead end and that, therefore, Christ, the Kingdom of God, is our only option.

This hellish circularity could have been easily avoided by trusting the words of Christ to begin with. Why did we have to convince ourselves scientifically that what Christ said was coming, was really coming? Why did we not trust him, and him alone? Why did we have to drive ourselves into despair? Or was all this trial and tribulation a doubtful prelude to the final trusting gesture of leaving everything in the hands of God, the gesture with which we began: "yes, yes, God is taking care of it"?

As I said, *Battling to the End* caught many Girardians by surprise. I was devastated. We had not talked the way we used to talk in the good old days at Buffalo, in a long time, although we never lost contact. My only personal contact with him after the publication of the book was a rather brief conversation at an annual meeting of COV&R in California. I did not know how to approach the subject. I made some general remark about being a bit surprised. I do not know whether he understood what I was trying to say. This is what he said: "Benoît has helped me a lot. I could not have done it all by myself. I no longer have the strength."

Others found the book "unsettling, eccentric" (Michael Kirwan, *Evolution and Conversion*, xx), "strikingly somber" (Kirwan, *Girard and Theology*, 145), and a "troubled work" (Scott Cowdell, *René Girard and the Nonviolent God*, 75). James

Williams, whose "Foreword" to *Resurrection from the Underground* in 1996 spoke of Girard as "a thinker . . . more positive and optimistic concerning human possibilities under God, could scarcely be imagined," now, after his encounter with the Girard of *Battling to the End*, finds him "with a more pessimistic view of the success of Christianity." "In this conversation with Benoît Chantre he makes a 180-degree turn to comment at length about the crisis of Western culture and civilization, although not at all in a hopeful, activist, fashion," which is really an understatement. "Do we dismiss his insights as the ramblings of a disillusioned sage, or do we recognize in their prophetic vehemence a strategic understanding of the in-between time of our 'modernity,' precariously advancing between Progress and Abyss?"[7]

Christian hope must be rescued from this scientific apocalypse. We must remember basic things, things which Girard knew perfectly well and yet rendered irrelevant in the context of mimetic anthropology. Christian things like those of which Father Kelly has recently reminded us in a marvelous article, which ought to be "ruminated" upon *morossisime*[8] by those of us who suffered through the reading of *Battling to the End*:

> The key element in the relationship of God to the world—that is, from "before the foundation of the world"—has been the presence of the crucified and risen One: "Do not be afraid; I am the first and the last, and the living one. I was dead, and see, I am alive forever and ever; and I have the keys of Death and Hades" (Rev. 1:17b–18). *Without this backdrop of a divine self-sacrificial love and our participation in it through mercy and forgiveness, history can seem like a dismal obituary. But any such conclusion based only on violence,*

7 Kirwan, "A New Heaven and a New Earth. Apocalypticism and Its Alternatives," in *Can We Survive Our Origins?* (East Lansing, MI: Michigan State University Press, 2015), 329.

8 An expression used by Saint Bonaventure in his *Itinerarium mentis ad Deum*: "non est harum speculationum progressus perfunctorie transcurrendus, sed morosissime ruminandus" (the development of these ideas is not to be run through in perfunctory fashion, but ruminated upon with the greatest of care) (*Prologus*).

> *hatred, and death as the drivers of our human history would be premature without the special energies of Christian love and hope* [my emphasis]. These virtues breathe with God's limitless self-sacrificial love, as it creates the universe, forms humanity, forgives sins, brings healing, and promises the transformed integrity of finding God "all in all."[9]

I could not have said it any better myself. Girard's scientific pessimism, or hope out of despair, was not always apparent. He sounded optimistic in *The Scapegoat* (1986):

> In reality, the world's lack of belief is perpetuated and reinforced only because the historical process is not yet complete, thus creating the illusion of a Jesus demystified by the progress of knowledge and eliminated with the other gods from history. History need only progress some more and the Gospel will be verified. "Satan" is discredited, and Christ justified. Jesus' victory is thus, in principle, achieved immediately at the moment of the Passion, but for most men it only takes shape in the course of a long history secretly controlled by the revelation.[10]

He also spoke of the "victory of the Cross," in *I See Satan Fall Like Lightning* (2000). It is true, as noticed by Dupuy, that the ground on which his anthropological pessimism is built was already there as early as *Things Hidden* (1978):

> Every advance in knowledge of the victimage mechanism, everything that flushes violence out of its lair, doubtless represents, at least potentially, a formidable advance for men in an intellectual and ethical respect but, in the short run, it is all going to translate as well into an appalling resurgence of this same violence in history, in its most odious and most atrocious forms, because the sacrificial mechanisms become less and less effective and less and less capable of renewing themselves.... Humanity in its entirety already finds itself confronted with an ineluctable dilemma: men must reconcile themselves for evermore

---

9 Anthony Kelly, "Love your enemies. God's new world order," in *Does Religion Cause Violence*, ed. Scott Cowdell et al. (New York: Bloomsbury Academic, 2018), 62.

10 *The Scapegoat*, 207.

> without sacrificial intermediaries, or they must resign themselves to the coming extinction of humanity.[11]

However, he expected that, eventually, universal knowledge of the victimage mechanism would prevail and move humanity toward some sort of global reconciliation, as he acknowledges in his last book. Nobody spoke of pessimism at that time. In fact, from what he told me, the 1978 book was very well received by the Catholic hierarchy, both in Paris and at the Vatican. It was not long thereafter that he was invited to a meeting with the Pope in the company of a few other French intellectuals, which I mentioned earlier. I seriously doubt that John Paul II would have had much interest in meeting with the author of *Achever Clausewitz.*[12] Let me bring up again those crucial words of the Holy Father's in *Crossing the Threshold of Hope*:

> *Of what should we not be afraid?* We should not fear *the truth about ourselves.* One day Peter became aware of this and with particular energy he said to Jesus: "Depart from me Lord, for I am a sinful man" (Luke 5:8).... Christ answered him: "Do not be afraid; from now on you will be catching men." (Luke 5:10)[13]

"*We should not fear the truth about ourselves.*" There it is, in a nutshell, the most radical antidote to what Girard says in *Achever Clausewitz.* But the truth about ourselves was revealed

---

11 *Things Hidden*, 150, 160.

12 As late as 2005 he was still remembered at the Vatican in the context of a homily about hope, delivered by Father Raniero Cantalamessa at the Good Friday service in Saint Peter's Basilica, in which he made reference to Girard's work, with which he was familiar. I kept that homily. He was preaching about the hope that the death of Christ brought into the world. He thought it was particularly appropriate to speak about this hope: "To overcome the horror of death and the mood of gloomy pessimism common in our society. So many reasons are put forward [today] for the desperate state of the world.... But God did not *reconcile the world to himself* only to abandon it to nothingness; *he did not promise to remain with us to the end of the world* [my emphasis] only to go, alone, back to his heaven." I take this opportunity to thank Gil Bailie for alerting me to the work of Father Cantalamessa, and for many other fruitful observations.

13 *Crossing the Threshold of Hope* (New York: Knopf, 1994), 5.

to us by the Crucified. Those creatures trembling under "the black Typhon or barbarous Ahriman," petrified with sacred horror, shrunk into themselves, must be something extraordinary, since they were loved by God to such an extreme, to be rescued by the Son of the Living God at such a price.

The amazing thing is that nobody has understood the extent of that price in human terms, its universal scope, better than Girard. After his conversion he did nothing but explore and explain to us what that price was from the beginning. What happened then? Was he overwhelmed by what he found? Did he faint? Was there a doubting moment when he felt that faith was not enough, that science must come to the rescue? Listen again to his words:

> BC: The more history tends toward the worst, the less we will be able to hide the need for a clear discussion of archaic religion.
>
> RG: Exactly. It is now time for that discussion. This is why mimetic theory does nothing but analyze archaic religion.[14]

What else could that mean if not that, in view of what the Gospels prophesy, it is urgent that we pay attention to what mimetic theory has been telling us? Girard was not trying to undermine the faith, of course. But in view of what he saw as the failure of the evangelical revelation, in view of the fact that we did not listen, it has become increasingly clear that a discussion of what mimetic theory has been doing from the beginning is urgent. There is something profoundly sincere, and incredibly naive, in this Girardian appeal for us to listen. There is something of the spirit of prophecy in it. He is not trying to be a substitute for Christ, of course. He would much rather be his prophet.

But to no avail. The scientific language of mimetic anthropology constitutes itself on the basis of an *a priori* expulsion, or absence, of any religious belief. It is not the Evangelical revelation, the word of Christ, that has failed; what has failed

14 *Battling to the End*, 79.

is mimetic anthropology. We wanted something scientific "without the slightest recourse to transcendence." And that is exactly what we got. We reap what we sow. Therefore, there is nothing between us and the Kingdom, except our violence, which is what has been revealed to us, according to mimetic anthropology. "The truth about violence has been stated once and for all. Christ revealed the truth that the prophets announced, namely, that of the violent foundation of all cultures."[15]

Let us review it once more. Girard said that it was Christ who revealed the truth about human violence. Christ gave us "universal knowledge of violence." He thought that that would lead to general reconciliation. It did not happen. Therefore, the Christian Revelation has failed historically. However, that knowledge of violence was the foundation of mimetic anthropology; it made mimetic anthropology possible. This being so, how can mimetic anthropology help where "universal knowledge of violence" failed? It does not make any sense. Mimetic theory will simply add another layer of futility to our hopeless predicament.

Nevertheless, by the mercy of God, we cannot manage to block the view completely. In spite of everything, the sound of hope can still be detected underneath the "sound and the fury" of the futile and meaningless surface:

> Apocalyptic thought recognizes the source of conflict in identity, but it also sees in it the hidden presence of the thought of "the neighbor as yourself" *which can certainly not triumph*, but is secretly active, secretly dominant under the sound and fury on the surface. Peaceful identity lies at the heart of violent identity as its most secret possibility.[16]

Is this not the moment of conversion? Similar, perhaps, to the conversion of the literary author. The end of the novel. The end of all novels, of literary fiction itself. Have we reached the end of theory in a similar way? Let us see:

---

15 *Battling to the End*, 105.
16 Ibid., 46. My emphasis.

> It is not the Father whom we should imitate, but his Son, who has withdrawn with his Father. *His absence is the very ordeal that we have to go through.* This is when, and only when, the religious should no longer be frightening, and the escalation to extremes could turn into its opposite. Such a reversal is nothing more than the advent of the Kingdom. *What form will that advent take? We cannot imagine it. We will be able to do so only if we abandon all our old rationalist reflexes. Therefore, once again, everything depends on the meaning we give to religion. The one that mimetic theory seeks to construct is relevant because it is anchored in a tradition and is also not incompatible with the advances of the "human sciences."*[17]

Obviously, we are not there yet. We are still trying to sell the higher merits of our theory. Are our new "rationalist reflexes, anchored in tradition and compatible with the advances of the 'human sciences,'" so different from the "old rationalist reflexes"? Should we not abandon them as well?

Then, all of a sudden, the entire argument in *Battling to the End* tilts silently out of its rationalist impasse toward individual conversion. In a book about the fate of humanity as a whole, which advises "to reason more and more at a global level, leave behind strictly individual perspectives, and consider things 'in big chunks,'" a most individual perspective, that of the poet Hölderlin's conversion, is placed at the center:

> This book is based on long discussions with Benoît Chantre, and has been entirely reworked and rewritten by him. We established the definitive version together. We follow Clausewitz's text very closely. Conversation's blessings include surprises and new connections. Little by little, we came to see that various authors, poets and exceptional people were crucial to our discussion. A whole constellation of writers and thinkers finally merged with our thinking. I consider this a little like the communion of saints. *The enormous problems that we have raised based on a single text have highlighted these people,* and the central thinker has seemed to us to be the poet Hölderlin.[18]

17 Ibid., 120. My emphasis.
18 Ibid., 17. My emphasis.

We have left our scientific anthropology behind. We have left behind the theory that tells us that individual conversions will not change anything at large. We are now talking about individual conversion, that of Hölderlin, "which will help us understand what is happening."[19] After all, the transition "from reciprocity to relationship, from negative contagion to a form of positive contagion [which] is what the imitation of Christ means . . . is on the level of a specific conversion."[20] There is no other way of meeting the Christ who saves, except individually. "I am not praying for the world but for those whom thou hast given me, for they are thine; all mine are thine, and thine are mine, and I am glorified in them" (John 17:9). Society at large is in a state of panic, "has gone crazy" at the approach of the truth:

> The reason that people fight more and more is that *there is a truth approaching* against which their violence reacts. The Christ is the Other who is coming and who, in his very vulnerability, arouses panic in the system. In small archaic societies, the Other was the stranger who brings disorder, and who always ends up as the scapegoat. In the Christian world, it is Christ, the Son of God, who represents all the innocent victims and whose return is heralded by the very effects of the escalation to extremes. What will he declare? That we have gone crazy, that the

19 This is an example of Hölderlin's testimony:
The only one (third version)
My master and lord!
O you, my teacher!
Why have you kept
Your distance? And when
Among the ancients, in the midst of the spirits
I saw the heroes and
The gods why were
You missing? And now my soul
Is full of sorrow as though
The immortals jealously competed
So that if I serve one
I will lack another.
(*Selected Poetry*, translated by David Constantine)

20 *Battling to the End*, 109.

> adulthood of humanity, which he announced through the cross, is a failure.[21]

The only way to escape the maddening failure of Christianity, which is the subject matter of *Battling to the End,* is an individual way. This is why Hölderlin's "withdrawal" is so significant:

> Hölderlin's withdrawal occurred at the very point when there was a frightening acceleration of history in Germany. In this, the poet was infinitely more lucid than his friend Hegel. It is as if he felt the terrifying future and saw that humanity would be unable to hear the truth. This is why I see in his distancing not only an apocalyptic attitude, but also a form of rediscovered innocence and, I dare say, holiness.[22]

This withdrawal, this distancing, is essential. He retreats from a vision that both terrifies and fascinates, from the spectacle of a society insanely trapped in reciprocal violence. "Some human beings resist desire and being carried away by mimetic violence.... To talk about freedom means to talk about man's ability to resist the mimetic mechanism."[23] We "resist desire," "being carried away," by averting our eyes from the object of desire; by withdrawing, by distancing ourselves from its powerful attraction. But human beings cannot cease to be mimetic. We will follow a model. We are free, however, to choose a model who will not only never become our rival, but who will also not take our freedom away. A god would take our freedom away. "The Greeks never thought to imitate gods"—nor heroes, I should add. But our God recedes into the distance, though he is still close enough to be our model and also to preserve our freedom. Christ is the perfect model, both God and man. Christ or Christ-like figures, saints.

This is the kind of reasoning behind the choice of Hölderlin as a model of behavior in the midst of an apocalyptic vision:

---

21 Ibid., 105.
22 Ibid., 124.
23 *Evolution and Conversion*, 159–60.

"The presence of the divine grows as the divine withdraws: it is the withdrawal that saves, not the promiscuity. . . . Hölderlin thus felt that the Incarnation was the only means available to humanity to face God's very salubrious silence."[24] "Resisting desire," "resisting being carried away," on one hand, and, on the other, following the perfect model at the perfect distance, imply each other.

Carl von Clausewitz fell silent before the madness of which he did not dare to talk, the maddening violence of endless reciprocity between polar opposites. The madness of which mimetic anthropology has been talking from the beginning. The maddening ambivalence of the sacred victim, in which it all began. The madness before which all knowledge disintegrates, including everything that mimetic anthropology had been saying from the beginning, always centered around the murder of the human victim. Knowledge is useless, powerless, before the collective madness. Girard knew this. Why should he keep talking about it? He pokes fun at himself: Oh! Those millions of victims, shouldn't God apologize to us? But he knows where the truth lies that can rescue a human from madness. It is inside, in the most intimate interiority, revealing, not only the interiority itself in its light, but the whole world in its light. The Christ who speaks in the intimacy of the soul is the Savior of the world, and vice versa, the Savior of the world can only be heard in the intimacy of the soul.

Clausewitz's silence, Hölderlin's withdrawal. In the end, mimetic anthropology becomes an exploration of the reasons for such a silence and withdrawal, which can only be the very reasons for mimetic anthropology itself to fall silent and withdraw. Enough is enough. It is the hour of truth. Let Christ speak. The rest is madness.[25]

---

24 *Battling to the End*, 122.

25 Kevin Mongrain has also noticed the striking difference between Girard's scientism and his profound spirituality. But I am not sure his view of this duality does justice to Girard's sincerity: "Because Girard is still primarily speaking to the academy, his agenda to reassert the value of Christian true gnosis inevitably suffers some obfuscation. His agenda is not completely

CHAPTER 11
Virgil

It is impossible to understand Virgil in all his fullness . . . without some reference to the oncoming faith, and to the part which that sense of something wanting played, and indeed still plays in the history of faith, as its natural, in contradistinction to its supernatural, foundation. To deny that Virgil did feel this lack of the Revelation and knew the longing consequent upon this want—to make of him simply the melancholy man wounded by eternity—is to make him only seemingly greater. It is to evade the real problem...

The essential unity and continuity of the human and natural foundations of the Graeco-Roman and the Christian Occident are laid bare to us at the critical moment in the person and work of a great poet; for not only has the *anima Vergiliana*, that most illustrious soul of ancient Rome, found for itself kindred spirits, such as Dante, Racine, and

---

hidden, however. If we look closely with the Balthasarian lens we see that Girard frames his religious thought as 'scientific anthropology' only so that he can get a hearing for his Catholic version of true gnosis from an audience generally biased against the claim that faith yields any form of real knowledge" (Mongrain, "Theologians of Spiritual Transformation," *Modern Theology* 28:1 [January, 2012]: 96). There is nothing devious here. It is simply a question of rhetorical or methodological adaptation of your speech to the audience. All we have to do is to expand our definition of theology: "Is *The City of God* a theological text? Do Ephrem the Syrian's writings count as theology? Is Hildegard of Bingen's *Scivias* a theological text? Is Dante's *The Divine Comedy* theology? Is Erasmus's *In Praise of Folly* theology? Did Charles Péguy write theology? Etc. The often-overlooked truth about Girard is that, while eschewing theology in the narrow senses of scholastic *disputatio* and modern academic *Wissenschaft*, he practices theology in the classical sense: speaking about God's relationship to the world in a genre that is intra-ecclesial, narrative, symbolic, panoramic, evocative, and even apocalyptic" (Mongrain, 84). I do not know if there is such a thing, historically, as a "theologian of spiritual transformation." In principle, I have no problem with applying such a title to Girard. "Spiritual transformation" is probably the one concept to which Girard remained faithful from beginning to end. But the relationship between his scientific demonstration and his religious faith was never an easy one. *Battling to the End* is a direct consequence of this uneasiness.

> Newman, throughout the centuries; but Christians have in their turn reflected the supernatural light of grace upon that most perfect *anima naturaliter Christiana* of antiquity, the soul of the great poet, Publius Vergilius Maro.[1]

IT IS UTTERLY AMAZING THAT GIRARD NEVER SPOKE OF Virgil in his work. And yet, it was Virgil of whom Saint-Beuve had famously said that "not even the coming of Christ is anything surprising after reading Virgil" (*La venue même du Christ n'a rien qui étonne quand on a lu Virgile*).[2] In fact, was this famous statement the reason why Georges Poulet would see Girard "as though [he] were the Sainte-Beuve of the twentieth century"?[3] I do not know if that was the reason, but it makes Girard's silence about Virgil all the more surprising. Girardian anthropology is uniquely qualified to read Virgil's *Aeneid*, in particular, its unexplained ending: the indignant protest of victim as it is killed and sent to the darkness below. Everything centers equally around the sacrificial victim both in Virgil and Girard. Before Girard, it was Chesterton, in our time, who noticed the dignity of "the defeated," the victim, in Virgil:

> We have already seen the first hint of it in the pathos of Homer about Hector. But Virgil turned it . . . into a legend. And it was a legend about the almost divine dignity that belongs to the defeated. This was one of the traditions that did truly prepare the world for the coming of Christianity.[4]

Sainte-Beuve and Chesterton are not the only ones among the best known Christian authors who have seen Virgil, in one way or another, as "a naturally Christian soul," *anima naturaliter Christiana*, some sort of pagan prophet, or precursor, of

1 Theodor Haecker, *Virgil, Father of the West* (New York: Sheed and Ward, 1934), 15–17. The notion of a *testimonium animae naturaliter christianae* appears in Chapter XVII of Tertullian's *Apology for the Christians.*

2 *Etude sur Virgile*, 78.

3 *Evolution and Conversion*, 22.

4 G. K. Chesterton, *The Everlasting Man* (San Francisco: Ignatius Press, 1993), 156.

Christianity. C. S. Lewis, T. S. Eliot must be included. "Lewis told Tolkien that he found similarities between the *Aeneid* and *The Lord of the Rings*—each one a 'great and hard and bitter epic' of reluctant heroes, 'men with a vocation, men on whom a burden is laid'; each one evoking a legendary past, marking a *novus ordo seclorum,* and foreshadowing beyond the ages of the world and the 'tears of things' something very like the gospel."[5] And T. S. Eliot remarked that "[Virgil] led Europe towards the Christian culture which he would never know."[6]

I believe there are profound reasons for this persistent Christian view of Virgil through the centuries. Perhaps the best way to approach this subject in the context of this book is to compare Virgil's attitude with that of his slightly older contemporary, Lucretius. First of all, we must be aware that Virgil's reading of Lucretius was, in the words of W. R. Johnson, "probably the most important thing in his life as a poet (to call that reading an event would be misleading since it is clear that the reading was habitual and unending)."[7] Let us read again those famous verses in *Georgics II:*

> felix qui potuit rerum cognoscere causas,
> atque metus omnis et inexorabile fatum
> subiecit pedibus strepitumque Acherontis avari.
> fortunatus et ille, deos qui novit agrestis,
> Panaque Silvanumque senem Nymphasque sorores.
> (II:490–94)

> (Blessed is he who has succeeded in learning the laws of nature's working, has cast beneath his feet all fear and fate's implacable decree, and the howl of insatiable Death. But happy, too, is he who knows the rural gods, Pan and aged Silvanus and the sisterhood of the Nymphs.)[8]

---

5 Carol Zaleski, "C. S. Lewis's *Aeneid,*" *The Christian Century*, June 2, 2011.
6 Eliot, "What is a Classic?" in *Selected Prose of T. S. Eliot*, ed. Frank Kermode (London: Faber, 1975), 131.
7 *Darkness Visible: A Study of Vergil's Aeneid* (Berkeley and Los Angeles: University of California Press, 1967), 151.
8 Virgil, *Eclogues, Georgics, Aeneid 1–6*, trans. H. R. Fairclough, rev. G. R. Goold (Cambridge, MA: Harvard University Press, 1999), 171.

Basically, this is what he is telling his admired Lucretius: yes, how fortunate is the one who can fight the terror of the sacred with the true knowledge of science; but no more fortunate than the one who prays to the familiar gods of the rustic, idyllic, countryside, and, by extension, any reassuring ritual of religious piety. Let us not forget that Aeneas is above all *pius Aeneas*, "a man distinguished for his piety," *insignem pietate virum*. And this is also what distinguishes Virgil from Lucretius: religious piety. There is really no such thing in Lucretius. His gods are real and exemplary precisely because they keep themselves completely detached from human affairs. Praying to the gods, petitioning the gods, makes no sense for Lucretius. The only conceivable piety is the one that keeps the gods where they really belong: away from human affairs. We might say that Lucretius's piety is scientific rather than properly religious. Virgil's piety is much more in line with what Cicero says about it in his book *On the Nature of the Gods*:

> [If the gods] have neither the power nor the wish to aid us, if they have no care at all for us and take no notice of what we do, if there is nothing that can find its way from them to human life, what reason is there for our rendering to them any worship, or honor, or prayers? On the other hand, in an empty and artificial pretense of faith piety cannot find a place any more than the other virtues; with piety it is necessary that holiness and religious obligation should also disappear, and when these are gone a great confusion and disturbance of life ensues; indeed, *when piety towards the gods is removed, I am not so sure that good faith, and human fraternity, and justice, the chief of all the virtues, are not also removed.* (*De natura deorum*, I. ii. 3–4. My emphasis)

There is nothing in Virgil which would disagree with that. However, he is also well acquainted with "sacred fear," *metus*, and the "howls of hungry Acheron," eager to swallow its victims. That is the nature of Virgil's problem. Everything that is decent and praiseworthy—piety, good faith, fraternity, justice—must have a sacred foundation; these are all the virtues that would disappear without the sacred. And yet, there is terrible violence, and horror, and devastation also at the very root of the sacred, which is to say, at the foundation of the city. For Virgil does not know any other god or gods but those of the city—not just any city, though, but Rome, *res maxima*, universal Rome, the city of man. The Epicurean garden is not the city of man. He is not Lucretius. He is not trying to find an impossible refuge from the horror of the sacred.

That is the truly important thing. He is not running away from the sacred. That is unprecedented. Lucretius is still running away from the sacred. Epicurus is not the god that his disciples see in him. His daring is remarkable, but he is still looking for a refuge. He takes refuge in the science of nature or in astronomy to keep his mind unperturbed by the terrors of the sacred. He still seeks the object, the thing out there, *hoc*, "neuter for gender, neuter for peace," as Michel Serres rightly saw, to escape the violence. Sophocles and Euripides appear to challenge the sacred for a moment, briefly, if Girard or Goodhart are right in what they saw in the tragic text. But this text immediately steps back at the edge of the abyss. The tragedians rejoin the crowd, they will follow the myth. Oedipus's expulsion from the city will take place as expected, and Oedipus himself will proclaim its sacred necessity. Dionysus will destroy Pentheus. This is the lesson to be learned: do not challenge the god or you will pay dearly. As it should be, says Plato himself in *The Laws*. It is a sacrilege to mourn—as the tragic poets do next to the sacrificial altar—when they bring on "Thyestes-figures or certain Oedipuses or certain Macareuses, who secretly have intercourse with their sisters, isn't it seen that they promptly inflict upon themselves the just punishment of death for their crime?"[9] Nothing but "auspicious" sounds should be heard next to the sacrificial altars. And yet, you hear those tragic choruses with mournful music and loud lamentation in almost all of our cities, says Plato:

9 See "Plato's Sacred Anxiety," in *The Sacred Game*, 50 ff.

> *Ath.* [Suppose] a sacrifice is going on, and the victims are being burnt according to law—if, I say, any one who may be a son or brother, standing by another at the altar and over the victims, horribly blasphemes, will not his words inspire despondency and evil omens and forebodings in the mind of his father and of his other kinsmen?
>
> *Cli.* Of course.
>
> *Ath.* And this is just what takes place in almost all our cities. A magistrate offers a public sacrifice, and there come in not one but many choruses, who take up a position a little way from the altar, and from time to time pour forth all sorts of horrible blasphemies on the sacred rites, exciting the souls of the audience with words and rhythms and melodies most sorrowful to hear. (*Laws*, VII, 800–1)

Plato is also terrified by the sacred. He blames the tragic poets for not knowing what they are doing.

Virgil's victim, on the contrary, will die protesting her death, in the case of Camilla, or his death, in the case of Turnus, with a groan of indignation:

> Vitaque cum gemitu fugit indignata sub umbris.

This is the last line of Virgil's *Aeneid.*[10] Nobody knows the particular reasons (if there were any) why Virgil did not go any further. It does not matter, all psychological explanations are irrelevant. Even if it were a mere accident, to end such a poem with a gesture of indignation of the sacrificial victim in the throes of death is, in itself, immensely significant. It sums up the entire meaning of the poem. Everything comes down to that, to the victim. The victim is at the beginning and at the end. The victim is the cornerstone of the entire sacrificial edifice. This is why it is as immensely significant to read Virgil in the light of Girard as it is to read Girard in the light of Virgil. I suspect that nothing that Virgil could

10 Such an abrupt ending of the poem has caused all kinds of speculations: is the poem really finished or not? Was this the reason why Virgil wanted, on his deathbed, to have his poem burnt? It does not really matter.

have said explicitly, in his own words, would say so much to us about the victim as his glaring silence. Silence is the final message. There is nothing else to say. Everything converges upon the victim. Nevertheless, after everything has been said, that groan of protest lingers on. And the question returns, why? Why does it have to be that way?

> Was it your will, Oh Jupiter, that in such a turmoil people should clash, who are destined to live in eternal peace? (*Tanton placuit concurrere motu, Iuppiter, aeterna gentis in pace futuras?*) (XII, 503–4)

"Such an enormous struggle to build the foundation of the Roman people" (*tantae molis erat Romanam condere gentem*) (I, 33). At one point even the gods feel pity over so much carnage: "The gods in Jove's halls pity the empty wrath of both sides, and so many toils that mortals must endure" (*di Jovis in tectis iram miserantur inanem / amborum et tantos mortalibus esse labores*) (X, 758–59). *Iram inanem*, empty, senseless, unnecessary fury on both sides, equally. Is that what you, Jupiter, you, the gods of the city, the protectors, want? The real question: how can such a senseless, empty, violence be sacred? One can see here the anxious historical question of an entire era straining for an answer. Neither what Simone Weil saw in the *Iliad* or Girard in Sophocles or Euripides come close to the "naturally Christian" quality of Virgil's intuition.

Virgil's attitude is not one of scandalized outrage. Once again, he is not Lucretius. He is profoundly sad because he does not understand. It is not the violence *per se* that bothers him; it is its sacred character. In mythical terms, how can that be the will of the gods? For example, how can savage, cruel resentment, be the driving force of a celestial creature like the supreme goddess, Juno?

> Tell me the reason, Muse: what was the wound to her divinity, so hurting her that she, the queen of gods, compelled a man remarkable for goodness to endure so many crises, meet so many trials? Can such resentment hold the minds of gods?

(Musa, mihi causas memora, quo numine laeso,
quidve dolens, regina deum tot volvere casus
insignem pietate virum, tot adire labores
impulerit. Tantaene animis caelestibus irae?)
(Book I, 8–11)[11]

Not just the violence, but the fact that the violence, being sacred, has the last word, is the last word. How can that be? And I do not think he would be satisfied at all if somebody were to show him the mimetic functioning of the scapegoat mechanism. I am sure it would sound quite familiar to him. But that would not answer his question either. Why is that sacred? As I have been trying to show, without Christ, mimetic anthropology does not have the answer either. Hypermimeticism, by itself alone, does not explain the sacred. In the final analysis, it is the presence of the sacred in man, perverted, corrupted, that explains hypermimeticism. Other than the implied, silent Christ, there is nothing that mimetic anthropology could teach Virgil.

Virgil knows what Lucretius also knows: behind the mythical sacrifice of Iphigenia, there is (or there was in the immediate past for a Roman) real horrible human sacrifice. Iphigenia's sacrifice is the symbol of a terrible worldwide reality. *Unum pro multis dabitur caput*, "one head will be given for the sake of many," is the implacable law of the land. Hence his surprise while he was guiding Dante through Hell, when he saw Caifas crucified on the ground (*Inferno* XXIII), for he was the one who told the Sanhedrin that "it was more expedient to kill one man than for a whole people to perish" (John 18:14). Not only is that the sacrificial law, without that one sacrificial head, there would be no city, no human civilization, as far as scientific anthropology can tell. The founding hero is first of all a victim. The victim is the incarnation of the sacred, which means that the victim is also the sacrificer. Aeneas personifies both the victim and the sacrificer. He is in the role of Hector and Achilles. In fact, Virgil will play ironically

11 Bantam Classics.

with this ambiguity. Who is Hector and who is Achilles in the duel between Aeneas and Turnus? Virgil's questioning will go even deeper: who is, in principle, by definition, the one destined? who is the victim? And here is the astonishing Virgilian answer: anybody, the choice may be the result of an accident. The victim may actually be, not only innocent, but exemplary. But how can that be? How could such an injustice be the very ground of justice? That is the unanswered question in the Palinurus episode, as we will see.

The distant origin of Rome lies in the devastated ruins of a city burned to the ground. Its distant hero is a victim, a defeated man, barely escaping the destruction of the city and the massacre of its people, an exile driven by inexorable fate, *fato profugo*, bitterly acquainted with grief, that is, with "the tears of things," *hic sunt lacrimae rerum*, said he; "the most untranslatable half-line in the whole of the *Aeneid*, and for that matter, in the whole of Roman literature," says Haecker. "Things themselves have tears. . . . There are things to which there is no answer but tears."[12] Isn't that what Christian tradition also says about us, human beings, *exules filii Evae gementes et flentes in hac lacrimarum valle* (exiles, children of Eve, sighing and weeping in this valley of tears)?

The future rested, literally, on the shoulders, of a defeated man, an exile (he is physically carrying his father and the household gods on his shoulders). He is the one appointed by an inscrutable and inexorable fate; *ego poscor Olympo* (It is I who am demanded of Heaven), he tells his host king Evander. He is the one, although reluctantly; he does not know why he is the one, but he has no choice. If it were up to him, he would much rather return home and rebuild Troy for the vanquished, as he tells grief-stricken and despairing Dido:

> Did the Fates suffer me to guide my life by my own auspices and order my sorrows by my own will, I would cherish first the town of Troy, the sweet remains of my own people. Priam's high house would still remain, and

12 *Virgil, Father of the West*, 93.

> my own hand should have revived Pergamus for the vanquished. (IV, 340–44)

Allen Mandelbaum, a modern translator of the *Aeneid*, notices how the critics' view of the poem has been changing recently:

> Much recent criticism has seen the ache and bite of doubt in the *Aeneid*, ever less—as we read more—a triumphant poem in praise of the *imperium* of Caesar Augustus.... I saw in the *Aeneid* the underground denial—by consciousness and longing—of the total claims of the state and history: the persistence in the mind of what is not there, as a measure of the present.[13]

There is much truth in what the critic says, but we must be careful not to turn Virgil into a modern sceptic. It is not "the ache and bite of doubt" that we find in the *Aeneid*, neither is there an "underground denial... of the total claims of the state and history." Virgil has no problem at all with Roman *imperium*. He knows that there is no other political and legal power in the world, at the time, comparable to it. But to the extent that we can talk about some sort of "denial," to use the critic's term, it is not exactly underground, but rather explicit.

Readers of the *Aeneid* may remember that Aeneas is allowed to enter Hades accompanied by the Sybil, the prophetess of Apollo, to visit the spirit of his dead father, Anchises. There, in Hades, Anchises reveals to his son the glory of that city, Rome, the first step in the foundation of which has been entrusted to him by fate. He hears of the coming of Julius Caesar, and his adopted son, Augustus Caesar (who was actually Virgil's friend and protector) and so many others. He hears of the extraordinary capacity of the future Empire to govern peacefully the vanquished and to bring down the proud (*parcere subiectis et debellare superbos*). To others, says Anchises (meaning, of course, the Greeks), were given the arts and sciences, but to you, Roman, remember, the rule

---

13 Introduction to his translation, 59.

of law: *tu regere imperio populos, Romane, memento* (VI, 851). These are not idle words. History is witness to their relevance. The enormous prestige and authority of Roman law survived for many centuries long after the Roman Empire as a political entity had disappeared. In many law schools throughout Europe, Roman Law is a required subject to this day. Emperor Justinian's Civil Code, the *Corpus Iuris*, from the sixth century, has been a model for countless civil codes throughout the West on matters of contracts, family law, property, inheritance, judicial process, etc. Every legal scholar is familiar with those famous Justinian principles of any rule of law: *honeste vivere, alterum non laedere, suum cuique tribuere* (to live honestly, not to injure another, to render to each one his own). And let us remember that Latin was the common language of all European scholars well into the modern era. The power of Rome was the power of peace, *pax romana*, through the rule of law, *pacique imponere morem*. It was the law tempered by prudence, because *summum ius, summa iniuria*, extreme justice is extreme injustice. These are not imaginary things, poetic inventions. These are not lies in the ordinary sense of the word.

And yet, as soon as Anchises' prophetic speech is finished, *his dictis*, "once these words were said," with which "he has fired the soul of his son with love of the fame that was to come," he takes him, together with the Sibyl, to their exit. But there are two doors through which to exit Hell:

> Sunt geminae Somni portae; quarum altera fertur
> cornea, qua veris facilis datur exitus umbris,
> altera candenti perfecta nitens elephanto,
> sed falsa ad caelum mittunt insomnia Manes.
> his ubi tum natum Anchises unaque Sibyllam
> prosequitur dictis portaque emittit eburna. (VI, 893–98)

> (There are two gates of Sleep, of which one is said to be of horn, through which easy passage is given to shades that are true; the other is shining white, made of perfectly polished ivory, through which the Spirits send false dreams

> to the upper world. That is where Anchises, "having said those words," takes his son and the Sibyl, and sends them up through the ivory gate.)[14]

Each gate, of course, assimilates the nature of that to which it gives passage. Opaque horn gives passage to "shady" truths; bright, shining ivory, to bright visions which are, however, false. The contrast between *veris umbris* and *candenti nitens... sed falsa insomnia* is remarkable. But we must understand that Virgil is performing a double operation here. By opening the shining gate to Aeneas's vision, he is also leaving the gate of horn closed to the "true shades." In other words, what he does not open is as important as what he does open.

It is usually assumed that Virgil echoes here what first appeared in Homer's *Odyssey* (XIX, 560–69), in the words of Penelope to the "stranger," who is, of course, Odysseus in disguise:

> Stranger, dreams verily are baffling and unclear of meaning, and in no wise do they find fulfilment in all things for men. For two are the gates for shadowy dreams, and one is fashioned of horn and one of ivory. Those dreams that pass through the gate of sawn ivory deceive men, bringing words that find no fulfilment. But those that come forth through the gate of polished horn bring true issues to pass, when any mortal sees them.[15]

But what can conceivably be false, "finding no fulfilment," in Anchises' words? What can be deceitful about prophesying a historical reality which had, indeed, happened already, or was in the process of happening before Virgil's own eyes? In what sense is the announced history of Rome, of Roman civilization, false? These things are historical facts. They are not fictions. Therefore, I think the question should be rephrased: it is not that Rome's power is not real, or that the Roman Empire did not happen; the question must be, what is it

---

14 What follows is an expansion and revision of what I already said in *The Sacred Game*. See Chapter 3, "Beyond Virgil."
15 Loeb Classical Library, book XIX, 560–69.

that the visible power and the shining glory of Rome are not telling? What kind of dark truth is there that the shining, the poetic, visibility of things blocks from view? Is the reassuring visibility of things compatible with the dark truth, or is the dark truth, by its very nature, unspeakable? Is it in itself dark? Can it be revealed in any other way than darkly, as in a haze, perhaps in some sort of altered state of consciousness, like the Sybil? And, if so, what shall we call it? Why is it not possible to pierce through the haze, to bring it up into the light of day? One thing is certain about it, it is deeply disturbing, far from reassuring. Virgil has a name for it, *fatum*, fate; but does he know what it is? This is what Theodor Haecker says about it:

> The typical theological term of the *Aeneid* is not any of the many names of the gods of Olympus, but the word *fatum*.... The *Aeneid* is grounded in this mystery.... Does Virgil anywhere tell us ... what fate is? He does not, for he does not know.... In the clearest language in all the world he speaks darkly, thereby clearly showing that he is talking about the darkest mystery of all being.[16]

At this point we must make an important distinction. Virgil clearly knows more about dark fate, shady truths (*veris umbris*), than his hero does, or even Father Anchises. There is not the slightest indication in the text of the poem that Aeneas is, in any way, aware that he is exiting Hades like a false dream, through the ivory door. The poet not only knows more than his character, as can always be expected, he also knows that in order for his character to be true to himself in his epic role as founder of what would eventually become the imperial city of Rome, he cannot know. If he did, such knowledge would become an impossible burden, too much to bear. Aeneas is an instrument of fate, and that is all he has to know. He must go where he is driven. He cannot bend what fate has decreed. That is one of the things he learns in Hell: *desine fata deum flecti sperare precando* (abandon any hope of bending the decrees of the gods by prayer) (*Aeneid*, VI, 376). He does not know why

16 *Virgil, Father of the West*, 83.

he has been chosen, or why what he is driven to do is what must be done. He does it because he has no choice.

Aeneas is the perfect symbol of the unremitting, pressing, question subjacent to the entire epic action: he is dutiful, obedient, he does well what he is supposed to do; his soul can even be "fired up" by the vision of the future glory of Rome. But he would have rather stayed home. He is an exile, and he feels it. He is not totally identified with his destiny. His destiny is not his choice. It weighs heavily on his shoulders. There is something dark, strange, about it, which he does not like or understand.

Underneath this reluctant epic hero, there is a reluctant epic writer. In a sense, Georg Lukács was right: Virgil is not really an epic writer. "Strictly speaking [Homer's works] alone are epics."[17] Let me quote what I said many years ago in *The Sacred Game*:

> [Lukács] does not care much for Virgil: "Virgil's heroes lead a cool and measured shadow-existence, nourished by the blood of a splendid ardour that has sacrificed itself, in order to conjure up what has vanished forever." And with good reason: what "Virgil's heroes conjure up" is what lies behind the "splendid ardour," what must be sacrificed in order to maintain that perfect, sacred, correspondence between immanence and transcendence, between the self and the world, that forms the surface of Homeric epic. As C. S. Lewis writes: "[But] an inch beneath the bright surface of Homer we find not melancholy [as in Virgil] but despair. 'Hell' was the word Goethe used of it. It is all the more terrible because the poet takes it all for granted, makes no complaint. It comes out casually, in similes."[18]

Lukács knew that it was the Christian *logos*, "The new spirit of destiny [that] would indeed seem 'a folly to the Greeks,'" that had opened an irreparable crack on that bright Homeric surface. He did not know why or how, because he never looked through the crack to see what lay hidden inside. All

17 Georg Lukács, *Theory of the Novel*, trans. Anna Bostock (Cambridge, MA: MIT Press, 1977), 30.
18 *The Sacred Game*, 182.

he knew is that in a world abandoned by the old gods and alienated from the sacred, the traditional epic form is an empty and essentially meaningless shell.

Lukács is right: "strictly speaking," only Homer's works are fully and unambiguously epic. Virgil is already a significant step in the direction of the Christian undermining of the epic model.[19]

There is no reluctance in Homer, no dark undercurrent. We are horrified by the level of violence, in the Iliad particularly; and doubly horrified by the naturalness with which it is narrated; that is the way it is; no questions, no questions at all. The horror hangs in the air, hovering equally, absolutely equally, over everybody; Greeks or Trojans, it does not make any difference; nothing makes any difference; they are both to be pitied equally. Simone Weil mistook that for Christian compassion; she saw in Homer an anticipation of Christ. But what does "compassion" mean when it does not make any difference whatsoever; when nothing counts except whatever tactics you may use not to draw the attention of the undifferentiating monster? The ritual expression of pity by the tragic chorus is the direct heir to Homeric pity. Expressions of pity before the inevitable are a way of humbling yourself in the face of the monster, of making yourself as inconspicuous as you can. You do not want to make a difference in front of that which destroys all differences.

Above all, you do not question. Homer's heroes are surface heroes; not by accident or authorial incompetence, but by design and necessity. This is how Auerbach described what he called "the basic impulse of the Homeric style":

> To represent phenomena in a fully externalized form, visible and palpable in all their parts . . . a continuous rhythmic procession of phenomena passes by, and never is there a form left fragmentary or half-illuminated, never a lacuna, never a gap, never a glimpse of unplumbed depths.[20]

---

19 Ibid.

20 See *A Refuge of Lies*, 17.

As I tried to demonstrate in *A Refuge of Lies*, that gapless surface is Homer's sacred refuge from an unspeakable, an unbearable truth that must be avoided with all the poetic, decoying, fictionalizing, skills of the greatest bard of all time, divine Homer, inspired by the Muses of Helicon, who knew the sacred art of "telling lies that look like the truth." Homer's art is Odysseus's art, cunning, crafty, devious Odysseus, capable of charming his audience like the best singer of tales. This is how Eumaios, the swineherd, describes his encounter with "the stranger":

> As when a man looks to a singer, who has been given from the gods the skill with which he sings for delight of mortals, and they are impassioned and strain to hear it when he sings to them, so he enchanted me in the halls as he sat beside me. (17:518–21)

He is a charmer and a master of disguise. These are Athene's words about her protégé:

> It would be a sharp one, and a stealthy one, who would ever get past you in any contriving; even if it were a god against you. You wretch, so devious, never weary of tricks, then you would not even in your own country give over your ways of deceiving and your thievish tales. They are near to you in your very nature.[21]

Virgil is the anti-Homer because he can read through the Homeric surface. He asks ultimate questions. There is an epochal difference. A Virgil-like poet would have been impossible in Homer's world. The Romans' willingness to question the unspeakable, the unbending power of a violent destiny, this profound historical difference with Homer, can only mean that the terrifying power of the dark truth, the old, the violent sacred, had relented to some degree, it was not quite as terrifying. This is the beginning of a liberation from the old sacred, untouchable, overwhelmingly undifferentiating violence. Enough of a distance from the horror to be able to see it for what it really is; enough of a distance to be able

21 See *A Refuge of Lies*, 22.

to identify it. Neither Lucretius nor Virgil were hopelessly bound to lie in order to survive. Theodor Haecker may have had a glimpse of this:

> The Homeric heroes can state plainly their truths and their falsehoods.... But Aeneas cannot do this. Like all reticent men, he speaks only the truth that is in him, and that only occasionally and darkly.[22]

It was much more than a question of individual personalities. As I said, there could be no Virgilian personality in Homer's time. But the new freedom, meagre though it was, had its pitfalls. It could give the wrong impression. Lucretius exemplifies the new danger, or rather, the new mistake: he thought he could defeat the old monster. Science would be his weapon, the science of things. Once you know the "causes of things," once you know that everything is natural, you can overcome the fear of death, which is at the root of all our fears. As we saw, his own description of the Athenian plague proved him wrong. The horrific violence of nature is just as bad as the horror of "religion." Actually, nature can be far crueler and more implacable than "religion." What Epicurus said about the system of the naturalist philosophers, "deaf to all entreaties," should be applied to nature itself.

Virgil is not trying to escape the sacred. He knows that is not a possibility for a human being. Besides, he, being the poetic father of *pius* Aeneas, also knows what Cicero knew: if you eliminate the sacred, you eliminate all the civic virtues that form the backbone of a civilized society. The problem for Virgil is, as we have seen already, the inexplicable double nature of the sacred. The problem is that *pius* Aeneas, an exemplary model of civic virtue, must also be the protagonist in a horrible and senseless violence to precisely create the foundation of all those civic virtues, the city itself. Virgil's problem is vividly condensed in Aeneas's heartrending lament when he sees in the sky the emblematic symbol of the

22 *Virgil, Father of the West*, 73–74.

fratricidal war that is about to begin, that is, the armor that Vulcan has made for him at the request of his mother, Venus:

> Alas, what carnage awaits the hapless Laurentines! What a price, Turnus [the Latin hero who will stand up against Aeneas], shalt thou pay me! How many shields and helms and bodies of the brave, shalt thou, O father Tiber, sweep beneath thy waves! (VIII, 535–40)

Aeneas had signed a peace treaty with king Latinus, including a formal engagement of his daughter, Lavinia, to Aeneas. There was peace between the Teucrians or Trojans and the Latins or Laurentines. But Amata, the queen, Latinus's wife, was opposed to the marriage. She wanted to marry Lavinia to Turnus, the chief of the Rutulians, close allies of the Latins. And, of course, Juno, the goddess, who never forgave the Trojan Paris for not choosing her as the most beautiful, in the famous judgement of Paris, in which the Trojan gained Helen, thereby triggering the Trojan war. She plotted against Aeneas and the Trojans, putting obstacles in their way constantly, in spite of the fact that she knows she cannot ultimately thwart his destiny. She is determined to destroy the peace and spread war all over Latium.

Virgil's description of how violence spreads, like a plague (he seems to be imitating Lucretius's description of the Athenian plague), is a perfect example of "hypermimeticism." I do not think Girard could have improved on it. What follows is a much-abbreviated version.

Allecto, a particularly horrible Fury from Hell, so evil she is hated even by her father Pluto and her Tartarean sisters, is the mythical embodiment of such a plague, the contagion of mimetic violence from one human being to another. This is how Juno, who wants to create as much turmoil as possible, addresses her:

> Thou canst arm for strife brothers of one soul, and overturn homes with hate . . . thou have a thousand names, a thousand means of ill . . . let men crave, demand, and seize the sword! (VII, 335 ff.)

First, she poisons Amata, the queen:

> On her [the Fury] flings a snake from her [Gorgonian] tresses, and thrusts it into her bosom, into her inmost heart, that maddened by the pestilence she may embroil the whole house. Gliding beneath her raiment and smooth breasts, it winds its way unfelt and unseen by the frenzied woman, breathes into her its viperous breath...
>
> When the serpent's maddening venom has glided deep into her veins and courses through her whole frame—then indeed the luckless queen, stung by monstrous horrors, in wild frenzy rages from end to end of the city. (345–77) Possessed by a Bacchic frenzy she goes into the woods with her daughter, Lavinia. Immediately,
>
> Fame flies abroad, and the matrons, their breasts kindled with fury, are driven on, all by the same frenzy, to seek new dwellings [in the woods]. (392–94)

Next the hellish fiend will visit the Latins' hero, Turnus:

> She hurled at the youth a torch, and fixed in his breast the brand.... A monstrous terror broke his sleep, and the sweat, bursting forth from all his frame, drenched bone, and limb. For arms he madly shrieks ... lust of the sword rages in him, the accursed frenzy of war, and resentment above all. (456–61)

His call for arms and war has an immediate impact on his people: "the Rutuli vie in exhorting one another to arms."

Next Allecto will fly to the Trojan camp, where Aeneas's son is hunting wild beasts with his hounds:

> Here the Hellish maid flings upon his hounds a sudden frenzy, and touches their nostrils with the well-known scent, so that in hot haste they course a stag. *This was the first source of ill*; this first kindled the rustic spirit to war. (479 ff.)

This stag, "of wondrous beauty," was a pet, a favorite, of Silvia, the daughter of Tyrrhus, "controller of the royal herds." Chased by the rabid hounds, the stag is wounded by an arrow shot by Ascanius, Aeneas's son. The animal fled "under familiar roof." Silvia, "beating her arms with her hands," calls for help. The incident will immediately escalate into a very bloody conflict. At which point Allecto sounds the alarm from "the topmost ridge . . . whereat forthwith every grove trembled, and the woods echoed to their depths." That was the beginning of full-scale war. Allecto reports back to Juno, and offers to continue expanding the conflict:

> with rumors I will draw bordering towns to battle and will
> kindle their minds with lust of maddening war. (549–50)

Bad news will travel fast from mouth to mouth, and everybody will believe it. Juno's response to Allecto's offer is revealing: No, she tells the fiend, that will not be necessary, there is already enough terror and deception; the momentum for war is already established; they are already engaged in hand-to-hand combat, *what mere chance started* (*quae fors prima dedit*) has now been stained by new blood.[23]

Juno's words are amazing. She is not simply responding to Allecto's offer, she is describing the internal self-feeding dynamic of human violence, the reality behind the mythical account. Once such violence has started, for any reason whatsoever, by accident,[24] it will immediately take root, it will feed on itself, "terror and deception" will continue to expand. Therefore, she tells the fiend, you can go back to Hell, there is already enough violence to keep it going indefinitely. It is as contagious as the plague.[25] As soon as one comes in contact with it, the poison will take over completely.

This being so, it is entirely useless to try to establish differences between the contending parties. They are all infected by

---

23 Tum contra Juno: "terrorum et fraudis abunde est.
stant belli causae, pugnatur comminus armis,
quae fors prima dedit, sanguis novus imbuit arma." (VII, 551–53)

24 Juno's words contradict the purely mythico-poetic account we have just heard, which tells us that Allecto engineered the whole thing. This type of literal contradiction will become particularly obvious and significant in the Palinurus episode, which we will examine presently.

25 The same dynamic was described in Book IV, when Rumour, "of all evils the fastest," spreads malicious talk about Dido's love affair with Aeneas: "she gains strength as she goes; small at first through fear, soon she mounts up to heaven" (174–76).

the same poison. They become mirror images of each other. They feed each other's violence. Violence will, therefore, oscillate between the two with no end in sight. In the words of the classical scholar Mario A. Di Cesare:

> The following passage portrays the alternating butchery of Aeneas and Turnus. The whole is epitomized in one line of the invocation: *inque vicem nunc Turnus agit, nunc Troius heros* (XII, 502) (now Turnus, now the Trojan hero takes its turn). Aeneas and Turnus are rhetorically juxtaposed, commingled, almost identified with each other. . . . The alternating movement gathers a stark inevitability.[26]

Jupiter himself acknowledges the perfect equilibrium between the two:

> Whatever the fortune of each today, whatever the hope each pursues, be he Trojan or be he Rutulian, no distinction shall I make. . . . Jupiter is king over all alike; the fates shall find their way. (X, 107–13)

Then he nodded assent in the direction of the Stygian waters, that is, in the direction of Hell, the realm of the dead. "And with the nod made all Olympus tremble." It is from Hell that "fate shall find its way" toward the victim; for the victim is the one marked with the sign of the sacred. One of the two will fall, not because of any differences between the two, but because sacred fate, or, if you will, the fate of the sacred, demands a victim.

In other words, the mimetic inevitability of self-feeding human violence was as clear to Virgil then as it has been to Girard in our days. "The slightest outbreak of violence can bring about a catastrophic escalation."[27] For Girard, this is where the victimizing mechanism of all against one must intervene, or the human community will self-destruct. It does not make any difference who the one, the victim, is, as long as the violence against it is unanimous. Just as any random incident, no matter how small, has the potential to trigger a war where

---

26 See *The Sacred Game*, 150.

27 *Violence and the Sacred*, 30.

thousands would be killed, any insignificant difference can turn everybody's violence towards the one, whose elimination will save the many. We might say that this reproduces at the level of human society the Lucretian "atomic" pattern, the way things are born from a random minimum disturbance in the perfect parallelism of the atoms falling through the void, *incerto tempore incertisque locis*, and will eventually be destroyed just as randomly. Except that now, the initial state of perfect equilibrium, maximum entropy, where all energy is wasted away, is the violent equilibrium of mimetically reciprocal human violence, perfect violent reciprocity. Unless a minimum deviation from perfect equilibrium occurs, *nec plus quam minimum*, everything will be wasted, the human city will not happen. Everything depends on that totally random one, the victim, that will attract toward itself all the collective violence and carry it away from everybody. The blind automatism of the Girardian scenario parallels that of Lucretius.

Virgil's insistence on the violent parallelism between the two contending parties is quite different from what we can see in the *Iliad*, for example. In Homer there is also a certain parallelism between the Greeks and the Trojans: now one party has the upper hand, now the other, depending on whom the fates happen to favor at any given time. Such a violent parallelism has nothing to do with what either party is doing; it all depends on the unpredictable inclination of a force that transcends both of them equally. In Virgil's battlefield, on the other hand, the parallelism is a result of the violent reciprocity between the two parties. Their actions mirror each other in endless alternation. Fate intervenes to put an end to this endlessness. One head must be given up for the sake of many. But fate's choice is necessarily arbitrary given the underlying equivalency of the two parties. And yet, fate's choice, fate's intervention, is sacred, untouchable, definitive, without appeal. Therefore, Virgil's question is not, "why did fate nod in the direction of this one rather than the other?" Virgil's question goes to the very root of the problem: why the need for the violent reciprocity to begin with; the need for the terminal, equalizing violence out of which the sacred choice emerges as the only, ultimate, definitive solution on which peace among human beings depends? Why the carnage?

Virgil's questioning reveals something else as well, something fundamental. The sacred character of the sacrificial victim has vanished. If the choice of the victim is clearly arbitrary; if the very violence out of which the fateful choice emerges is "insane," the sacred uniqueness of the victim disappears. The victim is just a human being like any other. It is shocking to kill an obviously innocent human being. This is why something like the sacrifice of Iphigenia becomes such a horrifying, scandalous outrage in Lucretius. Virgil also provides us with an example of a sacrificial victim, who is not only innocent of any wrongdoing, but a model example of loyalty and good faith, Palinurus, the helmsman. Contrary to Girard's insistence, "the victim's guilt" is not "the mainspring of the victim mechanism." The mythical guilt of the victim is a rationalization of the sacrificial practice. The victim mechanism itself is utterly indifferent to the guilt or innocence of the victim. The only difference that counts is the sacred difference, which is granted to the victim because it is the cornerstone, but anybody can be the cornerstone. Once the victim is identified as such, *qua* victim, it becomes sacred. The sacred is totally *sui generis*. It is unlike anything else. The archaic sacrificer believed that the sacred choice was always the correct one, the victim whose sacred identity had remained hidden until the infallible choice makes it manifest. Neither Lucretius nor Virgil believed in such an infallibility *a posteriori*. Anybody could be the sacred victim. Nevertheless, a sacred victim was still required, whoever that might be.

Which is why, before we proceed to analyze the famous episode, we should pause for a moment to reflect on what should be apparent by now. If the victim is no longer sacred the way it used to be, or only sacred in a purely functional way bordering the make-believe, according to mimetic theory, the scapegoat mechanism should disintegrate rather quickly, should stop working. If the hypermimetic mechanism fails to sacralize the victim, which is the root of the old sacred, how can the old sacred survive? How can it maintain its power in the light of reason? How can it still terrorize Epicurus and his devoted follower Lucretius? Indeed, why is it still capable of keeping Virgil in the grip of a very deep and somber pessimism? Virgil's insistence, time and again, on the irrational insanity of the whole thing, is a witness to the lingering power of the old sacred, apparently immune to rational progress. And, in this sense, the Palinurus episode is probably the best Virgilian example of sacrificial arbitrariness deliberately, purposely, emphasized: an implicit commentary on Lucretius's scientific proposal as an anti-sacrificial defense.

Let us, then, examine the famous episode. It happens during the last stretch of the, until then, frustrating meandering of the Trojan fleet up and down the Eastern Mediterranean. They have now left Sicily, where they have established a colony with the women and all those who were too tired to continue. Clearly it is no accident that it happens at the beginning of the last stretch. For what is at stake is precisely whether or not this is going to be the last stretch; in other words, whether or not they will ever get to their destination, a destination decreed by sacred fate. If they ever get there, it will not be for any other reason; certainly not by following any human rational design, knowledge, or expertise. Destiny determines where they will go, and the same destiny demands a victim to be fulfilled.

As they start their voyage, the weather looks favorable. But Venus is still suspicious of what Juno's anger, *gravis ira*, and insatiable heart, *exsaturabile pectus*, may be plotting against Aeneas and the Trojans. So, she pleads with Neptune, god of the sea, to grant them easy sailing to finally reach the Italian shore. Neptune agrees: *pelle timorem*, throw away your fear, he tells her,

> tutus, quos optat, portus accedet Averni.
> unus erit tantum, amissum quem gurgite queres;
> unum pro multis dabitur caput. (V, 812–15)

> (In safety, as you wish, shall he reach the haven of Avernus. One only shall there be whom, lost in the flood, thou shall seek in vain. One head will be given up for the sake of many.)

Meanwhile, "favoring breezes bear on the fleet."

> princeps ante omnis densum Palinurus agebat
> agmen; ad hunc alii cursum contendere iussi. (833–34)

> (First before all, leading the close column, was Palinurus; by him all the rest are ordered to keep their course.)

It is midnight. The sailors are all resting, except Palinurus, the leading helmsman. He keeps watch, looking at the stars, distrustful of the "monster" on whose waves the fleet is sailing, keeping the safety of Aeneas in mind, forever loyal to his leader.

Almost immediately after Neptune's words, we see Somnus, "in the semblance of Phorbas," come down from the sky in search of Palinurus:

> te, Palinure, petens, tibi somnia tristia portans *insonti*. (840–41)

> (In search of thee, O Palinurus, bringing thee baleful dreams, O guiltless one.)

Somnus tries to persuade Palinurus to take a rest from his duty. The helmsman resists; he cannot forget for a moment the safety of the fleet and of Aeneas. At which point the god sprinkles his temples with a "bow dripping with Lethe's dew and steeped in the drowsy might of Styx," thus forcefully putting him to sleep:

> Hardly had a sudden slumber begun to unbend his limbs when, leaning above, Sleep flung him headlong into the clear water, tearing away, as he fell, the helm and part of the stern. (V, 857–60)

Guiltless, loyal, Palinurus will manage to swim ashore, only to be killed by a group of savages who happened to be there and mistook him for some precious prey. In other words, Palinurus's death is not only unjust, because he is "innocent," *insonti*, but the specific circumstances of it are utterly unpredictable, a senseless accident. And yet, such a senseless and unjust death carries with it the seal, the mark, of the sacred. He is the one who must die for the sake of many; he fulfills the unbending, inexorable, demand of the sacred; the demand on which the sacred itself is grounded. Howsoever such a one may die is utterly irrelevant, as irrelevant as who he may be. The only crucial thing is that he be the one fated, designated, to die. Without such a sacred death, the city of man will not be founded, or, in the mythico-poetic language of Virgil, Aeneas will not get to the shores of Lavinia, Rome will not be founded. In the end, it is not human ingenuity or expertise, like that of incomparable Palinurus, *princeps ante omnis*, that will get to that historic destination, but fulfilling the sacred demand: one head must be given up. Virgil chose his poetic victim, the one given up, for a purpose. Palinurus is precisely the pilot, the one who knows the way and steers the course in the right direction. He and everything that he represents is replaced by the ultimate decider, the sacred, *fatum*. This is why, as soon as Somnus throws Palinurus overboard,

> the god himself flies easily away through the thin air,
> and no less safely does the fleet speed on the water
> unafraid, trusting in the promises of Father Neptune.
> (V, 861–63)

Fate itself is guiding the fleet. Human knowledge, expertise, or any other human value is utterly irrelevant, purely circumstantial, accidents that will not change Fate. If we keep this in mind, Palinurus's apparently strange words to Aeneas, when the latter encounters him, or rather his ghost, in Hell may sound less strange or surprising. Indeed, as soon as Aeneas arrives in Italy, he will visit the cave of the Sybil and, guided by her, will descend to the underworld with the intention of visiting the spirit of his father Anchises. Before he crosses the Stygian waters, he sees the spirit of Palinurus, who cannot cross over, because his body remains unburied on the beach where the savages killed him. Eventually the savages will be prompted by terrifying signs from heaven to cover his body. These are Aeneas's words, as he recognizes the spirit of Palinurus:

> What god, Palinurus, tore thee from us and plunged beneath the open ocean? O tell me! For Apollo, never before found false, with this one answer tricked my soul, for he foretold that thou would escape the sea and reach Ausonian shores. Is it thus his promise holds? (VI, 341–46)

And this is the surprising answer of Palinurus:

> Neither did tripod of Phoebus fail thee, leader, son of Anchises, nor did a god plunge me in the deep. For by chance (*forte*) the helm to which, as my charge, I clung, steering our course, was violently torn from me, and I, dropping headlong, dragged it with me. (VI, 347–51)

Of course, literally, Phoebus did not lie, since Palinurus did "reach Ausonian shores." But his promise was clearly deceitful. On the other hand, what does it mean to say that "no god plunged me in the deep," it was just an accident? For we have just seen the god Somnus, a creature of Hades, do precisely that. In other words, what does it mean to say, on the one hand, "the gods have not failed you," and on the other, "my death was just an accident"? What did Somnus, the gods' emissary, do then when he approached Palinurus and pushed him overboard? For his hand is the hand of the gods. Quite simply, he designates the victim. When he pushes him, it is as if the gods were saying, "that is the one." We did not know, until then, "whose head had to be given up for the sake of many." As soon as Somnus approaches Palinurus, we know. He does not stay to make sure that Palinurus is dead. He knows that he is going to die. In fact, he did not even have to push him as a designating gesture. Palinurus was already half asleep when he fell overboard.

We could psychologize about Palinurus's state of mind when he fell; could he remember later that he had been pushed? But I do not think Virgil would care one way or the other. Beyond psychology, what interests Virgil is the role the character plays in the fated founding of the city. Palinurus is the designated victim who must be sacrificed. But the designation itself, Virgil makes perfectly clear, is unjust and arbitrary. Virgil insists on the injustice and the randomness, the unpredictable sequence of events of the whole episode. And yet, it is what sacred fate demands. Here, as everywhere else throughout the poem, is the underlying question: why? For which he cannot find an answer. How can it be sacred and also random, unjust, unfair, deceitful, implacable, indifferent to anything that human beings aspire to, long for?

On the one hand, everything of value to humankind rests on the sacred, which is the reason why an exemplary citizen must be a *pius* citizen, the model of which is Aeneas himself. And yet the sacred is ultimately indifferent to such exemplary behavior. Virgil longs for something which is ultimately not there. Hence the hero's reluctance, his perennial questioning: why does it have to be that way? And the tears of things, and the "indignant" protest of the victim. Palinurus's seeming contradiction—"it was an accident, and yet, sacred fate, the gods, have not failed you in your mission"—is only a more explicit formulation of the underlying questioning, an indicator of Virgil's profound pessimism, and equally profound insight. An insight which is perfectly clear to us, because we are looking at it within the context of Girardian theory. Girard never said anything about Virgil, but gave us the key to his poetic text.

Perhaps now we can fathom the depth and complexity of Virgil's distinction between the bright surface of things and the opaque, dark, truth, with which we started our analysis. These two levels are not in opposition to each other in reference to the founding of the city; quite the contrary, the bright surface, that which everybody sees, the glory of Rome, the magnificence of civilized institutions, rests on a sacred truth, which is dark, because its sacred character is ultimately irrational in the sense of being violently indifferent to rational differentiations.

A VIRGILIAN EPILOGUE

IN HIS STUDY ON VIRGIL, C.A. SAINTE-BEUVE HAD famously said that "not even the coming of Christ is anything surprising after reading Virgil" (*La venue même du Christ n'a rien qui étonne quand on a lu Virgile).*[1] This can be profoundly misleading, but there is also a profound truth behind it. We could say of such a statement what T.S. Eliot said of the notion of Virgil's soul being *naturaliter Christiana*: "he just falls short."[2] Let me repeat here what I said in *The Sacred Game*: "One can see the *Aeneid* as the poem of fallen man, man as the sacrificial founder of his own *civitas terrena* (earthly city), thereby caught in the vicious circle of his own violence, struggling to separate good from evil, in other words, the poem of fallen man *without the promise of redemption*."[3]

But what does that have to do with Girard? Girard himself tells us in *Evolution and Conversion* that George Poulet saw him as the "Sainte Beuve of the twentieth century."[4] Could that have anything to do with Sainte Beuve's famous *dictum*? I do not know what Poulet had in mind, because, as far as I can tell, the name of Virgil is as absent from Girardian anthropology as the name of Christ. In fact, what is no surprise after reading Virgil is this Christless Girard. On strictly rational grounds, there is nothing in Girard which was not already, and in general quite explicitly, in Virgil. But the absence of Christ is one thing in Virgil and quite another in Girard. In Virgil it is the end result of a long historical journey; in Girard it is a purely epistemological postulate. We should add that there is no scapegoat theory in Virgil, as there is none either in Cervantes, in spite of their profound understanding of mimetic desire.

---

1 *Étude sur Virgil* (Paris: Garnier, 1857), 78.
2 *On Poetry*, 130.
3 *The Sacred Game*, 183.
4 *Evolution and Conversion*, 22.

It is a long journey from Homer to Virgil, as it is from Homer's world to Virgil's Rome. There are no questions in Homer. Everything is a question in Virgil. Nothing alters the bright surface in Homer; not even the most terrible violence in the *Iliad*, rivers of blood, endless fields of dead bodies, food for vultures and dogs. There is lamentation; it is ritually required, the same for everybody, Greek or Trojan, it doesn't make any difference. Each one of those killed was a father, or a son, or a friend; each one has a name, details can be remembered. But it doesn't make any difference. Nothing makes any difference in the face of that which is overwhelming. Simone Weil called it "might" or "force." In the *Iliad* it is called "the will of Zeus," or "the anger of Achilles," to which the hero himself must submit, as we have already seen. In our Girardian context we may just call it "the sacred," unbending, terrifying. No questioning at all: "It is all the more terrible because the poet takes it all for granted, makes no complaint. It comes out casually, in similes."[5] Divine Homer, God-like, is the human voice of the old sacred, no dissent.

The situation has changed significantly by the time we reach classical Athenian tragedy. According to Girard, the tragic poet's inspiration runs counter to "Mythological and ritual values."[6] In *Oedipus the King*, for example, a very dangerous question hangs in the air: "were there many who killed Laios or was it just one?" If there were many, then Oedipus is in the clear. It was not he who did it, as the myth and the ritual affirm, and as the victimizing mechanism requires to function properly, according to Girard. But "Sophocles stopped just short of framing the question and concludes by reaffirming the compromised mythological values." The same thing, but even more clearly, happens with Euripides:

> But this time the backing off is not performed in silence. His tragedies contain numerous passages whose emphatic tone and repetition of theme clearly mark

5 See *The Sacred Game*, 182.
6 *Violence and the Sacred*, 129.

> them as expressions of the poet's decision to retreat and his attempts to justify himself: "Human wisdom is not wisdom, and to aspire to more than a man's due is to shorten life, is to sacrifice the fruit at hand for what is out of reach."[7]

There is no such retreat in the case of Virgil. His entire *Aeneid* is a perfectly clear and explicit question, repeated time and again, "Why?" Why does it have to be this way? Virgil's standing is unique. There is nothing in the classical pagan world that comes even close. He knows the fear (*metus omnis*); he has heard the terrifying howls of hungry Acheron (*strepitum Acherontis avari*). With Aeneas, he knows "the tears of things" (*lacrimae rerum*). In the beginning of a long foundational struggle was the victim, a defeated man, barely escaping the destruction of his city and the massacre of his people. That was the first stone in what will end up being the glory of Imperial Rome: a fugitive driven by a fate he has not chosen. If it were up to him, he would go back and rebuild his city. He knows the horror of the sacred; the terrible price that must be paid for the founding of the city; the dark irrationality at the bottom of it all, the inanity of fratricidal violence, the sacrifice of the innocent, one head for the sake of many. But he stays, he doesn't look for a refuge. He admires Lucretius, but he is not a member of the Epicurean Garden. His Aeneas is not a rebel, but a deeply pious man, *insignem pietate virum.* He understands Cicero's objection: if you remove the gods, you also remove "good faith, and human fraternity, and justice, the chief of all the virtues." You also eliminate the idyllic country gods, "Pan, the old Silvano, and the Nymphs." Why the terrible violence at the bottom of it all? How could that be divine? In mythical terms, "how can the Queen of the gods hold such a violent resentment against an exemplary man such as Aeneas?" Why the dark truth?

---

7 Ibid.

He, the poet, does what Plato did not do. Plato blamed the poets for lamenting the fate of the victim, the one so designated by the sacred tradition of myths and rituals. Why lament the wholly merited expulsion from the city of an incestuous parricide such as Oedipus? It is a sacrilege to turn those stories into tragedies, that is to say, poetic lamentations. That is why those poets have no place in the ideal republic; they do not know what they are doing, they toy dangerously with ambiguity. Philosophy, not poetry, should rule the ideal republic. Plato does not ask questions either. But Virgil, the poet, knows very well what he is doing. He is not playing ambivalent sacrilegious games. He confronts ambivalence directly. Why is the good tied to the bad? He is not playing games, he wants an answer. But the answer that broke the ambivalence by transforming evil into good had not been revealed yet. And Virgil does not have a scapegoat theory. He asked the fundamental question that Cervantes would ask sixteen centuries later. But Cervantes knew where to go to get the answer, the miraculous answer—you may remember—by the mercy of God, who was used to remedy humanity's problems "from way back," as we saw in the allegorical "drowning" of Sinforosa in the *Persiles.* Virgil did not know. This is why I think it is more than melancholy. What we see in Virgil is a profound and somber pessimism. Tradition has it that on his death bed he ordered his *Aeneid* to be destroyed. The intervention of his friend Octavius Augustus prevented the order from being carried out. But Virgil's rational and profoundly pessimistic self-awareness was the closest thing to the Christian truth that the pagan world ever produced, *anima naturaliter Christiana.*

Yes, but did he, could he anticipate the coming of Christ, is it true that "even the coming of Christ is no surprise after reading Virgil"? It is one thing to say that Christ explains Virgil, and quite another to say or imply that Virgil explains Christ. Theodor Haecker was right in the words with which we began the Virgil chapter: "It is impossible to understand Virgil in all his fullness . . . without some reference to the oncoming faith." The oncoming faith reveals the reason for Virgil's pessimism. Virgil's pessimism, by itself, is a dead end, by definition. Only the Biblical prophecies anticipate the coming of Christ; Virgil was not a prophet. There are no pagan prophets. Nevertheless, Virgil's question is the right question at the right moment. The very last line of the *Aeneid* sums up the questioning that, either explicitly or implicitly, has governed the poem from the beginning. As Aeneas deals the fatal blow to Turnus, thus "sacrificing" him to atone for the earlier killing of Pallas, Turnus's life, with a moan, runs away *indignant* into the darkness below, *vitaque cum gemitu fugit indignata sub umbras.*

Such an abrupt ending for the long poem. It is strange, to say the least. Occasionally critics have thought that Virgil did not finish his poem; and, in some sense, they may be right. But was that an accident, something purely circumstantial? Could that be the reason why he wanted his poem destroyed, simply because he did not have the time to finish? That would seem unreasonable. Literally the poem makes perfect sense as it is. We could imagine all sorts of psychological explanations. As we said, it does not matter. We just don't know. But, even if such an ending occurred for purely accidental circumstances, its meaning within the demonstrable sacrificial character of the poem is loud and clear: there is nothing more to say. Everything begins and ends with the sacrifice of the human victim. And the spirit of the victim rushes to the dark underworld "indignant" (*indignata*). Virgil repeats here exactly the same words used in the killing of Camila by Arruns, the priest of Apollo (XI, 831).

But the indignation felt by Virgil's poetic victims is not the indignation first felt by Peter, who drew Jesus's rebuke, and in our time the indignation typified by Ivan Karamazov. Virgil is not scandalized. That is the huge difference. He is frustrated. He wants to know why. Why is the sacred, the source of all that is good, rooted in a violence for which he cannot find a reason? He must follow and obey a fate he does not like, and engage a battle which he feels is unnecessary. He would much rather sign a permanent peace with the Latins than go to war. He does not see himself as conqueror:

> If Victory grants battle to us and ours . . . I will not bid Italy obey my Teucrians, nor do I claim the realm for mine; let both nations, unconquered, join treaty for ever under equal law. (XII, 187–91)

This is extraordinary. Even if he wins the battle he will not take anything from the defeated enemy; nobody will be declared conqueror; enemies will no longer be enemies but equals under the law.

> And let the Sun and the Earth be witness, and the gods; not only Almighty Father (*pater omnipotens*), but even you, his wife, divine daughter of Saturn, at last, I pray, more favourable, and you mighty Mavors, lord of warfare, and on the Springs and Rivers I call, and the Dread of high heaven, and the divinities of the blue seas: if haply victory fall to Turnus the Ausonian, the vanquished make covenant to withdraw to Evander's city; Iülus shall quit the soil; nor ever hereafter shall the Aeneadae return in arms to renew warfare, or attack this realm with the sword. (XII, 176–85)

Why, then, the battle, for heaven's sake? But to no avail. Neither gods nor humans, with the exception of king Latinus, is paying attention. Everybody is getting ready to kill the enemy. Aeneas makes a final effort to stem the spreading violence:

> But good Aeneas, his head bared, kept stretching his unarmed hand and calling loudly to his men: "Whither run you? What is this strife that so spreads and swells? Ah, restrain your wrath! truce is already stricken, and all its laws ordained." (XII, 311–14)

The warriors on both sides are restless and ready for battle. Then they see an omen in the sky involving the giant bird of Jupiter, which Turnus's Rutulians interpret favorably, and march into battle. This is the final confirmation of how irrelevant Aeneas's desire for peace really is. There will be massacre all over the place, ending with the duel between Aeneas and Turnus, in which Aeneas in the role of high priest will sacrifice his rival and his equal. Aeneas, the reluctant hero, obediently follows his destiny, but never found an answer to his constant and urgent question: why the violence, what is the link between violence and the sacred? Why is the best rooted in the worst?

We claim that mimetic theory is made possible by the coming of Christ. Is mimetic theory no surprise after reading Virgil? The answer must be an unequivocal affirmative: yes, it is no surprise. Virgil does not anticipate Christ, but he does anticipate Girard's theory. This is why mimetic theory is the perfect instrument to read Virgil, and *vice versa*. And yet, Girard insisted all along that, ultimately, there is no reason to despair. Ultimately, we have a choice, there is hope. Where does that hope come from? Mimetic theory does not teach us anything that Virgil wouldn't know as well. Virgil's insight into the overwhelming mimetic contagion that makes the spread of human violence inherently open-ended, endless, is as profound and as revealing as that of Girard at its best, as we have seen in the description of the terrible wars on Italian soil. The ultimate knowledge of violence, defined by Girard as the fundamental identity, sameness, of all contenders, their perfect violent reciprocity, is explicitly brought out even with a tinge of irony, by Virgil. The human element, the historical facts of the case, are the same in Virgil and in Girard. They are both looking at the same thing. What makes the difference? Where does Girardian hope come from? Hope, in spite of an anthropological assessment as bleak, at times, as anything in Virgil. Hope out of hopelessness upon the realization that the Christian revelation has failed, "has not been heard"? The answer is still Christ. In fact, our hope in Christ, he told us in his last book, will not be genuine unless, or until, we realize that the revelation has actually failed. This realization is conceived as a form of *askesis* along which everything which is not the person of Christ and nothing but Christ is shed. We must face the abyss in order to fully realize how absolutely unique the hope offered by Christ, really is. Reading Girard's *Battling to the End*, one may get the impression that his message is something like this: we must go through Hell before we can reach Heaven. Christ has left, said Girard, and will not come back until we realize that his revelation has failed. He came, revealed himself to us, and we did not pay attention. So he left.

The time has come, says Girard, for a serious discussion of what mimetic theory has been saying about archaic religion. In other words, we did not listen to Christ, perhaps we should now listen to anthropological science, that is to say, the scientific discourse of mimetic theory. And remember, we call it scientific because it makes no recourse to any kind of religious belief. But Girard's purely epistemological Christianity, which does not require Christ's direct involvement, is really a fake, and a very superficial one. The scientifically required absence of Christ does not exist. Christ has already come, he has been revealed already. The world is no longer what it used to be. His absence for methodological reasons is totally artificial, a make-believe. You can no longer say anything fundamental about humanity without involving Christ, whether you know it or not, whether you are nominally a Christian or not.

If we are looking for profound rational knowledge about mimetic desire, without Christ, then our best bet is Virgil. For Virgil is truly the one closest to us. He knows everything about mimetic desire. Virgil's lack of hope, his pessimism, is genuine. He doesn't know Christ, our source of hope. Girard's scientific independence from Christ is totally artificial. Whether Christ is mentioned or not by mimetic theory doesn't change anything. As Girard himself told us, mimetic theory would not exist without Christ.

And again regarding Sainte Beuve's dictum, "The coming of Christ is no surprise when one has read Virgil," is there any truth in it? It depends. If we mean to say that Virgil would not have been surprised, then it is not true. Neither Virgil nor any other pagan could have imagined God becoming human so that we could be saved. However, he could have been extremely well-pleased because he would have seen Christ as the perfect solution to the problem that had burdened him from the beginning: the link between violence and the sacred, the two sides of his destiny. But he would have also learned that his destiny was not the founding of the city, but something far more exalted than that: discovering the divine in the human, that is to say, a universal transcendence that the sacrificial religion of the city could never have. The true sacred is not concerned with the defense of the city but with the ultimate destiny of each and every one of its inhabitants. He would have seen God, and perhaps learned what Girard had also learned, that it is all a question of sanctity.

BIBLIOGRAPHY

Alberg, Jeremiah. "Scandal." In *The Palgrave Handbook of Mimetic Theory and Religion*. Edited by James Alison and Wolfgang Palaver. New York: Palgrave Macmillan, 2017.

Alison, James. *Jesus the Forgiving Victim. Listening for the Unheard Voice*. Doers Publishing, 2013.

————. *Knowing Jesus*. London: SPCK, 1993.

————. *Raising Abel. The Recovery of the Eschatological Imagination*. New York: The Crossroad Publishing Co., 1996.

———. *The Joy of Being Wrong. Original Sin Through Easter Eyes*. New York: The Crossroad Publishing Co., 1998.

————. and Wolfgang Palaver, editors. *The Palgrave Handbook of Mimetic Theory and Religion*. New York: Palgrave Macmillan, 2017.

Anspach, Mark R. *Vengeance in Reverse. The Tangled Loops of Violence, Myth, and Madness*. East Lansing, MI: Michigan State University Press, 2017.

Antonello, Pierpaolo, and Paul Gifford, editors. *How We Became Human. Mimetic Theory and the Science of Evolutionary Origins*. East Lansing, MI: Michigan State University Press, 2015.

Aquinas, Thomas. Mulligan Translation. "The 29 Questions on Truth." http://www.documentacatholicaomnia.eu.

Bailie, Gil. *An Excerpt from The Work in Progress*. The Cornerstone Forum, Thanksgiving 2013.

———. *God's Gamble. The Gravitational Power of Crucified Love*. Brooklyn, NY: Angelico Press, 2016.

———. "Making Peace through the Blood of his Cross." *Communio* (2018): 471–93.

———. "On Paper and in Person." In *For René Girard. Essays in Friendship and Truth*. Edited by Jorge Jorgensen, Tom Ryba, James G. Williams, and Sandor Goodhart. East Lansing, MI: Michigan State University Press, 2009: 179–87.

———. *Violence Unveiled. Humanity at the Crossroads*. New York: Crossroad, 1995.

Balthasar, Hans Urs Von. *Theo-drama. Theological Dramatic Theory. Vol IV: The Action*. San Francisco: Ignatius Press, 1994.

Bandera, Cesáreo. *A Refuge of Lies: Reflections on Faith and Fiction*. East Lansing, MI: Michigan State University Press, 2013.

———. "The Doubles Reconciled," *MLN* 93 (3): 1009-12.

———. *The Humble Story of Don Quixote. Reflections on the Birth of the Modern Novel*. Washington, DC: The Catholic University of America Press, 2006.

———. *Mímesis Conflictiva. Ficción Literaria y Violencia en Cervantes y Calderón*. Madrid: Gredos, 1975.

———. *The Sacred Game. The Role of the Sacred in the Genesis of Modern Literary Fiction*. University Park, PA: The Pennsylvania State University Press, 1994.

Bandera, Pablo. *Reflection in the Waves*. East Lansing, MI: Michigan State University Press, 2019.

Barberi, Maria Stella. "Les trois règnes ou la crise de la représentation sacrificielle." In *La spirale mimetique. Dix-huit leçons sur René Girard*. Edited by Maria Stella Barberi. Paris: Desclée de Brouwer, 2001.

Bellinger, Charles K. *The Genealogy of Violence. Reflections on Creation, Freedom, and Evil*. Oxford, New York: Oxford University Press, 2001.

Besterman, Theodore. *Voltaire*. New York: Harcourt, Brace, and World, 1969.

Boas, Georg, and Lovejoy, Arthur O. *Primitivism and Related Ideas in Antiquity*. Baltimore, MD: Johns Hopkins University Press, 1997.

Brenk, F., S.J. "Unum pro multis caput: Myth, History, and Symbolic Imagery in Vergil's Palinurus Incident." *Latomus* 43 (1984): 776–801.

Bright, David F. "The plague and the Structure of De Rerum Natura." *Latomus* 30 (1971) (3): 607–632.

Bubbio, Paolo Diego. *Intellectual Sacrifice*. East Lansing, MI: Michigan State University Press, 2018.

Catholic Church, International Theological Commission. "Human Persons Created in the Image of God." http://www.vatican.va/roman_curia/congregations/cfaith/cti_documents.

Cayley, David. *The Ideas of René Girard. An Anthropology of Violence and Religion*. Independently published, 2019.

Cervantes, Miguel de. *Obras Completas*. Edited by Rodolfo Schevill and Adolfo Bonilla.

Chantre, Benoït. *Les derniers jours de René Girard*. Paris: Grasset, 2016.

Chesterton, G.K. *The Everlasting Man*. San Francisco: Ignatius Press, 1993.

Chilton, Bruce. *Abrahan's Curse*. New York, London: Doubleday, 2008.

Cicero, M.T. *On the Nature of the Gods*. Translated by Francis Brooks. n.p., 1896.

Cowdell, Scott. *René Girard and the Nonviolent God*. Notre Dame, IN: University of Notre Dame Press, 2018.

———. *Does Religion Cause Violence?* Edited together with Chris Fleming, Joel Hodge, and Carly Osborn. New York / London: Bloomsbury Publishing, 2018.

Dawson, Christopher. *The Historic Reality of Christian Culture*. New York: Harper and Brothers, 1960.

de Sahagún, Fray Bernardino. *Historia General de la Nueva España*.

Deacon, Terrence W. *The Symbolic Species: The Co-evolution of Language and the Brain*. New York: Norton, 1997.

Domenach, Jean-Marie. "Voyage to the End of the Sciences of Man." In *Violence and Truth*. Edited by Paul Dumouchel. Stanford: Stanford University Press, 1988: 152–59.

Dumouchel, Paul. "A Covenant among Beasts: Human and Chimpanzee Violence in Evolutionary Perspective." In Pierpaolo Antonello and Gifford, Paul: *Can We Survive Our Origins?* East Lansing, MI: Michigan State University Press, 2015: 1–24.

———. "A Theory of Everything? A Methodological Tale." In *The Palgrave Handbook of Mimetic Theory and Religion*. Edited by James Alison and Wolfgang Palaver. New York: Springer Nature, 2017: 424–27.

———. *The Barren Sacrifice. An Essay in Political Violence*. East Lansing, MI: Michigan State University Press, 2015.

———. ed. *Violence and Truth*. Stanford, CA: Stanford University Press, 1988.

Dupuy, Jean-Pierre. *A Short Treatise on the Metaphysics of Tsunamis*. East Lansing, MI: Michigan State University Press, 2015.

———. *La Jalousie. Une géométrie du désir*. Paris: Éditions du Seuil, 2016.

———. "Neither Dawkins nor Durkheim: On René Girard's Theory of Religion." In *Mimetic Theory and World Religions*. Edited by Wolfgang Palaver and Richard Schenk. East Lansing, MI: Michigan State University Press, 2018.

———. *Pour un catastrophisme éclairé. Quand l'impossible est certain*. Paris: Editions du Seuil, 2002.

———. *The Mark of the Sacred*. Stanford, CA: Stanford University Press, 2013.

———. *René Girard et le problème du Mal*. Edited by Dupuy and Michel Deguy. Paris: Grasset, 1982.

Fiddes, Paul S. *Past Event and Present Salvation*. Louisville, Kentucky: Westminster/John Knox Press, 1989.

Fornari, Giuseppe. *Fra Dioniso e Cristo. La sapienza sacrificale greca e la civiltà occidentale*. Bologna: Pitagora, 2001.

Gans, Eric. *The Origin of Language. A Formal Theory of Representation*. Berkeley: University of California Press, 1981.

Gardner, Stephen L. *Myths of Freedom. Equality, Modern Thought, and Philosophical Radicalism*. Westport, CT and London: Greenwood Press, 1998.

Girard, René. *A Theater of Envy. William Shakespeare*. New York, Oxford: Oxford University Press, 1991.

———. *Battling to the End. Conversations with Benoît Chantre*. Translated by Mary Baker. East Lansing, MI: Michigan State University Press, 2010.

———. *Deceit, Desire, and the Novel. Self and Other in Literary Structure*. Translated by Yvonne Freccero. Baltimore, MD: The Johns Hopkins University Press, 1965

———. *Evolution and Conversion. Dialogues on the Origins of Culture*. London: Bloomsbury Academic, 2008.

———. *I See Satan Fall Like Lightning*. Translated by James G. Williams. Maryknoll, NY: Orbis Books, 2001.

———. *Job: The Victim of His People*. Stanford, CA: Stanford University Press, 1987.

———. *The One By Whom Scandal Comes*. East Lansing, MI: Michigan State University Press, 2014.

———. *Resurrection from the Underground. Feodor Dostoevsky*. East Lansing, MI: Michigan State University Press, 2012.

———. *Sacrifice*. Translated by Matthew Patillo and David Dawson. East Lansing, MI: Michigan State University Press, 2011.

———. *The Girard Reader*. Edited by James Williams. New York: The Crossroad Publishing Company, 1996.

———. *The Scapegoat*. Translated by Yvonne Freccero. Baltimore, MD: The Johns Hopkins University Press, 1989.

———. *Things Hidden Since the Foundation of the World*. Stanford, CA: Stanford University Press, 1987.

———. *Violence and the Sacred*. Translated by Patrick Gregory. Baltimore, MD: The Johns Hopkins University Press, 1977.

———. *La voix méconnue du réel*. Paris: Grasset, 2002.

———. *When These Things Begin*. Translated by Trevor Cribben Merrill. East Lansing, MI: Michigan State University Press, 2014.

Giuseppe, Riccardo di. "L'Eucaristia nel banquetto mediterraneo.pdf." http://www2.unime.it/cover2011/Forum.

Goodhart, Sandor. *The Prophetic Law. Essays in Judaism, Girardianism, Literary Studies, and the Ethical*. East Lansing, MI: Michigan State University Press, 2014.

———. "René Girard and the Innocent Victim." In *Violence Renounced. René Girard, Biblical Studies, and Peacemaking*. Edited by Willard M. Swartley. Telford, PA: Pandora Press US, 2000: 200–17.

Green, Garrett. *Imagining God. Theology and the Religious Imagination*. New York, Cambridge, Philadelphia: Harper and Row, 1989.

Grivois, Henri. *Le Fou et le mouvement du monde*. Paris: Grasset, 1995.

———. and Proust, Joëlle. *Subjectivité et conscience d'agir. Approches cognitive et clinique de la psychose*. Paris: Presses Universitaires de France, 1998.

———. *Tu ne seras pas schizophrène*. Paris: Éditions du Seuil, 2001.

Guardini, Romano. *El comienzo de todas las cosas*. Translation of *Der Anfang Aller Dinge*. Bilbao: Desclée de Brouwer, 2013.

Haecker, Theodor. *Virgil, Father of the West*. New York: Sheed and Ward, 1934.

Hamerton-Kelly, Robert. *Politics and Apocalypse*. East Lansing, MI: Michigan State University Press, 2007.

———. *Sacred Violence. Paul's Hermeneutic of the Cross*. Minneapolis: Fortress Press, 1992.

Hardin, Michael. *Reading the Bible with René Girard: Conversations with Steven E. Berry*. Lancaster, PA: JDL Press, 2016.

Haven, Cynthia L. *Evolution of Desire*. East Lansing, MI: Michigan State University Press, 2018.

Heidegger, Martin. *"Only a God Can save Us": The Spiegel Interview*. Translated by William J. Richardson, S.J. *Der Spiegel* (31 May 1976).

John Paul II. *Crossing the Threshold of Hope*. New York: Alfred A. Knopf, 1994.

Johnson, W.R. *Darkness Visible: A Study of Virgil's Aeneid*. Berkeley: University of California Press, 1967.

Journet, Charles. *The Meaning of Grace*. New York: Scepter Publishers, 1996.

Juilland, Alphonse. "To honor René Girard." *Stanford French Review* Vol. X, 1–3. Anma Libri & Co., 1986.

Kaplan, Grant. "New Paths for a Girard/Lonergan Conversation." *Method: Journal of Lonergan Studies* 4.1 (2013): 23–38.

Kelly, Anthony J. *Eschatology and Hope*. Ossining, NY: Orbis Books, 2006.

———. "A multidimensional disclosure: Aspects of Aquinas' Theological Intentionality." *The Thomist* 67.3 (2003): 335–74.

à Kempis, Thomas. *The Imitation of Christ*. Translated by Aloysius Croft and Harold Bolton. Milwaukee, WI: Bruce Publishing, 1949.

Kermode, Frank. *Selected Prose of T. S. Eliot*. London: Ecco, 1975.

King, Chelsea Jordan. "Girard Reclaimed: Finding Common Ground between Sarah Coakley and René Girard on Sacrifice." *Contagion* 23: 63–73.

Kirwan, Michael. *Girard and Theology*. London, New York: T&T Clark, 2009.

Livingston, Paisley. "Disorder and Order. Proceedings of the Stanford International Symposium (Sept. 14–16, 1981)." In *Disorder and Order*. Stanford, CA: Anma Libri, 1984.

———. *Models of Desire*. Baltimore, MD: Johns Hopkins University Press, 1992.

Lonergan, Bernard. *The Redemption*, Vol. 9 of *The Collected Works of Bernard Lonergan*. Toronto: University of Toronto Press, 2018.

Lucretius. *On the Nature of Things*. Translated by H.A.J. Munro. Delphi Classics, 2015.

Lukács, Georg. *Theory of the Novel*. Translated by Anna Bostock. Cambridge, MA: MIT Press, 1977.

Lusvardi, Anthony R. "Girard and the Sacrifice of the Mass." *Contagion* 24: 159–90.

McKenna, Andrew J. *Violence and Difference. Girard, Derrida, and Deconstruction*. Urbana and Chicago: University of Illinois Press, 1992.

Mellinkoff, Ruth. *The Mark of Cain*. Berkeley and Los Angeles: University of California Press, 1981.

Merleau-Ponty, Maurice. *L'oeil et l'esprit*. Paris: Gallimard, 1964.

Mongrain, Kevin. "Theologians of Spiritual Transformation." *Modern Theology* 28.1 (2012): 81–111.

Oakes, Edward T., S.J. *The Theology of Grace in Six Controversies*. Grand Rapids, MI: William B. Eerdmans Publishing Company, 2016.

Oesterdiekhoff, Georg W. "www.richarddawkins.net/2014/11/what-is-religion-and how-is-it-explainable/." www.richarddawkins.net. November 21, 2014.

Oughourlian, Jean-Michel. *The Mimetic Brain*. Translated by Trevor Cribben Merrill. East Lansing, MI: Michigan State University Press, 2016.

Palaver, Wolfgang. *René Girard's Mimetic Theory*. East Lansing, MI: Michigan State University Press, 2013.

Paz, Octavio. *El Laberinto de la Soledad*. Mexico City: Fondo de Cultura Económica, 1999.

Pietsch, Thomas. "René Girard, Anthropologist of the Cross." *Lutheran Theological Journal* 51.2 (2017): 119–34.

Pope Paul VI. "Gaudium et Spes. Pastoral Constitution of the Church in the Modern World." Vatican, 7 December 1965.

Ratzinger, Joseph Cardinal. *God and the World*. San Francisco: Ignatius Press, 2002.

———. *Introduction to Christianity*. San Francisco: Ignatius Press, 2004.

———. *Must There Be Scapegoats? Violence and Redemption in the Bible*. New York: The Crossroad Publishing Co., 2000.

Rocha, João Cezar de Castro and Pierpaolo Antonello. *René Girard. Evolution and Conversion*. London, New York: Bloomsbury, 2008.

Rosenzweig, Franz. *The Star of Redemption*. Notre Dame, IN: University of Notre Dame Press, 1985.

Sabourin, Léopold and Stanislas Lyonnet. *Sin, Redemption, and Sacrifice. A Biblical and Patristical Study*. Rome: Pontificio Istituto Biblico, 1998.

Sainte-Beuve, C.A. *Étude sur Virgil*. Paris: Garnier, 1857.

Salay, Sean, S.J. "Anselm, Girard, and Sacramental Theology." *Contagion* 18: 100–3.

Schwager, Raymund, S.J. *Jesus of Nazareth. How He Understood His Life*. Translated by James G. Williams. New York: The Crossroad Publishing Co., 1998.

———. *Banished from Eden. Original Sin and Evolutionary Theory in the Drama of Salvation*. Translated by James G. Williams. Leominster: Gracewing, 2006.

Scubla, Lucien. "The Christianity of René Girard and the Nature of Religion." In *Violence and Truth*. Edited by Paul Dumouchel. Stanford University Press, 1988: 160–78.

———. *Giving Life, Giving Death. Psychoanalysis, Anthropology, Philosophy*. East Lansing, MI: Michigan State University Press, 2016.

Serres, Michel. *The Birth of Physics*. London: Rowman and Littlefield International, 2018.

Stroumsa, Guy G. *The End of Sacrifice. Religious Transformations in Late Antiquity*. Chicago and London: The University of Chicago Press, 2009.

Swartley, William M., editor. *Violence Renounced. René Girard, Biblical Studies, and Peacemaking*. Telford, PA: Pandora Press, 2000.

Tester, S.J. *Fides Quaerens Intellectum. Medieval Philosophy from Augustine to Ockham*. Bristol: Bristol Classical Press, 1989.

Vico, Giambattista. *The New Science of Giambattista Vico*. Ithaca and London: Cornell University Press, 2006.

Vincent, Marvin R. *Word Studies in the New Testament*, Vol. 1. New York, 1887.

Virgil. *The Aeneid of Virgil* (Mandelbaum verse translation). New York: Random House (Bantam Classics), 2003.

———. *Eclogues, Georgics, Aeneid 1–6*. Translated by H.R. Fairclough, rev. G.R. Goold. Cambridge, MA: Harvard University Press, 1999.

Voltaire, "Poème sur le désastre de Lisbonne." In *Œuvres Complètes*. Paris: Garnier, 1877.

William, James G. *The Girard Reader*. New York: The Crossroad Publishing Co., 1996.

Zachhuber, Johannes and Julia Meszaros. *Sacrifice and Modern Thought*. Oxford: OUP, 2013.

Zaleski, Carol. "C.S. Lewis's Aeneid." *Christian Century Online/Magazine* (2 June 2011).

Zúñiga, Santiago. "Psychose et restructuration du corps vécu: L'analyse de Blankenburg et Pankov à la lumière du transcendental." *Acto Universitatis Carolinae* 1–2: 194–211.

INDEX

CESÁREO BANDERA is University Distinguished Professor Emeritus of Romance Languages at the University of North Carolina, former Director of the Program in Comparative Literature at SUNY Buffalo, and former President of the Colloquium on Violence and Religion. His previous works include *Mimesis Conflictiva*, *The Sacred Game*, and *A Refuge of Lies.*

www.ingramcontent.com/pod-product-compliance
Lightning Source LLC
Chambersburg PA
CBHW021140090426
42740CB00008B/873

* 9 7 9 8 8 9 2 8 0 0 2 9 7 *